# REVENGE PORNOGRAPHY

Facilitated by developments in technologies, the non-consensual posting of sexually explicit images of someone else for revenge, entertainment or political motive – so-called revenge porn – has become a global phenomenon. This groundbreaking book argues that fundamental and recurring issues about how victims are violated can be understood in terms of gender and sexual dynamics and constructions, binary gender and sexual positioning and logics, and the use of sexual meanings.

Using a discourse analytical approach the authors examine revenge pornography through the words of the perpetrators themselves and study the complex ways in which they invoke, and deploy, gender- and sexuality-based discourses to blame the victim. They explore strategies to curb the phenomenon of revenge porn, and by placing their research in a broader social and political context, the authors are able to examine the effectiveness of current legislative frameworks, education and awareness raising, victim support and perpetrator re-education programmes, along with wider political considerations.

This enhanced understanding of the perpetrator mindset provides important insights into the use of social media to facilitate gender violence, and holds the promise of more effective interventions in future. This is a unique resource for students, academics, researchers, and professionals interested in revenge pornography and related issues.

**Matthew Hall** is Research Associate at Ulster University and an Associate Academic at the University of Derby. He is also an editor for the *Journal of Gender Studies*. His research has focused on gender, sexuality, body image, beauty cultures, online violences, substance (mis)use and veterans' health and well-being.

**Jeff Hearn** is Professor of Sociology, University of Huddersfield, UK; Senior Professor, Gender Studies, Örebro University, Sweden; and Professor Emeritus, Hanken School of Economics, Finland. His research focuses on gender, sexuality, violence, organisations and transnationalisations.

# REVENGE PORNOGRAPHY

## Gender, Sexuality and Motivations

*Matthew Hall and Jeff Hearn*

Routledge
Taylor & Francis Group

LONDON AND NEW YORK

First published 2018
by Routledge
2 Park Square, Milton Park, Abingdon, Oxon OX14 4RN

and by Routledge
711 Third Avenue, New York, NY 10017

*Routledge is an imprint of the Taylor & Francis Group, an informa business*

*British Library Cataloguing-in-Publication Data*
A catalogue record for this book is available from the British Library

*Library of Congress Cataloging-in-Publication Data*
Names: Hall, Matthew, 1968– author. | Hearn, Jeff, 1947– author.
Title: Revenge pornography: gender, sexuality and motivations /
Matthew Hall and Jeff Hearn.
Description: Abingdon, Oxon; New York, NY: Routledge, 2018. |
Includes index.
Identifiers: LCCN 2017015819 | ISBN 9781138124394
(hardback: alk. paper) | ISBN 9781138124400 (pbk.: alk. paper) |
ISBN 9781315648187 (ebook)
Subjects: LCSH: Computer sex—Moral and ethical aspects. |
Internet pornography. | Revenge. | Sexual ethics. | Sex crimes—
Psychological aspects.
Classification: LCC HQ66 .H35 2018 | DDC 176/.4—dc23
LC record available at https://lccn.loc.gov/2017015819

ISBN: 978-1-138-12439-4 (hbk)
ISBN: 978-1-138-12440-0 (pbk)
ISBN: 978-1-315-64818-7 (ebk)

Typeset in Bembo
by codeMantra

# CONTENTS

# ACKNOWLEDGEMENTS

While almost all of the material is published here for the first time, related versions of Chapter 4 'Online interactions' and Chapter 5 'A discursive approach to revenge porn' have appeared in *Metrosexual Masculinities* (Hall, 2014). We are grateful to the editors and publishers at Palgrave Macmillan for permission to reproduce this material here in revised form. We would also like to thank the following individuals and organisations for their permission to quote from their material verbatim:

Danica Johnson, (2013). 4 Ways to Take a Stand against Revenge Porn. *Everydayfeminism.com*. December 3. http://everydayfeminism.com/2013/12/revenge-porn-and-internet-exploitation.

Emily Baker, (2016). An Egyptian woman posted a video of her dancing to own her "shame": Ghadeer Ahmed's boyfriend tried to shame her by posting a video of her dancing online, but she wasn't going to let that happen. *The Pool*. October 27. https://www.the-pool.com/news-views/latest-news/2016/43/an-egyptian-woman-posted-a-video-of-her-dancing-to-own-her-shame.

*Iceland Monitor*, (2015). Women gather in the sunshine for #FreeTheNipple. June 13. http://icelandmonitor.mbl.is/news/news/2015/06/13/women_gather_in_the_sunshine_for_freethenipple/.

Mary Anne Franks, (2015). Drafting an Effective "Revenge Porn" Law: A Guide for Legislators. Cyber Civil Rights Initiative. *Cyber Civil Rights Initiative*. https://www.cybercivilrights.org/guide-to-legislation/.

Sam Dylan Finch, (2015). 6 Reasons Why Revenge Porn Is Really F★cked Up (And How One Woman Is Pushing Back). *Everydayfeminism.com*. June 16. http://everydayfeminism.com/2015/06/6-reasons-why-revenge-porn-is-actually-really-fcked-up-and-how-one-woman-is-pushing-back/.

*Scientific American*: Elizabeth Svoboda, (2014). Virtual Assault. *Scientific American Mind*, 25(6), 46–53.

*Taylor & Francis*: Jonathon W. Penney, (2013). Deleting revenge porn. *Policy Options Politiques*, August 21. http://policyoptions.irpp.org/fr/issues/vive-montreal-libre/penney/.

We would also like to thank Kristian Daneback, Linn Egeberg Holmgren, Ásta Jóhannsdóttir and Annadís G. Rúdólfsdóttir for advice and information, and Elizabeth Rankin, Eleanor Reedy and Alex Howard at Routledge, who waited patiently for the manuscript and who saw it through to publication, along with Rebecca Dunn and Will Tyler for working on the final production. We would also like to thank the anonymous reviewers at Routledge for their constructive feedback.

On a more personal note, Matthew would like to thank his co-author Jeff for his guidance and support in putting this book together; his encyclopaedic knowledge was both invaluable and impressive. He would also like to say thank you to his family who continually support and enrich his life, and, in particular, to his partner Tracy for her support throughout the project.

Jeff would like to thank Matthew for working together so congenially and productively, even if at a distance and having only met a couple of times, the last occasion unexpectedly sharing a taxi at 5:30 in the morning in Iceland in June 2014, that led to this very cooperation ... and also for doing most of the work.

# DISCLAIMER AND TERMINOLOGY

Revenge pornography is a heinous act that can devastate the lives of victims and those around them. This is so much so that, as a result, victims have been known to take their own lives. It is a phenomenon to be opposed and stopped.

Immediately, there are questions of terminology and definition. "Revenge pornography" has become a well-used term in contemporary media, discourse and society; this is often shortened to "revenge porn". Even though we use both terms, a more accurate term is "non-consensual pornography". We address these issues of terminology and definition in more detail later in the book (see pp. 13–16, ch. 2).

In order to be able to access perpetrators' electronic accounts to examine the motivations behind the acts that devastate lives, we viewed several websites that contained explicit revenge pornography material. The data in this book are drawn primarily from what is claimed to be the largest specific revenge porn site MyEx.com. While we sought permission to reproduce material for analysis from MyEx.com on several occasions, no response was received. For analytical purposes we reproduce perpetrators' written electronic data in full. The reader should therefore be aware that the electronic text in this book is reproduced verbatim, and as such, some readers might find its content upsetting.

Child pornography is illegal in the United Kingdom under the Protection of Children Act 1978 (PCA 1978) and section 160 of the Criminal Justice Act 1988 (CJA 1988) (Crown Prosecution Service, 2015). Given a significant amount of 'sexting' involves minors and some 'sexting' is reported to end up on revenge porn websites, we have made every effort to confine the research to text and related images where it was claimed that the victim was over 18 years of age and also where the victim appeared so.

This book is also designed to provide information to readers only. It is sold with the understanding that the publisher is not engaged to render any type of psychological, legal or any other kind of professional advice. The content of each chapter is the sole expression and opinion of the authors, and not that of the publisher. Neither the publisher nor the author shall be liable for any physical, psychological, emotional, financial or commercial damages, including, but not limited to, special, incidental, consequential or other damages.

# INTRODUCTION

> The Internet never forgets. And that permanent digital record, a blessing when it summons a moment we want to recall with the click of a mouse, can be a weapon in more sinister hands when it preserves ones we would like to forget. Controlling the distribution of the acts we want back, from mere silly poses for a camera to the most intimate deeds, has become a fact of life in the digital age, taking us into uncharted legal and ethical territory. And few expressions of this exploitative power are as disturbing as what is known as revenge porn, the posting online of sexually explicit photos or videos by a former partner seeking retribution.
>
> *(Penney, 2013, p. 1)*

Jonathon Penney's (2013) warning about the misuse of the Internet is demonstrable by what has become known as *The Fappening* (Moloney & Love, 2017). In August 2014, the non-consensual disclosure of nude and sexually explicit photos of around 100 female celebrity A-listers appeared on the online image-based bulletin board 4chan, many of which were pay-per-view (Radhika, 2014). The famous women involved included Jennifer Lawrence, Kim Kardashian, Rihanna, Scarlett Johansson, Kaley Cuoco-Sweeting, Kirsten Dunst, Meagan Good, McKayla Maroney, Vanessa Hudgens and Ariana Grande (see Strang, 2014, for the full list).

Making public sexually explicit (consensual and non-consensual) images and videos of others with new technology is nothing new. Communication technologies, whether labeled as 'new' or not, have repeatedly been taken up by those wishing to represent sex and sexuality, and pornographers, in particular, have done so in a more or less organised way. Rosen's (2010) *Beaver Street: A History of Modern Pornography* points out that throughout history, pornography and technology have enjoyed a symbiotic relationship. Increasingly complex technologies have developed from the peep show, photography and film, and associated histories of 'the real', the glossy image, the pin-up, the film star and the film icon. Early filmmakers were not slow to exploit the sexual display on the screen, with sexual themes figuring in clear, conscious and sometimes less conscious ways. Telephones brought 'call girls'; specialist telephone sexual services, sex lines, and telephone sex followed.

Video and television technologies have led on to sex videos, sex channels and sex pay TV. Johnson (1996) points out the pornography industry always accelerated the growth of new technologies such as video recorders and cameras, and more recently the Internet and smartphone, because they appealed to creators and consumers of pornography. Their appeal centered on being able to produce explicit photos in the privacy of one's home without having to go to the store to get a film developed. "Videotape first emerged as a cheap and efficient alternative to film (later kinescope) for TV production. Its development for home use owes its birth to Sony and Betamax but its maturity to porn" (Johnson, 1996, p. 222). Conversely, new technologies such as the Internet allow the consumption of explicit material at home, and, as such, the porn industry has gained a new audience of people willing to watch their films; "[i]nstead of travelling to a disreputable store, viewers could watch films at their convenience at home" (Johnson, 1996, p. 222).

Information and computer technologies (ICTs), and specifically the Internet, have raised possibilities of techno-sex, high-tech sex, non-connection sex, mobile phone sex and virtual sex. New forms of sex, sexual storytelling, sexual genres, sex talk shows and digital sexual media have mushroomed. Indeed, ICTs are themselves part of the broader histories of the publicisation (Brown, 1981) of sexuality and technologies of the senses. There are daily reports of how ICTs are changing how sexuality is done and experienced in chat lines, Internet dating, email sex, cybersex, cyberaffairs and falling in love on the Net, so providing new channels for sexuality, sexual communication, sexual citizenships and sexualised violence (Hearn, 2006). Speed and ease of ICTs create many possibilities for new forms of cybersexual experimentation, such as mixed or multi-media sex, interactive sex and interactive pornography.

There are many further ways in which people use ICTs and the Internet for sexual purposes. These may draw on the increasing range of online information and discussion forums on all manner of sexual aspects that are to be found on the Internet. In addition, their growing moves from more passive use of the Internet information to more active engagement and creation on interactive sites by those who might be described as competent online sexual agents (Döring, 2009). Above all, the Internet has brought all this and more into one "single medium to which a still increasing number of people have access due to technological advances and decreasing prices" (Daneback & Ross, 2011, p. 3).

Online uses of ICTs for sexual purposes are now normalised in many parts of the world, and especially so, but not only, for younger people. For example, in one recent four-country (Canada, Germany, Sweden the United States) study of 2,690 college students' sexuality-related activity online, 89.8% reported accessing sexual information, 76.5% experiencing sexual entertainment, 48.5% browsing for sexual products and 30.8% having engaged in cybersex (Döring, Daneback, Shaughnessy, Grov, & Byers, 2015; also, see Cooper, Månsson, Daneback, Tikkanen, & Ross, 2003; Cooper, Scherer, Boles, & Gordon, 1999; Shaughnessy, Byers, & Walsh, 2011).

Some representative samples of adult populations have indicated much lower figures of using the Internet for sexual purposes, with estimates ranging between 15% and 33% (Cooper, Morahan-Martin, Mathy, & Maheu, 2002). For example, a representative Swedish study estimated that 17% of adults had visited a website with sexual content (Findahl, 2010). However, this may neglect Internet use for some other kinds of sexual purposes such as educational purposes, ambiguities in what is meant by "sexual content", and whether use implies any relation to sexual arousal. They also do not take account of likely under-reporting by some people, particularly some women, who claim *not* to use the Internet for sexual purposes, but still report that they engage in online sexual activities (Daneback & Ross, 2011). Under-reporting may be for a variety of further reasons, including gendered and sexual taboos, cultural notions of sexual respectability and normalisation of everyday ICT use, whether sexual or not. Also, such generalised figures can obscure some broad demographic tendencies, for example, in some surveys, women's lesser and men's greater use, younger people's greater and older people's lesser use and bisexuals' greater use than heterosexuals and homosexuals.

Of particular relevance for our current concerns is the normalisation of access to, and use of, pornography. Men tend to access and use pornography, online or not, more than women, with less gender difference for younger people, and declining use with age. According to a recent UK study (Puccio & Havey, 2016), the average age for first exposure to online pornography is 11, and, of 3,000 13- to 18-year-old boys surveyed, 81% said they had looked at online pornography. Another recent UK study, *Young People as Critical Users of Online Pornography* (Martellozzo et al., 2016), commissioned by the National Society for the Prevention of Cruelty to Children (NSPCC) and the Children's Commissioner for England, based on focus groups and an online survey of 1,001 young people between ages 11 and 16, found that the majority of 11-year-olds (72%) had not seen online pornography, while almost two-thirds of 15-year-olds (65%) had. This study also provided information on sexting and related activities, reporting on how relatively few young people had taken naked or partly naked photographs of themselves (13%–14%) or others (3%–4%), and sent them to other people (c.7.5%) (also see Ringrose et al., 2012, 2013).

Such broad tendencies have multiple effects, especially on younger people. For example, the 2014 UK Institute of Public Policy Research (IPPR) study, *Young People, Sex and Relationships: The New Norms* (Parker, 2014), surveyed a representative sample of 500 18-year-old young people: "Seven out of 10 say 'accessing pornography was seen as typical' while they were at school; the consensus view is that this is typical between the ages of 13 and 15"; and "Almost eight out of 10 young women (77%) say 'pornography has led to pressure on girls or young women to look a certain way', while almost as many (75%) say 'pornography has led to pressure on girls and young women to act a certain way'." (also see Martellozzo et al., 2016). It is now clear that pornography – that is, online pornography – is part and parcel of many children's, young people's and indeed adults' lives.

At the same time, the Web and ICTs more generally have facilitated, in many ways, new forms of relatively easy and virtual violation and abuse (Hearn & Parkin, 2001), by Twitter, social networking sites (SNSs) or other means. The European Union's Fundamental Rights Agency (FRA, 2014) interview survey of 42,000 women in all 28 EU countries on experiences of violence against women addressed three types of acts that could be considered cyberstalking – that is, which involve the use of the Internet, email or mobile phones:

- sending emails, text messages (SMS) or instant messages that are offensive or threatening;
- posting offensive comments about the respondent on the Internet; and
- sharing intimate photos or videos of the respondent, on the Internet or by mobile phone.

They add that to be considered as stalking, these and all the other acts described in the survey must take place repeatedly and be perpetrated by the same person. Based on these definitions, the FRA survey authors estimate that 5% of women in the European Union have experienced one or more forms of cyberstalking since the age of 15, and 2% have experienced it in the 12 months preceding the survey. Taking the victim's[1] age into consideration, the 12-month rates vary from 4% among 18- to 29-year-olds to 0.3% among women 60 years old or older. Not surprisingly, there appear again to be important variations across age and generation.

There would appear to be both significant differences and significant continuities between the ubiquity of what might be called stranger pornography online, and its widespread negative pressures and effects, especially on young women, but also young people more generally, and the more personally directed and repeated online violations, including revenge pornography, from known others. An important caveat here is that what has been hitherto a basic distinction between knowing and not knowing someone is becoming blurred, especially for younger generations. Similarly, notions of privacy, anonymity and confidentiality are not so absolute for some people. At the risk of over-generalisation, Daneback and Ross (2011, p. 7) put it:

> It has … been suggested that younger and older people (in relative terms) have different concepts of anonymity with regard to sexually related activities on the Internet. It seems that by anonymity, young people mean not having to express sexually related details face to face (but they have no problems displaying a picture of themselves while doing it), whereas older people equate anonymity with not being seen or known.

Pornography, online pornography and online violation can indeed be intertwined in complex ways, both societally and individually. It should be added that, for some people, these developing and unstable connections can be intensified in and through what have become known, in psychological parlance, as 'Internet addiction' (Young, 1996), 'virtual addiction', 'cyber addiction' or indeed 'pornography addiction'. Some studies report young men's greater propensity for 'compulsive use of the Internet', and also how this may in turn link with psychological tendencies towards, for example, depression, loneliness, low self-esteem, experience of low parental involvement or conflict (for example, Ayas & Horzum, 2013; Aydin & Sari, 2011; Wiederhold, 2016), and co-addictions, and at times also psycho-sexual problems (Sussman, Lisha, & Griffiths, 2011).

Furthermore, various forms of online abuse have a socio-spatial and geo-political aspect that can be both local and global. Once on the Web, they can be accessed from anywhere in the world, the global digital public space. Incipient 'globalisation' of sexuality and abuse through ICTs can be produced through local and globalised social practices. ICTs have multiple impacts on sexuality, with changing forms locally and globally. Although this relationship has, in strictly quantitative and commercial terms, been mutually beneficial for the porn industry, some sectors of the porn industry have, as a consequence, stagnated or declined. For example, the speed and relative anonymity of the Internet, and especially in the Dark Net, has meant that the distribution and viewing of child pornography have been extended. One of the more recent consequences of the relationship between pornography and the development of Internet and smartphone technologies has the number of people reporting harassment, humiliation, invasion of privacy and loss of reputation with what has become termed 'revenge porn' (Parliament.UK, 2015).

Hasinoff (2015) suggests that the development of smartphones with built-in cameras has led to the explosion in 'sexting' – people texting explicit images of themselves to others. Smartphone technologies provide a false sense of security by giving people a sense of privacy, making them feel comfortable taking and sending explicit pictures and videos. Indeed, a survey conducted by Match.com (2012) found that out of 5,000 adults, 57% of men and 45% of women had received an explicit photo on their phone and 38% of men and 35% of women had sent one. Yet these pictures and videos can easily be uploaded to the Internet by anyone who has access to them. As Penney (2013) points out in the quote above, once this happens, those seemingly 'private' pictures are then available for the world to see. It is the uploading of such private pictures with text onto revenge porn specific websites, motivated by revenge, that is the focus of this book.

In Chapter 1 *Mapping the terrain* we explore the parameters of revenge porn. This chapter is divided into four sections. The first explores uses of the term 'revenge porn', and looks at what is covered in the various definitions of the term in dictionaries, by organisations such as the UK Safer Internet Centre (2015), and in legislation such as the UK Criminal Justice and Courts Act 2015 (Parliament.UK, 2015). In combining these, we provide a more comprehensive definition of what can be deemed revenge pornography, who commits this crime and who the victims are.

The second part of the chapter looks at where revenge porn is posted, for example, specific pornographic websites such as Cliphunter, specific revenge porn sites such Anonymous Image Board and social media sites such as Tumblr. We also look at the multiple linkages and convergences between e-media that mean that revenge porn is able to circulate with ease and speed. The relationship between 'sexting' (Hasinoff, 2015) and revenge porn is also explored, in particular, the reported increase in 'sexting' in younger generations and the risks of doing so.[2] We look at the geographical scope of revenge porn and where the vast majority of victims and perpetrators reside. Given its increasing popularity, we look at how lucrative it can be for host websites.

The third section looks at who produces revenge porn. While male ex-partners are reported to be the main perpetrators (McAfee, 2013), we show that current partners, (ex)friends of both victims and perpetrators, people known to the victim, complete strangers and Internet hackers are also involved. We explore some of the motivations perpetrators provide for posting explicit images of another, for example, reported infidelity, to brag, revenge for a reported crime, rejection and many others. Our broad definition implicates some sections of the media such as the paparazzi, and celebrities.

The final section of this chapter looks at who the victims are and the impact of revenge porn. While 90% of victims are reported to be women from teens to thirties, we show that younger and older people do also fall victim. We provide examples where victims have experienced physical and psychological health issues. For example, victims report experiencing humiliation, shame, embarrassment, concerns for personal safety and so on (Lichter, 2013).

Chapter 2 *Responses* is divided into two sections. The first explores the legal and governmental responses to revenge porn. We look at issues related to ownership of the images, in particular, the ownership of photographer, and how that might impact on perpetrator perspectives. Although some revenge porn laws exist, these are not universal and limited to a handful of countries. In countries where they do exist the collection of data is often sparse. While people are now being convicted of this crime, we show that it is still difficult for victims to bring lawsuits or take action against the perpetrators and the host websites.

We examine what resources and support are available to victims, such as the UK government's launch of the Revenge Porn Helpline offering victims free downloadable resources on legislation, how to limit the effects of revenge porn, the use of social media platforms and how to remove images and report offenses. Other not-for-profit organisations such as Woman's Aid, Broken Rainbow and the National Stalking Helpline also provide assistance to victims, including dealing with the fallout of revenge porn. In addition to, and overlapping with, legal and governmental responses, we explore various other responses in the second section. These are largely technological and political responses. Technological responses are shown to be more poster-orientated and more focused on online processes, whereas overtly political responses are shown to focus more on the victim. We also explore some of the campaigns against revenge porn (Penny, 2014), for example, *The Guardian*'s campaign project, 'the web we want' and feminist-led websites fighting revenge porn directly (Johnson, 2013).

In Chapter 3 *Situating revenge porn* we show how revenge porn can be understood from several different traditions and perspectives: (1) revenge porn can be seen as a relatively new form or genre of publicly displayed pornography which coincides with the 'pornografication' (Attwood, 2009) or 'mainstream-ification' (Empel, 2011) of pornography in society; (2) a form of interpersonal revenge, involving, in particular, what motivates people to seek revenge, how they express it and what happens after they act. Revenge can thus be seen as an extension of well-developed strategies and tactics for dealing with, and coping with, emotions and social relations (Yoshimura, 2007). And, as we show in Chapter 1 and Chapters 6–8, revenge can be understood in relation to a variety of motivators, which may include, and be framed in terms of, gender and sexuality, and gender-sexual dynamics; (3) since it tends to be committed by former intimate partners it can be understood as another form of gendered violence and abuse that ranges across femicide, rape, stalking and non-contact harassment (Blumenstein & Jasinski, 2015); (4) given revenge porn is largely facilitated by information and computer technologies, it can be viewed as another part of the multifarious possibilities for virtual/online socialities, sexualities and violences, specifically cyberabuse (Slonje, Smith, & Frisén, 2013); (5) the publicisations of revenge porn notably amongst national newspapers, government ministers and some activists in the United Kingdom. This general perspective might also be seen as an example of a complex, unstable and rhizomic nexus of postings, violations, media interest, law and regulation, and further postings and violations, and so on (Holehouse, 2014) and; (6) revenge porn can also be seen as gendered, gender-sexual, or intersectionally gendered, practices, especially as it is largely the practices of men and masculinities.

Since revenge porn is largely facilitated by online platforms, Chapter 4 *Online interactions* explores how people communicate in cyberspace. We show that people interact on multiple levels such as narrative, interactive, communicative, adaptive and productive, as well through a variety of media such as email, social media, forums and chat rooms. The vast array of ways people can engage with online sources and each other can influence how people present themselves when surfing the web (Tyler & Feldman, 2005). We argue this has important implications for the study of revenge pornography since it allows us to see what motivates people to undertake this activity and how they account for their actions. We explore how people present themselves, which includes discussions around online deception and 'real' identities that mirror offline identities. This chapter concludes with us outlining our position in which we see identities, as co-constructed in interactions regardless of the online or offline medium.

Chapter 5 *A discursive approach to revenge porn* sets out philosophical and methodological position in which we analyse our datasets. Beginning with ethnomethodological enquiry (Garfinkel, 1967), we argue that people perceive social life to be relatively stable in order to make sense of their experiences, even though this stability or certainty does not actually exist in itself. Garfinkel (1991) argued these social 'facts' could be observed and studied through available data on talk and action. The method we draw upon in our analytical chapters is discourse analysis (Potter, 1996), as this method lends itself well to interrogating the online electronic text accompanying the posting of explicit images. We discuss the background to our dataset, our analytical process and steps, concluding with ethical considerations.

We begin our analytical chapters by looking at how heterosexual men account for posting explicit images of others. Chapter 6 *'She took my kids, ruined my life': Heterosexual men's accounts* shows the complex ways in which masculinities, manhood acts, femininities and sexualities are invoked by men to account for their practices. We show the various types of response and, in particular, non-consensual posts. Several emergent masculine discourses were identified in our analysis: intimate relationship control, power over other men, heterosexuality, homosexuality, financial status, power and fatherhood. Our analysis shows that, overall, revenge porn was reported positively as a supposedly equalising action that downplayed any culpability. We conclude this chapter by discussing how these can be understood in the traditions set out in Chapter 3.

Chapter 7 *'Just wants to use you for sex': heterosexual women's accounts* examines women's electronic talk to see how they account for posting explicit images of others. These women claimed the men deserved being posted because they were reported to have been violent, a poor father, a sexual predator (both online and offline), homosexual, effeminate, a liar and not fulfilling their intimate partner sexual duties. We show that many of these reported or alleged misdemeanors are linked, even tied, to and invested in notions of appropriate gender and sexual interactions from a gendered perspective. Similarly, to heterosexual men, women posters tended to frame revenge porn as a positive and legitimate way to reclaim equality.

In Chapter 8 *'...Cheater! liar! thief!': Gay and lesbian accounts*, we examine texts by posters who either self-identified as, or orientated to, gay or lesbian. Five gay and five lesbian texts are analysed and show similarities to heterosexual posts, such as sexual promiscuity and intimate relationship control. There were, however, sexuality-related differences such as challenging someone's 'true' sexuality. For example, some heterosexual posters challenged sexuality as a way to directly abuse (for example, 'he's gay'), whereas some same-sex poster could be seen to challenge their ex-partner's sexuality as a way to deny them group membership (for example, 'pretesbian'). But despite these differences, both heterosexual and same-sex posters worked up accounts in which they, themselves, are positioned as the victim with a legitimate right to seek revenge.

Our ninth chapter *Discussion* summarises the key points made in the previous chapters. This is followed with a discussion on the more general perspectives on revenge porn, and what it is and is not. Incorporating the findings from our analytical chapters, we further develop and contextualise some of the perspectives highlighted in Chapter 3. We argue that the fundamental and recurring issues about how revenge porn violates victims and survivors can be understood in terms of gender and sexual dynamics and constructions, binary gender and sexual positionings and logics and the use of sexual meanings. These we suggest are further complicated by technology, thus revenge porn needs to be placed within the wider context of contemporary socio-technological conditions.

Our final chapter *Future interventions* builds on, and develops, some of the points raised in Chapter 2 about what is being done, and what else might be done, to curb revenge porn. We begin by looking at the effectiveness of current legislative frameworks. While these have clearly had an impact on revenge porn and gender violences more generally, we argue that there should be a more specific focus on online gender and sexuality offences, especially since these are reported to be on the rise. While there is currently a patchwork of laws addressing revenge porn in the United Kingdom and some other countries, this kind of response is far from global. Thus, arguably, laws are required at the regional, national and international levels, since revenge porn can easily cross national boundaries, and include various forms of pornography, as we outline in Chapter 1 (Tyler, 2016). Such laws might apply to both individuals and organisations, and in criminal and civil contexts.

But even with the growth of legal means to either prosecute perpetrators or host websites, or provide the means for victims to bring civil lawsuits, we suggest that more could, and should be done to prevent this crime, for example, including content on national sex and relationship curricula on how to deal with, and appropriately conduct, when relationships end (Eckhardt et al., 2013). Such interventions could help to avoid a lifelong trajectory of violence, either as victims or perpetrators.

We discuss also how support for the victim might be improved. Existing specialist support services could develop protocols of cooperation between themselves and the relevant authorities, for example, by sharing best practices and promoting cooperation and multidisciplinary networking. More could also be done to re-educate perpetrators, especially since criminalisation does not act as a deterrent for all.

We conclude our final chapter by looking at the political aspects of revenge porn: that is, revenge porn is part and parcel of the gender-sexual-violation visual culture. While legislative and technological responses, support for those violated, punishment and re-education for those violating are all positive, it is through broader political and gender-sexual-feminist political action and activism that lasting change is most likely to happen. We suggest this will need to take new forms, given that revenge porn and other online abuses are likely to continue. Thus, we argue that more attention is needed to the future of gender and sexuality as an arena of policy, politics, research and action.

## Notes

1 'Victim' and 'survivor' are at times used interchangeably by some of the sources we draw upon. We recognise that the correct term should be determined by context, and that 'survivor' or 'victim-survivor' is more appropriate than 'victim' in many instances (see Kelly et al., 1996, for a major discussion on this issue in relation to sexual violence more generally).
2 It was reported in July 2017 that police in England and Wales had over the previous three years investigated nearly 400 children under the age of 12 for sexting, including a boy as young as five (Perraudin, *The Guardian*, 12 July 2017).

## References

Attwood, F. (Ed.) (2009). *Mainstreaming sex: The sexualization of Western sex*. London: I.B. Tauris.

Ayas, T., & Horzum, M. B. (2013). Relation between depression, loneliness, self-esteem and internet addiction. *Education*, *133*(3), 283–290.

Aydin B., & Sari, S. V. (2011). Internet addiction among adolescents: The role of self-esteem. *Procedia Social & Behavioral Sciences*, *15*(1), 3500–3505.

Blumenstein, L., & Jasinski, J. L. (2015). Intimate partner assault and structural-level correlates of crime: Exploring the relationship between contextual factors and intimate partner violence. *Criminal Justice Studies*, *28*(2), 186–210.

Brown, C. (1981). Mothers, fathers, and children: from private to public patriarchy. In L. Sargent (Ed.) *Women and revolution: The unhappy marriage of marxism and feminism* (pp. 239–267). New York/London: Maple/Pluto.

Cooper, A., Månsson, S-A., Daneback, K., Tikkanen, R., & Ross, M. W. (2003). Predicting the future of Internet sex: Online sexual activities in Sweden. *Sexual and Relationship Therapy*, *18*(3), 277–291.

Cooper, A., Morahan-Martin, J., Mathy, R., & Maheu, M. (2002). Toward an increased understanding of user demographics in online sexual activities. *Journal of Sex & Marital Therapy*, *28*(2), 105–129.

Cooper, A., Scherer, C. R., Boles, S. C., & Gordon, B. L. (1999). Sexuality on the Internet: From sexual exploration to pathological expression. *Professional Psychological Research*, *30*(2), 154–164.

Daneback, K., & Ross, W. M. (2011). The complexity of internet sexuality. In R. Balon (Ed.), Sexual dysfunction II: Beyond the brain-body connection. *Advances in Psychosomatic Medicine*, *31*, 1–14.

Döring, N. (2009). The Internet's impact on sexuality: A critical review of 15 years of research. *Computers & Human Behavior*, *25*(5), 1089–1101.

Döring, N., Daneback, K., Shaughnessy, K., Grov, C., & Byers, E. B. (2015). Online sexual activity experiences among college students: A four-country comparison. *Archives of Sexual Behavior*, Online December 10, doi:10.1007/s10508-015-0656-4.

Eckhardt, C. I., Murphy, C. M., Whitaker, D. J., Sprunger, J., Dykstra, R., & Woodard, K. (2013). The effectiveness of intervention programs for perpetrators and victims of intimate partner violence. *Partner Abuse*, 4(2), 196–231.

Empel, E. (2011). (XXX) potential impact: The future of the commercial sex industry in 2030. *Manoa: Journal for Fried and Half Fried Ideas (About the Future)*. December. Retrieved November 27, 2014 from www.friedjournal.com/xxxpotential-impact-the-future-of-the-commercial-sex-industry-in-2030.

Findahl, O. (2010). *Svenskarna och internet 2010. [Swedes and the interrnet 2010]*. Stockholm: Stiftelsen för Internetinfrastruktur.

FRA (Fundamental Rights Agency). (2014). *Violence against women: An EU-wide survey.* Vienna: FRA.

Garfinkel, H. (1967). *Studies in ethnomethodology.* Cambridge: Polity Press.

Garfinkel, H. (1991). Respecification: Evidence for locally produced, naturally accountable phenomena of order, logic, reason, meaning, method, etc. in and as of the essential haecceity of immortal ordinary society (I) an announcement of studies. In G. Button, (Ed.), *Ethnomethodology and the human sciences* (pp. 10–19). Cambridge: Cambridge University Press.

Hasinoff, A. A. (2015). *Sexting panic: Rethinking criminalization, privacy, and consent.* Champaign, IL: University of Illinois Press.

Hearn, J. (2006). The implications of information and communication technologies for sexualities and sexualized violences: Contradictions of sexual citizenships. *Political Geography, 25*(8), 944–963.

Hearn, J., & Parkin, W. (2001). *Gender, sexuality and violence in organizations: The unspoken forces of organization violations.* London: Sage.

Holehouse, M. (2014). Cameron backs curbs on revenge pornography. *The Daily Telegraph.* 14 July. Retrieved November 27, 2014 from www.telegraph.co.uk/news/politics/david-cameron/10956790/David-Cameron-backs-crackdown-on-revenge-pornography.html.

Johnson, P. (1996). Pornography drives technology: Why not to censor the Internet, *Federal Communications Law Journal, 49*(1), 217–227.

Johnson, D. (2013). 4 Ways to take a stand against revenge porn. Everydayfeminism.com. December 3. Retrieved August 1 from http://everydayfeminism.com/2013/12/revenge-porn-and-internet-exploitation.

Kelly, L., Burton, S., & Regan, L. (1996). Beyond victim or survivor: Sexual violence, identity and feminist theory and practice. In L. Adkins & V. Merchant (Eds.), *Sexualizing the social: Power and the organization of sexuality* (pp. 77–101). Basingstoke: Palgrave.

Lichter, S. (2013). Unwanted exposure: Civil and criminal liability for revenge porn hosts and posters. JOLT Digest: *Harvard Journal of Law and Technology.* May 28. Retrieved April 4, 2015 from http://jolt.law.harvard.edu/digest/privacy/unwanted-exposure-civil-and-criminal-liability-for-revenge-porn-hosts-and-posters.

Martellozzo, E., Monaghan, A., Adler, J. R., Davidson, J., Leyva, R., & Horvath, M. A. H. (2016). *"I wasn't sure it was normal to watch it": A quantitative and qualitative examination of the impact of online pornography on the values, attitudes, beliefs and behaviours of children and young people.* London: Middlesex University. Retrieved November 22 from www.mdx.ac.uk/__data/assets/pdf_file/0021/223266/MDX-NSPCC-OCC-pornography-report.pdf.

Match.com. (2012). More on sexting and texting from SIA 3. *UpToDate.* February 5. Retrieved February 15, 2016 from http://blog.match.com/2013/02/05/more-on-sexting-and-texting-from-sia-3.

McAfee. (2013). Love, relationships, and technology: How we expose ourselves today. December. Retrieved April 3, 2015 from http://promos.mcafee.com/offer.aspx?id=605366.

Moloney, M. E., & Love, T. P. (2017). # The fappening: Virtual manhood acts in (homo) social media. *Men and Masculinities,* doi:1097184X17696170.

Parker, I. (2014). *Young people, sex and relationships: The new norms.* London: Institute for Public Policy Research.

Parliament.UK. (2015). Criminal Justice and Courts Act 2015. Lords Amendments. November 12. Retrieved April 3, 2015 from www.publications.parliament.uk/pa/bills/cbill/2014–2015/0120/15120.pdf.

Penney, J. (2013). Deleting revenge porn. *Policy Options Politiques*. November. Retrieved August 21, 2015 from http://policyoptions.irpp.org/fr/issues/vive-montreal-libre/penney.

Penny, L. (2014). *Unspeakable things: Sex, lies and revolution*. London: Bloomsbury.

Perraudin, F. (2017). Boy of five among nearly 400 sexting cases dealt with by police. *The Guardian*. 12 July. Retrieved 12 July, 2017 from www.theguardian.com/society/2017/jul/12/sexting-boy-five-400-police-children-explicit-pictures

Potter, J. (1996). *Representing reality: Discourse, rhetoric and social construction*. London: Sage.

Puccio, D., & Havey, A. (2016).*Sex, likes and social media: Talking to our teens in the digital age*. London: Vermilion.

Radhika, S. (2014). Jennifer Lawrence photo leak: Let's stop calling this hacking 'The Fappening'. *The Telegraph*. September 2. Retrieved April 20, 2015 from www.telegraph.co.uk/women/womens-life/11069829/Jennifer-Lawrence-photo-leak-Lets-stop-calling-this-hacking-The-Fappening.html.

Ringrose, J., Gill, R., Livingstone, S., and & Harvey, L. (2012). *A qualitative study of children, young people and sexting*. London: NSPCC.

Ringrose, J., Harvey, L., Gill, R., and Livingstone, S. (2013). Teen girls, sexual double standards and *sexting*: Gendered value in digital image exchange. *Feminist Theory*, *14*(3), 305–323.

Rosen, R. (2010). *Beaver street: A history of modern pornography: From the birth of phone sex to the skin mag in cyberspace: An investigative memoir*. London: Headpress.

Shaughnessy, K., Byers, S. E., & Walsh, L. (2011). Online sexual activity experience of heterosexual students: Gender similarities and differences. *Archives of Sexual Behavior*, *40*(2), 419–427.

Slonje, R., Smith, P. K., & Frisén, A. (2013). The nature of cyberbullying, and strategies for prevention. *Computers in Human Behavior*, *29*(1), 26–32.

Strang, F. (2014). Celebrity 4chan shock naked picture scandal: Full list of star victims preyed upon by hackers. *The Mirror*. September 22. Retrieved May 4, 2015 from www.mirror.co.uk/3am/celebrity-news/celebrity-4chan-shock-naked-picture-4395155.

Sussman, S., Lisha, N., & Griffiths, M. (2011). Prevalence of the addictions: A problem of the majority or the minority? *Evaluation and the Health Professions*, *34*(1): 3–56.

Tyler, J. M., & Feldman, R. S. (2005). Deflecting threat to one's image: Dissembling personal information as a self-presentation strategy. *Basic & Applied Social Psychology*, *27*(4), 371–378.

Tyler, M. (2016). All porn is revenge porn. *Feminist Current*, February 24. Retrieved August 20, 2016 from: http://www.feministcurrent.com/2016/02/24/all-porn-is-revenge-porn/

UK Safer Internet Centre (2015). Revenge Porn Helpline. March 19. Retrieved April 11, 2016 from: http://www.saferinternet.org.uk/news/revenge-porn-helpline.

Wiederhold, B. K. (2016). Low self-esteem and teens' internet addiction: What have we learned in the last 20 years? *Cyberpsychology, Behavior, and Social Networking*, *19*(6), 359.

Yoshimura, S. (2007). Goals and emotional outcomes of revenge activities in interpersonal relationships. *Journal of Social and Personal Relationships*, *24*(1), 87–98.

Young, K. S. (1996). Internet addiction: The emergence of a new clinical disorder. *CyberPsychology & Behavior*, *1*(3), 237–244.

# 1

# MAPPING THE TERRAIN

## What is revenge porn?

Despite the relatively recent media attention, revenge porn has been around for years. The term *revenge pornography*, or its abbreviated colloquial usage, *revenge porn*, appears to have originated in the last decade or so, although people have participated in this activity for some time (Rosen, 2010). For example, the 1980 *Hustler Magazine* started Beaver Hunt, 'a contest that published reader-submitted images of naked women. Beaver Hunt photos were often accompanied by details about the woman: her hobbies, her sexual fantasies, and sometimes her name. Some of the photos were stolen. Exes submitted many more' (Levendowski, 2014, p. 1). According to Levendowski, women sued *Hustler* for publishing their photos without their permission throughout the 1980s. In the 1990s, ex-Olympic figure skater, Tonya Harding, had her video *Tonya and Jeff's Wedding Night* made public by her husband, Jeff, after they split up (Hillyer, 2004, p. 57). In 2000, the Italian researcher Tsoulis-Reay (2013) identified a new genre of pornography where explicit pictures of ex-girlfriends were being shared in Usenet groups.[1] Yet a search of the newspaper archive Nexis indicates that the term 'revenge pornography' appears to have been first used in the mass media by Richard Morgan in the magazine *Dossier* (2008).

Online, the term first seems to have appeared a year earlier in the Urban Dictionary (2007). JonasOooohyeah (a user's pseudonym) defined it as 'Home-made porn uploaded by an ex-girlfriend or (usually) ex-boyfriend after parti-cularly vicious breakup as a means of humiliating the ex or just for own amusement.' What is immediately noticeable in JonasOooohyeah's definition is that pornography is classified as amateur, 'Homemade': it's mainly com-mitted by men and boys 'ex-girlfriend or (usually) ex-boyfriend'; it happens outside a relationship 'after particularly vicious breakup'; and the motivations for doing so are 'a means of humiliating the ex or just for own amusement'. However, the non-consensual aspect of revenge porn is only implicit in this definition. Yet other definitions do incorporate this; for example, Dictionary.com (2015) defines the act as 'sexually suggestive images of someone, typically a former romantic partner that are posted online or otherwise shared without the person's consent'. Arguably, a strength of this definition is that pornography is broadened from sexually explicit material to 'sexually suggestive images' thus potentially capturing more forms of Internet crime such as cyberstalking (see Weisskirch & Delevi, 2011, p. 1697). What is only implied is the perpetrator's motivation, as in 'typically a former romantic partner'. We do get a sense from the inclusion of 'typically' that revenge porn might not only be committed by ex-partners. Similar definitions are offered by other organisations, such as

- the UK Safer Internet Centre (2015): 'Revenge Porn is a term used to describe sexually explicit media that is publicly shared online without the consent of the pictured individual';
- the Speech Project (2016): *Cyber-exploitation, Nonconsensual Photography or 'Revenge Porn'*: 'The distribution of sexually graphic images without the consent of the subject of the images. The abuser obtains images or videos in the course of a prior relationship, or hacks into the victim's computer, social media accounts or phone';
- the UK Criminal Justice and Courts Act (2015): 'revenge porn – usually following the breakup of a couple, the electronic publication or distribution of sexually explicit material (principally images) of one or both of the couple, the material having originally been provided consensually for private use' (Parliament.UK, 2015); and
- the US National Conference of State Legislatures (2014): 'the posting of nude or sexually explicit photographs or videos of people online without their consent, even if the photograph itself was taken with consent. It can follow a spurned spouse, girlfriend, or boyfriend seeking to get revenge by uploading photographs to websites, many of which are set up specifically for these kinds of photos or videos'.

At the time of writing, September 2016, there is no definition of 'revenge pornography' or 'revenge porn' in the *Oxford English Dictionary*.

Combining these provides us with a more comprehensive definition of the revenge pornography act (non-consensual), mode of pornography (mostly homemade sexually suggestive or explicit images and/or videos, but also includes those commercially produced), perpetrators (largely male ex-partners), victims (predominantly female ex-partners) and context (post-relationship revenge, but also including hacking and commercial pornography), location of the act (online largely from offline practices) and motivations (revenge, entertainment or political motive).

It should be noted, at this point, that sexually suggestive or explicit images and videos of someone do not need to be of the person in question. For example, in 2014 a woman from Houston, Texas, began a lawsuit against her ex-partner for superimposing images of her head onto naked body shots of someone else and posting them on Facebook as if they were 'really' her (Mazza, 2014). This suggests that one can become a victim of revenge porn despite never having participated in the production of sexually explicit material. Thus, any definition needs to incorporate the experiences of victims and the motivations of perpetrators as well as types of perpetrator such ex-partners, current partners, ex-friends, people known to the victim, others distributing others' revenge posts and Internet hackers, both as individuals or as groups such as 'human flesh search groups'[2] (Citron & Franks, 2014; Lyons et al., 2016, p. 1; Stroud, 2014; Tungate, 2014). Thus, in this book we refer to revenge porn as the online and offline non-consensual distribution, or sharing, of genuine or fake explicit images of someone else by ex-partners, partners, others or hackers in order to seek revenge, for entertainment or for political motives.

## The problem of naming

In this book, we generally use the term 'revenge porn', as these are the most well-used words to describe the phenomena and actions under examination. However, we need to state early on an important major caveat to this analysis, namely, that the terms 'revenge porn' and 'revenge pornography' are themselves open to severe critique. This is made clear by Franks:

> The term "revenge porn" is misleading in two respects. First, perpetrators are not always being motivated by vengeance. Many act out of a desire for profit, notoriety, or entertainment, including hackers, purveyors of hidden or "upskirt" camera recordings, and people who distribute stolen cellphone photos. The term "revenge porn" is also misleading in that it implies that taking a picture of oneself naked or engaged in a sexual act (or allowing someone else to take such a picture) is pornographic. But creating explicit images in the expectation within the context of a private, intimate relationship – an increasingly common practice[3] – is not equivalent to creating pornography. The act of disclosing a private, sexually explicit image to someone other than the intended audience, however, can accurately be described as pornographic, as it transforms a private image into public sexual entertainment.
>
> *(Franks, 2016, p. 2)*

For these reasons, there is a strong case for using the term 'non-consensual pornography', or even often the more elaborated 'online non-consensual pornography for the purposes of revenge', even though the purposes may not always be clearly for revenge or solely for revenge, but rather for other reasons and motivations. Other namings and framings include: cyber-exploitation, hate speech and hate crime.

In addition, another broader set of arguments disputes the specificity of revenge porn, and instead argues that all pornography is revenge porn (Tyler, 2006). Furthermore, some feminists and gender activists argue against both labels: 'revenge pornography' and 'pornography'. For example, in the project on online violence against women organised by the Women's Rights Association in Iceland, the survivors of 'revenge porn' oppose the use of the words, as they felt it was degrading to talk about such acts of violence as pornography. This suggests that the very labelling and naming itself elaborates and extends the violating actions initially into language use, and then beyond into further social degradation. Thus, in using the term 'revenge porn', we do so throughout, in a sense, in inverted commas, as the cultural reference that it has become, not as a distinct analytical or political category.

## Revenge porn websites

Revenge porn can appear in various different online and offline locations and formats. Unsurprisingly, it can be found on pornographic websites such as Cliphunter, Xvideos and PornHub that allow the uploading of amateur personal images and videos, as well as specific revenge porn sites such as Anonymous Image Board; Expic Net; Ex-Girlfriend Pictures, MyEx.com, My Fucking Ex-Girlfriend and Revenge Porn Net. There are also some women-specific sites that include revenge porn, such as 'She's A Homewrecker' (http://shesahomewrecker.com/), which features individual women who are alleged to have, usually deliberately, broken up previous marriages and relationships. However, non-consensual sexually explicit material can also be found on more mainstream platforms, such as Facebook and Tumblr, although there seems to be a move by some of these large organisations to tackle this problem. Until recently, Twitter also hosted revenge porn specific pages, 'Twitter bans revenge porn and vows to stop pervert stalkers publishing their victims' home addresses' (Hamill, 2015, *The Mirror*, March 12). Non-consensual category specific websites are also available for groups such as older mothers (colloquially known as MILF) *SubmitYourMom* (www.submityourmom.com/) and girlfriends/wives *PsVoyeurOfWives* (http://psvoyeurofwives.tumblr.com/).

There are also other media for the creation and distribution of revenge porn: some are close relations to bespoke sites, such as cheating sites; some in the process of rapid change and development; some not so new forms of media, for example, a man was found guilty of auctioning a CD with his ex-partner's naked images on eBay (Miller, *Miami New Times*, 2013). And increasingly, there are multiple linkages and convergences between e-media: for example, Internet via mobile telephones; interactive television with Internet, video-chat and telephone; tablets with Internet access, video distribution; audio-visual communication on the Internet and so on. Thus, revenge porn can circulate with ease and speed.

While a significant amount of revenge porn happens online, the explosion of 'sexting' (DoSomething.org, 2015; GuardChild.com, 2015; Hasinoff, 2015) means images and videos can be circulated solely by texting, or shown to others in the perpetrators' and victims' social circles in person by electronic devices. Indeed, the Internet security company McAfee (2013) found more than 50% of adults shared sexually explicit material through their mobile devices, about 50% also said they stored these images online and 16% said they had shared sexually explicit images and videos with complete strangers. Apparently, one in ten ex-partners have threated to expose risqué images online, and 60% of those who threatened this course of action carried out their threat. It appears from examining the various websites hosting revenge porn that the vast majority of victims and perpetrators reside in the more developed nations of Europe, North America and Australasia and in particular the United States and the United Kingdom. However, revenge porn can also be found in smaller quantities for those reported to be living in the Asian, South American and African countries as dispersed as Armenia, Belize, Bahrain, Ecuador, Guam, Ghana, India, Pakistan, Malaysia, Thailand, South Africa, and so on.

Revenge porn is popular. Hunter Moore's notorious website IsAnybodyUp, before being closed down by the anti-bullying organisation, BullyVille, in April 2012, averaged between 150,000 and 240,000 unique page views per day (Dodero, 2012, April 4). The site received approximately 35,000 submissions of photo content each week, although 50% of these were claimed to be consensual (Hill, 2012). Even after Hunter had sold the website to BullyVille he still received submissions for use on Twitter and Tumblr. The popularity of this revenge porn site is mirrored by what is currently the largest revenge porn website, MyEx.com. The Internet monitoring and analytic web organisation, Alexa (2016, August 30, p. 1), ranks MyEx.com as 22,023 in the United States and 41,789 in the world, up 9,223 places on the previous year. The top five visitor locations are the United States 36.6%, United Kingdom 16.6%, India 14.2%, Canada 7.5% and Austria 5.9%, suggesting that the website has global interest. The majority of visits are by men from their home or work, and more than half of these men are reported to be educated to college level or higher. The statistics and analytics service Hype Stat (2016, September 1, p. 1) claim My Ex.com 'receives about 7,400 unique visitors and 153,180 (20.70 per visitor) page views per day'.

Revenge porn can also be highly lucrative, for some. Hunter Moore, who was arrested for running the site 'IsAnyoneUp' was claimed to have been earning between $8,000 and $30,000 per month in advertising revenue (Stroud, 2014). 'Revenge porn sites such as SeeMyGF or MyEx charge $100 a year to access private photos and videos of non-porn stars, almost invariably women, usually posted by spurned ex-lovers' (Tynan, *The Guardian*, April 26, 2016). According to Tynan (2016), this is only one part of a much larger story in which every adult site appears to have an entire ecosystem supporting it. For example, organisations such as domain registrars and web hosting services get financial rewards for their services. Indeed, Tynan (2016, p. 1) argues that 'Scores of businesses routinely scrape law enforcement sites for mugshots of recent arrestees, republish them, then charge $400 or more to remove them'.

Many websites demand fees for 'take-down services.' UGotPosted.com site and changemyreputation.com owner, San Diego resident Kevin Bollaert, was recently convicted on 27 felony counts of identity theft and extortion, and given an 18-year prison sentence for charging victims to have their images removed from his revenge porn website (Collier, *The Daily Dot*, February 3, 2015; Associated Press in San Diego, *The Guardian*, April 4, 2015). He had published more than 10,000 nude photos on his first website, linked them to the women's social media accounts, and then directed them to his second website, where he charged them $350 or more to have the images expunged (Tynan, *The Guardian*, April 26, 2016), as part of so-called 'sextortion'.

Companies and sites such as Reputation Stars, Remove My Name, and Online Defamation Defenders offer to remove negative material more generally for between a few hundred and a few thousand dollars: 'Reputation Repair charges $1,459 for "expedited removal" from cheater sites and "future attack prevention"' (ibid.). MyEx.com currently charges $500 take-down fees, helping to make it worth an estimated $450,000 (Alexa, 2016). Many revenge porn websites also charge viewers. Revenge Porn Net charges for membership. A two-day trial membership costs $1.95, a 1-month membership is $24.95, a 3-month membership is $49.95 and a 6-month membership costs $57.50 (www.revengeporn.net/home.html). UGotPosted.com was also reported to be receiving $900 per month from advertising (Collier, *The Daily Dot*, February 3, 2015).

## Who posts revenge porn?

Although male ex-partners are reported to be the main perpetrators (McAfee, 2013), an examination of electronic text on currently the largest revenge porn site MyEx.com shows current partners, (ex)friends of both victims and perpetrators, people known to the victim, complete strangers and Internet hackers are also involved. For example, Kayla Law took revealing photos of herself for her eyes only and sent them to her own email. However, her email was hacked, and the pictures were posted online (Honeywood, *The Current*, 2014). Some of the reasons reported by those were posting sexually explicit images of others include:

- *apathy*: 'Just an ex thought I'd show his small dick to the world!';
- *bragging*: 'The Best Shag I have ever had, dirty, will do anything x';
- *cheated on*: 'She cheated on me several times';
- *conned*: 'This guy is slimy piece of shit that uses girls for their money';
- *exposing*: 'not an ex, just someone I know':
- *genital size*: 'Guy with baby dick';
- *immorality*: 'She took my kids, ruined my life';
- *rating*: 'my hubby's small dick what do you ladies think';
- *recognition*: 'An old friend of mine';

- *regret*: 'The sex was awful, I was able to pleasure myself more with a cocktail sausage';
- *reminiscing*: 'Would love to sleep with her again';
- *retribution*: 'He went to prison for attacking me, cracking my head open, and fracturing a rib';
- *romantic intentions*: 'Pretends he cares but fucks women on pof all the time';
- *payback*: 'Payback to a closetted gay cocksucker who posted me';
- *providing a service*: 'Her friends all wanted to see these';
- *sharing*: 'I'm sharing her with you guys, but please don't tell her about this post';
- *trolling*: 'Another Silly Model using her Real Name on her profile!'; and
- *unsafe sex*: 'likes nothing more than to meet as many guys as possible from (identifier omitted) and other apps usually asking for Bareback sex'.

Other examples include people seeking revenge for their friends, posting images of someone interested in one's current partner, someone finding images and sharing them and friends sharing explicit images for entertainment.

Our broad definition implicates some sections of the media such as the paparazzi. For example, the Duchess of Cambridge had her naked breasts photographed and circulated by some international media outlets (Moore, *Mail Online*, 2012). Indeed, there have been several other high-profile celebrity victims, including Prince Harry (*The Mirror*, 2012); *Twilight* actor Kiowa Gordon (Chen, *Gawker*, 2012); *Hunger Games* film star Jennifer Lawrence (Glenza, 2014); and the singer–songwriter, actress and television personality Tulisa Contostavlos. Conversely, the celebrities have also been accused of revenge porn. For example, in 2014 the wife of former NFL player Jeffrey Roehl filed a lawsuit seeking damages for him uploading explicit images of her on several websites (CBS Chicago, 2014). Singer Curtis Jackson (stage name 50 Cent) stood trial in June 2015 for allegedly uploading a video of Rick Ross's former partner Lastonia Leviston having sex with ex-partner Maurice Murray. The video is reported to have been watched by 3.2 million people worldwide (Nianias, 2015).

## The impact of revenge porn

The negative impact revenge porn has on its victims is significant and profound in terms of physical and psychological health and well-being, as is the case with many other forms of violence and abuse. There is, however, an additional complication with online revenge porn that, in some cases at least, there is an element of *not knowing* what has been done, where the images or text have been placed and replicated. This follows as some posting is done to be viewed by the victim, the postee, while some is directed more to friends and acquaintances, or even a more diffuse, unknown and imagined audience.

The online survey 'Effects of Revenge Porn' conducted in 2013 by Cyber Civil Rights Initiative and EndRevengePorn.org (Cyber Civil Rights Initiative, 2014; Franks, 2016) found that 90% of victims are women. As one might expect, given the increase in 'sexting' – sending sexually explicit photographs or messages via mobile phone (DoSomething.org, 2015; GuardChild.com, 2015; Hasinoff, 2015) – the typical age group is teens to thirties. However, there are reports of victims as young as 11 (Ridely, *Huffington Post UK*, 2015). A scan of the 30 or so UK websites hosting revenge porn (BBC, 2014a) also showed people who appear to be, or are reported to be, older – that is, older than middle-aged.

Victims of revenge porn report a host of negative effects. Pointing out the majority of victims are women, the former UK culture secretary Maria Miller said, 'When you speak to the victims of these crimes, many say that it feels as if you've been virtually raped' (BBC, 2015). Similar words are echoed on several online sites such as NoBullying.com, WithoutMyConsent.org, EndRevengePorn.org, The Mary Byron Project and others. Victims report experiencing various problems, including humiliation, shame and embarrassment with intimate partners, family, friends, work colleagues and in public; sexual shame and sexual problems; body image issues; education and employment disruptions; concerns for personal safety; becoming paranoid and hyper-vigilant and having trust issues. Lichter's (2013, p. 1) study of the revenge porn legislation found that victims had experienced 'embarrassment, reputation ruination' and some had also faced stalking, harassment and threats of being gang raped because their personal information was also out in the public domain. Indeed, some victims had taken their own life. As a consequence, some victims had 'resorted to changing their names and phone numbers'.

A victim with the username 'my_ex_is_a_dick' explains how devastating revenge porn can be:

> When I was married, my then husband and I made a homemade porn. I thought it was a good idea at the time and I was very wrong. Not too long after we made said porn, I found out he had been cheating and I left him. I had completely forgot that we had even had a video until a co-worker came to me and said he got a very interesting email from my ex (they were friends) and showed me the link. That f\*\*king asshole uploaded the video to porn site. He sent the link to everyone we know, including family. I was completely mortified to find out he had done this. Needless to say, I had to quit my job and move back to my home province. I was being harassed at my job (I worked in a factory, it was mostly men that worked there). I couldn't bear to see or hang out with any of my friends.
>
> *(Reddit, 2014)*

A 24-year-old victim, Anisha, talking on BBC *Newsbeat* (2014b) says when her boyfriend asked her to take some photos of her naked, she trusted him when he said he would be the only person to see them. After their relationship ended he posted them on a couple of websites, and now they are on over 200 websites across the globe. She says people recognise her in public and turn up at her door as well as contact her by phone, text messages, emails and through Facebook claiming they have spoken to her when it was her ex whom they had spoken to. She now struggles to find a job because an employer can see the images of her from a simple Google search. Even when victims have attempted to switch schools, move to another community and try therapy, they may remain taunted like Nova Scotia teenager Rehtaeh, who eventually took her own life (Thanh Ha & Taber, *The Globe and Mail*, 2013). Anisha talking on BBC *Newsbeat* (2014b) points out, experiences can be amplified if the perpetrator also provides the victim's personal information along with their images, also known as 'doxing'.[4]

McAfee's (2013) survey research found 2% of victims had their social security number made public; 14% had their work address and 16% their home address posted with their images. A further 26% of posts included their email address, while 49% had social media information and further 59% also include the victim's full name. Other information provided to the notorious IsAnyoneUp included profession, social media profile and city of residence (Stroud, 2014). In providing this information viewers are then able to crowdsource[5] the contact information for the victim and victim's family, friends, boss and colleagues before forwarding them the images and image hyperlinks and making contact with the victim (Goldberg, 2014).

While victims report devastating and life-altering effects, increasing numbers of victims are reported to have either felt suicidal (Britton, *Macclesfield Express,* December, 17, 2014) or committed suicide as a result. For example, the California teenager Audrie Pott was sexually assaulted while passed out drunk at a party. Naked photos of her were then circulated around school and online before she took her own life (Plank, *Huffington Post*, 2013). Other suicide cases include a Brazilian woman after a sex tape of her with a male and female friend was posted online (Berger, *BuzzFeed News*, 2013). The Canadian teenager Amanda Todd also took her own life after being blackmailed by a Dutch man into videoing herself naked. She then faced harassment after he posted the video on YouTube, which was reported to have been watched by millions around the world (Keneally, *Mail Online*, 2012). Indeed, some perpetrators are reported to aim for their victim's suicide (Examiner.com, 2015).

One reason that victims report feeling isolated is that many people blame them for allowing the photos and videos to be taken (BBC, 2014c). Such sentiment is easily viewed on webpages where victims have been posted or talk about their experiences. For example, responding to revenge porn victim Anisha talking about her experiences on BBC *Newsbeat* (2014b), people have said,

> It is your fault…you sent the pictures, and you should have known what would happen when you broke up.
>
> There's no protection against being immorally STUPID!

Some readers responding to the *Daily Mail*'s (2014) article about Hunter Moore said,

> I really feel bad for the women who have their photos leaked but this should be a huge lesson. Don't under any circumstances let anyone take photos or videos of you naked or performing sex acts. Once it ever gets out

there is no going back! Unless you are a vile person like Kim Kardashian it will be devastating.

The moral: Don't put nude pictures of yourself on your computer idiots!!!!!

These types of sentiments mirror common public perceptions of victim blaming and culpability in rape, sexual assault, sexual harassment and domestic abuse cases in which the victim is often blamed rather than the culprit (see Franks, 2013; Citron & Franks, 2014). In light of such perceptions, organisations such as EndRevengePorn.org (www.endrevengeporn.org/help-us-educate-the-public/) aim to tackle these through their public outreach programmes, which aim to encourage victims and their families to anonymously tell their stories so that others might think twice before participating. Individuals' experiences reported in the media contribute to changing public perceptions. Others such as Scottish Women's Aid (www.scottishwomensaid.org.uk/node/4592) advocate the inclusion of revenge porn in sex education programmes. They believe in providing guidance on what a healthy relationship looks like and what is appropriate conduct when a relationship ends. An additional way of discouraging others from engaging with revenge porn is to make it illegal. We discuss additional measures in more detail in our final chapter. We now examine some of the current legislation and other governmental responses that have been developed to deal with this crime.

## Notes

1 Usenet groups are worldwide computer-based distributed discussion systems. Users read and post messages to categories, known as groups or newsgroups. They resemble bulletin boards and are early versions of Internet forums.
2 Human flesh search groups use the Web to identify and expose individuals in order to publicly humiliate them. This has been termed as a form of online vigilantism.
3 In a 2014 survey of 1,100 New Yorkers, nearly half (45%) reported that they had recorded themselves having sex. *New York Post*, New Yorkers Reveal What Their Sex Lives Are Really Like, September 3, 2014.
4 Also, termed 'doxing' – the Web-based practice of the non-consensual broadcasting of private or identifiable information about a person.
5 Crowdsourcing is the process of obtaining content by soliciting financial contributions from a large group of people, and especially from an online community.

## References

Alexa. (2016). How popular is myex.com? August 30. Retrieved September 1 from www.alexa.com/siteinfo/myex.com.

Associated Press in San Diego. (2015). Revenge porn website operator jailed. *The Guardian*. April 4. Retrieved April 7, 2015 from www.theguardian.com/us-news/2015/apr/04/revenge-porn-website-operator-jailed.

BBC. (2014a). Is revenge porn already illegal in England? December 28. Retrieved April 10, 2015 from www.bbc.co.uk/news/uk-england-30308942.

BBC. (2014b). Revenge porn victim: I trusted him, now I'm on 200 sites. *Newsbeat*. April 3. Retrieved April 2, 2015 from www.bbc.co.uk/newsbeat/26852254.

BBC. (2014c). Revenge porn victim speaks out. April 3. Retrieved April 7, 2015 from www.youtube.com/watch?v=z6zAWWvwE5I.

BBC. (2015). 'Revenge porn' illegal under new law in England and Wales. February 15. Retrieved April 7, 2015 from www.bbc.co.uk/news/uk-31429026.

Berger, M. (2013). Brazilian 17-year-old commits suicide after revenge porn posted online. *BuzzFeed News*. November 20. Retrieved April 7, 2015 from www. buzzfeed.com/miriamberger/brazilian-17-year-old-commits-suicide-after-revenge-porn-pos#.ub79oaJLZ.

Britton, K. (2014). Woman left suicidal after 'revenge porn' style attack. *Macclesfield Express*. December 17. Retrieved September 1, 2016 from www.macclesfield-express.co.uk/news/local-news/woman-left-suicidal-after-revenge-8299561.

CBS Chicago. (2014). Suit: Former NFL player published explicit images of ex-wife without permission. March 4. Retrieved April 8, 2015 from http://chicago.cbslocal.com/2014/03/04/suit-former-nfl-player-published-explicit-images-of-ex-wife-without-permission/.

Chen, A. (2012). Did a *Twilight* star's penis pic shut down is anyone up? *Gawker*. April 23. Retrieved April 7, 2015 from http://gawker.com/5904343/did-a-twilight-stars-penis-pic-shut-down-is-anyone-up.

Citron, D. K., & Franks, M. A. (2014). Criminalizing revenge porn. *Wake Forest Law Review, 2014*(1), 345–391.

Collier, K. (2015). California man faces 20 years in historic revenge-porn conviction. *The Daily Dot*. February 3. Retrieved September 1 from www.dailydot.com/layer8/you-got-posted-revenge-porn-bust-felony-extortion/.

Cyber Civil Rights Initiative. (2014). Victims' stories. January 27. Retrieved September 1, 2016 from www.cybercivilrights.org/page/5/?s=revenge+porn.

*Daily Mail*. (2014). 'Most hated man on the Internet' busted on federal identity theft charges after 'paying hacker to steal naked photos' for his 'revenge porn' website. January 23. Retrieved April 7, 2015 from www.dailymail.co.uk/news/article-2544968/Most-hated-man-Internet-busted-federal-identity-theft-charges-paying-hacker-steal-naked-photos-revenge-porn-website.html#ixzz3WczW8oUl.

Dictionary.com. (2015). Revenge porn. Retrieved April 4, 2015 from www. dictionary.com/browse/revenge-porn?s=t.

Dodero, C. (2012). Bullyville has taken over Hunter Moore's is anyone up? *Village Voice*. April 19. Retrieved April 8, 2015 from http://blogs.villagevoice.com/runninscared/2012/04/bullyville_isanyoneup.php.

DoSomething.org. (2015). 11 facts about sexting. Retrieved April 5, 2015 from www. dosomething.org/facts/11-facts-about-sexting.

Examiner.com. (2015). Mich. man sentenced for revenge porn photos of ex, wanted her to commit suicide. January 14. Retrieved April 7, 2015 from www.examiner.com/article/mich-man-sentenced-for-revenge-porn-photos-of-ex-wanted-her-to-commit-suicide.

Franks, M. A. (2013). Adventures in victim blaming: Revenge porn edition. *Concurring Opinions* February 1. https://concurringopinions.com/archives/2013/02/adventures-in-victim-blaming-revenge-porn-edition.html.

Franks, M. A. (2016). Drafting an effective 'revenge porn' law: A guide for legislators. *Cyber Civil Rights Initiative*. Retrieved March 19, 2017 from www.cybercivilrights .org/guide-to-legislation/.

Glenza, J. (2014). Jennifer Lawrence denounces nude photos hack as 'sex crime'. *The Guardian*. October 7. Retrieved November 27, 2014 from www.theguardian.com/film/2014/oct/07/jennifer-lawrence-nude-photo-hack-sex-crime.

Goldberg, M. (2014). Revenge porn is malicious and reprehensible: But should it be a crime? *The Nation*. October 1. Retrieved April 5, 2015 from www.thenation.com/article/181829/war-against-revenge-porn.

GuardChild.com. (2015). Teenage sexting statistics. Retrieved April 5, 2015 from www.guardchild.com/teenage-sexting-statistics/.

Hamill, J. (2015). Twitter bans revenge porn and vows to stop pervert stalkers publishing their victims' home addresses. *Mirror*. March 12. Retrieved April 5, 2015 from www.mirror.co.uk/news/technology-science/technology/twitter-bans-revenge-porn-vows-5318025.

Hasinoff, A. A. (2015). *Sexting panic: Rethinking criminalization, privacy, and consent*. Champaign, IL: University of Illinois Press.

Hill, K. (2012). Why we find Hunter Moore and his "identity porn" site, is anyone up, so fascinating. *Forbes*. April 5. Retrieved April 8, 2015 from www.forbes.com/sites/kashmirhill/2012/04/05/hunter-moore-of-isanyoneup-wouldntmind-making-some-money-off-of-a-suicide/.

Hillyer, M. (2004). Sex in the suburban: Porn, home movies and the live action performance of love in *Pam and Tommy Lee: Hardcore and Uncensored*. In L. Williams (Ed.) *Porn studies*. (pp. 50–77). Durham: Duke University Press.

Honeywood, N. (2014). Revenge porn. *The Current*. May 12. Retrieved April 7, 2015 from www.arcurrent.com/top-stories/2014/05/12/revenge-porn.

Hype Stat. (2016). Myex.Com – Info. Retrieved September 1 from http://myex.com.hypestat.com.

Keneally, M. (2012). Tragedy as girl, 15, kills herself just one month after posting desperate YouTube plea begging bullies to stop tormenting her. *Daily Mail*. October 12. Retrieved September 1, 2016 from www.dailymail.co.uk/news/article-2216543/Amanda-Todd-Canadian-teen-kills-desperate-video-plea-begging-bullies-stop.html.

Levendowski, A. (2014). Our best weapon against revenge porn: Copyright law? *The Atlantic*. February 4. Retrieved September 1 from www.theatlantic.com/technology/archive/2014/02/our-best-weapon-against-revenge-porn-copyright-law/283564/.

Lichter, S. (2013). Unwanted exposure: Civil and criminal liability for revenge porn hosts and posters. *JOLT Digest: Harvard Journal of Law and Technology*. May 28. Retrieved April 4, 2015 from http://jolt.law.harvard.edu/digest/privacy/unwanted-exposure-civil-and-criminal-liability-for-revenge-porn-hosts-and-posters.

Lyons, K., Phillips, T., Walker, S., Henley, J., Farrell, P., & Carpentier, M. (2016). Online abuse: How different countries deal with it. *The Guardian*. April 12. Retrieved October 15 from www.theguardian.com/technology/2016/apr/12/online-abuse-how-harrassment-revenge-pornography-different-countries-deal-with-it?CMP=share_btn_link.

Mazza, E. (2014). Facebook sued for $123 million over 'revenge porn'. *Huffington Post*. July 30. Retrieved April 20, 2016 from www.huffingtonpost.com/2014/07/30/facebook-sued-over-revenge-porn_n_5632865.html.

McAfee. (2013). Love, relationships, and technology: How we expose ourselves today. Retrieved April 3, 2015 from http://promos.mcafee.com/offer.aspx?id=605366.

Miller, M. E. (2013). Revenge porn victim Holly Jacobs "Ruined My Life," Ex Says. *Miami New Times*. October 17. Retrieved April 5, 2015 from www.miaminewtimes.com/news/revenge-porn-victim-holly-jacobs-ruined-my-life-ex-says-6393654.

Moore, S. (2012). A princess's breasts are NOT for leering at (and neither are anybody else's). *The Daily Mail.* September 16. Retrieved April 5, 2015 from www.dailymail.co.uk/debate/article-2203949/Kate-Middleton-topless-photos-The-Duchess-Cambridges-breasts-NOT-leering-at.html#ixzz3WqdZdZeb.

Morgan, R. (2008). Jilted lovers are posting sex tapes on the Web—And their exes want justice. *Dossier, 96*(27), 96.

my_ex_is_a_dick. (2014). Those who have naked pictures on the internet; how did they get there and how has it affected your life? *AskReddit.* Retrieved March 28, 2017 from www.reddit.com/r/AskReddit/comments/1upmim/those_who_have_naked_pictures_on_the_internet_how/ceknbt0/.

Nianias, H. (2015). 50 Cent given court date for allegedly uploading a revenge porn video of Rick Ross' ex-girlfriend to YouTube. *The Independent.* March 17. Retrieved April 8, 2015 from www.independent.co.uk/news/people/50-cent-given-court-date-for-allegedly-uploading-a-revenge-porn-video-of-rick-ross-ex-girlfriend-to-youtube-10114018.html.

Parliament.UK. (2015). Criminal Justice and Courts Act 2015. *Lords Amendments.* November 12. Retrieved April 3, 2015 from www.publications.parliament.uk/pa/bills/cbill/2014-2015/0120/15120.pdf.

Plank, E. (2013). Audrie Pott rape: Viral rape is trending, and we should all be very worried. *Huffington Post.* April 13. Retrieved September 1, 2016 from www.huffingtonpost.co.uk/elizabeth-plank/rape-viral_b_3076545.html.

Ridely, L. (2015). Revenge porn victims are children as young as 11, new figures reveal. *Huffington Post.* September 30. Retrieved April 5, 2015 from www.huffingtonpost.co.uk/2014/09/30/revenge-porn-children_n_5905554.html.

Rosen, R. (2010). *Beaver street: A history of modern pornography: From the birth of phone sex to the skin mag in cyberspace: An investigative memoir.* London: Headpress.

Speech Project (2016). Online abuse 101. Retrieved September 1 from http://wmcspeechproject.com/online-abuse-101/#cyber_exploitation.

Stroud, S. R. (2014). The dark side of the online self: A pragmatist critique of the growing plague of revenge porn. *Journal of Mass Media Ethics: Exploring Questions of Media Morality, 9*(3), 168–183.

Thanh Ha, T., & Taber, J. (2013). Bullying blamed in death of Nova Scotia teen. *The Globe and Mail.* April 9. Retrieved April 3, 2015 from www.theglobeandmail.com/news/national/bullying-blamed-in-death-of-nova-scotia-teen/article10940600/.

*The Mirror.* (2012). Naked Harry photos. August. Retrieved April 5, 2015 from www.mirror.co.uk/all-about/prince-harry-naked-pictures.

Tsoulis-Reay, A. (2013). Brief history of revenge porn. *New York Magazine.* Retrieved August 23, 2015 from http://nymag.com/news/features/sex/revenge-porn-2013-7/.

Tungate, A. (2014)._Bare necessities: The argument for a 'revenge porn' exception in Section 230 immunity. *Information & Communications Technology Law, 23*(2), 172–188.

Tyler, M. (2016). All porn is revenge porn. *Feminist Current,* February 24. Retrieved August 20, 2016 from www.feministcurrent.com/2016/02/24/all-porn-is-revenge-porn.

Tynan, D. (2016). Revenge porn: The industry profiting from online abuse: Sites charge $100 a year to access private photos and videos of non-porn stars in the nude, usually posted by spurned ex-lovers – but it doesn't end there. *The Guardian.* April 26. Retrieved September 1 from www.theguardian.com/technology/2016/apr/26/revenge-porn-nude-photos-online-abuse.

UK Safer Internet Centre. (2015). Revenge porn helpline. March 19. Retrieved April 11, 2016 from www.saferinternet.org.uk/news/revenge-porn-helpline.

Urban Dictionary. (2007). Revenge porn. September 25. Retrieved April 4, 2015 from www.urbandictionary.com/define.php?term=revenge%20porn&utm_source=search-action.

US National Conference of State Legislature. (2014). Revenge porn. Retrieved April 4, 2015 from www.ncsl.org/research/telecommunications-and-information-technology/state-revenge-porn-legislation.

Weisskirch, R. S., & Delevi, R. (2011). 'Sexting' and adult romantic attachment. *Computers in Human Behavior, 27*(5), 1697–1701.

# 2

## RESPONSES

### Legal and governmental[1]

Clearly, there are a variety of motivations for revenge porn, such as for commercial profit, increasing peer status, revenge, entertainment, opportunity, empowerment, and so on. Yet what underlies all revenge porn is that, in law, those who *take* the photographs and videos own them. This right is lawful. The UK Intellectual Property Office (2014) and the US Constitution and the Federal Copyright Act (2011) both state that the author of the image – the person who took the photo – retains copyright and as such can do what they wish with the     photograph even if the person in the photo or video does not consent to this. One US survey indicated that 80% of revenge porn victims took the pictures in question themselves, thus giving them the legal rights to the photographs in question (Johnson, 2013).

Many websites offering take-down services such as MyEx.com state, 'Send us the copyright registration number that you received from the copy right office after you registered the photos. If you do not have a copy right registration number we will ignore your emails' (MyEx.com, 2015: www.myex.com/faq/). We wonder what the probability is of a couple seeking joint copyright after taking sexually explicit images and photographs? In the United States, the Digital Millennium Copyright Act of 1998 (DMCA) means that victims can submit a DMCA 'take-down' request to offending websites that are using their photographs without consent. The rights protection group DMCA Defender provides relatively low-cost services to victims seeking assistance to submit a claim. Photographer ownership right claims can be viewed quite easily in various online communication mediums. For example, a poster on the website IsItNormal.com (2015) where people discuss taking secret pictures of their wives, girlfriends and others, states, 'It's my wife's ass, I took it with my camera, I should be able to use them as I see fit.' This is patriarchal ownership in marriage made explicit. This also means that when victims of revenge porn report their ex-partner to police forces, where it is not yet a crime, they often face responses such as, 'The police said the most they could do was file a domestic incident report in case his behaviour escalated' (BBC, 2014). While the United Kingdom now has legislation to tackle this crime, many countries around the globe do not.

Universal laws able to convict revenge porn perpetrators do not exist. Mary Anne Franks (2016: 3) reports:

> In 2009, the Philippines became the first country to criminalize nonconsensual pornography, with a penalty of up to 7 years' imprisonment.[2] The Australian state of Victoria outlawed non-consensual pornography in 2013. In 2014, Israel became the first country to classify non-consensual pornography as sexual assault, punishable by up to 5 years' imprisonment; Canada criminalized this conduct the same year.[3] Germany and Japan have now made revenge porn a criminal offence. England and Wales joined these countries in February 2015. New Zealand outlawed the practice in July 2015. Northern Ireland and Scotland followed suit in February and March 2016, respectively.

In other countries, the legal frameworks for prosecuting revenge porn perpetrators are either non-existent, or cultural aspects make it difficult to secure convictions. For example, Lyons et al. (2016, p. 1) found that in China there is no specific law for revenge porn or for countering cyberbullying. As such, the 'human flesh search engine' has grown in notoriety. In Russia, the government is reported to either be behind the online abuse, for example, homophobia is indirectly encouraged by the 2013 laws on homosexual propaganda, or abuses are rarely investigated as securing a conviction is unlikely due to the relative absence of evidence. Although Russia has no specific laws against revenge porn or online abuses, in theory online abuses could be covered by standard laws against the threatening of violence. However, in a culture where online violence is rarely investigated by police, it is reported that many victims of revenge porn are reluctant to report revenge porn or other online abuses.

A somewhat different context has been reported in Colombia. Online sexual abuses in Colombia are often linked to political motives by paramilitary groups. Lyons et al. (2016) report Olga Paz Martinez, coordinator of the Take Back the Tech project in Colombia, as saying 'online violence is often directed against women's rights campaigners and in particular those who speak out about sexual violence against women'. They also suggest that the situation is further complicated by a deep-seated culture of *machismo* based on patriarchal power and dominance. Paz Martinez is reported to have claimed, 'In this culture, many women who are the victims of revenge pornography, return to their former partners or give in to other blackmail demands to protect their reputation and safety'. The Democratic Republic of Congo is reported (Lyons et al., 2016) to be much worse since sexual violence and online abuse against women are either not taken seriously or are completely dismissed.

In the 'more developed' nations such as Australia and Sweden, the picture is also reportedly mixed (Lyons et al., 2016). For example, there are no specific revenge porn laws in Australia, although there are broad criminal laws that can be used to prosecute online abuses. Currently, the states of Victoria and South Australia have their own laws to criminalise the sharing of intimate photos without consent, and in February 2016 a Senate committee recommended this should be introduced nationally. Similarly, Sweden does not currently have specific revenge porn laws, but people have been tried for defamation. However, according to the Swedish National Council for Crime Prevention report, *The Swedish Crime Survey* (2015), even though approximately 44% of online abuses reported by women are by a current or ex-partner, only 4% of complaints result in prosecution, because in more than 40% of cases it has been difficult to identify the perpetrator or obtain evidence.

In the United States, too, the picture is also mixed, with 27 US states and the District of Columbia having laws barring non-consensual pornography; some states, for example, Texas, Alaska and New Jersey, have broad privacy laws that can be interpreted to encompass revenge porn. However, criminal penalties vary between states, and prosecutions are still rare, not least as many law enforcement agencies are not fully equipped to deal effectively with such allegations and crimes. In addition, almost all US states have some form of legislation against online harassment. In California, these extend to the power to suspend or expel college students from their educational institution for online bullying (Svoboda, 2014). Mary Anne Franks (2016, pp. 4–5) has provided further details of differential treatment among US states:

> In the U.S. only three states – New Jersey, Alaska, and Texas – had criminal laws that could be directly applied to nonconsensual pornography before 2012. Between 2012 and May 2016, 32 states and Washington D.C. passed criminal legislation to address this conduct: Arizona, Arkansas, California, Colorado, Connecticut, Delaware, Florida, Georgia, Hawaii, Idaho, Illinois, Kansas, Louisiana, Maine, Maryland, Michigan, Minnesota, Nevada, New Hampshire, New Mexico, North Carolina, North Dakota, Oklahoma, Oregon, Pennsylvania, Tennessee, Texas (to supplement previous law), Utah, Vermont, Virginia, Washington, and Wisconsin, bringing the total number of states with "revenge porn" laws as of August, 2016, to 24. ... CCRI's Legislative and Tech Policy Director, Mary Anne Franks, has been working with the offices of U.S. Representative Jackie Speier (D-CA) on a federal criminal bill in 2013. The bill titled the Intimate Privacy Protection Act was introduced with bipartisan support in Congress on July 14, 2016.

Arguably, the United Kingdom's journey to criminalising revenge porn began with several national charities, including the National Stalking Helpline, Women's Aid and the UK Safer Internet Centre reporting, in April 2014, due an increase in revenge porn activity. Apparently, there were 149 allegations of revenge porn made between January 1 2012 and July 1 2014 across eight police forces in England and Wales. On November 12, 2014, an amendment was included in the Criminal Justice and Courts Bill, later receiving Royal Ascent on February 16, 2015 (Parliament.UK, 2015); and Scotland's the Abusive Behaviour and Sexual Harm Bill came into force on October 8, 2015. These new laws cover images sent on social networks, including Facebook and Twitter as well as those sent by text. Offenders now face up to two years in prison. In early 2016 Northern Ireland also passed a bill criminalising revenge porn.

Luke King was the first person to be convicted of this crime in the United Kingdom. Southern Derbyshire Magistrates' Court found King guilty after he had posted explicit images of his ex-lover online after their three-year relationship had ended. He was remanded in custody for 12 weeks (*Nottingham Post*, November 12, 2014). In November 2015 Samantha Watt became the first woman to be sent to prison for posting sexually explicit images of her ex-girlfriend on Facebook. She was remanded in custody for 16 weeks (Matharu, 2015).

Israel's Knesset outlawed revenge porn at the beginning of 2014 and offenders face up to five years in prison. Israeli politician and social worker MK Yifat Kariv (Yesh Atid) led the Knesset amendment to the 15-year-old Sexual Harassment Prevention Bill after 'a young woman was filmed having sexual relations with her partner, only to have the video uploaded to the mobile chat application WhatsApp and forwarded to thousands of people after the couple broke up' (Y Net News, 2014). Following in Israel's footsteps, Germany made revenge porn illegal in May 2014 after a man was found guilty by a Koblenz higher regional court for distributing several erotic photographs of his ex-partner. However, only erotic photographs of the woman could be deleted (*The Guardian*, May 22, 2014). Japan's criminalisation of revenge porn was also spurred after a Tokyo man killed his former girlfriend in 2013 and then posted photos and videos of her on the Internet (*The Japan News,* 2015). Whereas laws in Israel, Germany, the United Kingdom and Japan are national, there is no federal bill yet on revenge porn covering the whole of the United States. Currently there are a mix of laws that may cover revenge porn or that cover revenge porn in general, such as those covering nudity, and have either been passed or are pending in US states: Alaska, Arizona, California, Colorado, Delaware, Georgia, Hawaii, Idaho, Illinois, Maryland, New Jersey, Pennsylvania, Texas, Utah, Virginia and Wisconsin (Goldberg PLLC, 2015). New Jersey and California were the first states to criminalise the practice.

Due to the popularity and money-making potential of revenge porn (Ridley, *Huffington Post*, February 12, 2015) it is likely to be difficult to halt its growth without universal international laws because many revenge porn sites are hosted in countries other than where they operate. MyEx.com service and website is reported to be operated by several anonymous US individuals in coordination with colleagues in the Philippines (Steinbaugh, 2014). The platform has been hosted by Web Solutions B.V., Netherlands, where there was no specific revenge porn law. Hype Stat (2016, p. 1) claims it is now hosted in San Francisco, California, and links to network IP address 104.20.4.158. Given the site shifts and is operated in countries without revenge porn legislation and has a global reach, it makes either closing the site or removal of images difficult. While sites such as MyEx.com claim to adhere to laws, these can be manipulated to work in the perpetrators' favour. As noted earlier, victims are required to produce a copyright registration number before the images are removed, and requesting their removal might lead to more attention being brought to the images.

Although now illegal in the United Kingdom the majority of the 43 individual police forces had not collected revenge porn data even though '149 allegations of crimes involving revenge porn were recorded by eight police forces in England and Wales in two-and-a-half years' (Kelsey, 2015). In light of these difficulties victims still face in bringing perpetrators to justice, some have sought alternative routes. For example, the US support group Women Against Revenge Porn (2015) suggests, in the absence of legislation, victims could either attempt to file a lawsuit for invasion of privacy or intentional infliction of emotional distress or submit a Digital Millennium Copyright Act (DMCA) if the images can be shown to be taken by the victim as 'selfies'. Indeed, revenge porn site MyEx.com, along with Google and Yahoo! were being 'sued for copyright infringement in the Federal District Court for the Eastern District of Texas' (Steinbaugh, 2014). Google settled the revenge porn copyright case while those against Yahoo! and MyEx.com were dismissed. In the United Kingdom, the victim can potentially sue for copyright infringement. However, currently UK 'law absolves internet companies of responsibility for content posted by users, in order to safeguard free speech' (Barrett, 2015, *The Telegraph*, April 13). Ellie Hutchinson of Scottish Women's Aid (2014) points out for many women this means they 'spend days, nights, weeks, months, years searching for their name and image, with a monumental impact on their mental health, jobs and relationships.' During this protracted process there are several forms of support for victims.

The former UK Women and Equalities Minister Nicky Morgan launched the Revenge Porn Helpline in February 2015 (www.revengepornhelpline.org.uk/). This website offers victims a free downloadable resource that contains information on UK legislation, limiting its effects, what can be done to limit its effects, using social media platforms such as Facebook, Twitter and Tumblr and how to remove images and report offenses to Internet search engines such as Google and Yahoo. There are several other organisations that can assist victims with removal of images, dealing with the fallout of revenge porn, or its hangover effects, such as with new intimate partners. These organisations include Woman's Aid, Broken Rainbow, the National Stalking Helpline, Victim Support, End Revenge Porn, Victims of Internet Crime and Digital Trust. The help organisations provide victims can be invaluable.

In addition, there is the possibility, in theory at least, of using civil law in some jurisdictions; however, in practice this remains very difficult, not least because of the questions of personal ownership and (contested) consent. There have been a few headline civil lawsuits. Tynan (*The Guardian*, April 26, 2016) draws our attention to a Texas court decision in December 2015 which awarded Bindu Pariyar $7.25 million damages from her former husband because he posted explicit images of her in various online platforms. However, Pariyar was reported to have said she did not believe she would collect much of the award and thought the damage done to her was irreparable.

To conclude this section, we cite Franks' (2016) recommendations for a model law on revenge porn, written in a US context (also see Cooper, 2016):

> An actor may not knowingly disclose an image of another person who is identifiable from the image itself or information displayed in connection with the image and whose intimate parts are exposed or who is engaged in a sexual act, when the actor knows that or consciously disregarded a substantial and unjustified risk that the depicted person has not consented to such disclosure [and under circumstances in which the actor knew or consciously disregarded a substantial and unjustified risk that the depicted person reasonably expected that the image would remain private. A person who has consented to the creation or distribution of an image described in this section within the context of a confidential relationship retains a reasonable expectation of privacy beyond that relationship. A person who did not consent to the creation, distribution, or access to an image described in this section has reasonable expectation of privacy in that image.][4]
>
> A. Definitions. For the purposes of this section,
>
> 1   "Disclose" includes transferring, publishing, distributing, or reproducing;
> 2   "Image" includes a photograph, film, videotape, recording, digital, or other reproduction;
> 3   "Intimate parts" means the naked genitals, pubic area, anus, or female post-pubescent nipple of the person;
> 4   "Sexual act" includes but is not limited to masturbation; genital, anal, or oral sex; sexual penetration with objects; or the transfer or transmission of semen upon any part of the depicted person's body.
>
> B. Exceptions. This section does not apply to
>
> 5   Images involving voluntary exposure in public or commercial settings; or
> 6   Disclosures made in the public interest, including but not limited to the reporting of unlawful conduct, or the lawful and common practices of law enforcement, criminal reporting, legal proceedings, or medical treatment.
>
> C. Severability.
>
> 7   The provisions of this section are severable. If any provision of this section or its application is held invalid, that invalidity shall not affect other provisions or applications that can be given effect without the invalid provision or application.

These kinds of stipulations need to be translated into legal and governmental action in the specific societal and cultural contexts across the world.

## Technological and political responses

In addition to, and indeed overlapping with, legal and governmental responses, there are various further responses against revenge porn to consider here. Some of these are primarily technological, others focus more on support structures, and some are more publicly political. These strands are of course interconnected, and indeed technological responses and support are often themselves forms of politics, even if they do tend to lead in somewhat different directions. Technological responses tend to be more poster/producer-orientated, and more focused on online processes; support responses tend to focus more on the victim/postee, both online and offline; the more overt political responses are both postee/consumer-orientated and poster/producer-orientated, with both online and offline activity.

In the first case, we are concerned with the ways in which those who own and run websites, web forums and mobile technologies, such as 3–5 G mobiles, of various kinds control their content, either by specified explicit rules or implicit algorithmic solutions. YikYak, the anonymous social chat app, has adopted stricter rules in recent years to combat harassment; Reddit now allows members to report offensive content to moderators, in response to fears that harassment might turn away new users. Another simple measure here is to increase the number and expertise of moderators. There are also various technologies to monitor online activity without direct human moderators; for example, some online games can be programmed to detect negative behaviour so that gamers are automatically sent warning messages. Of course, such measures only apply to online sites or activities not designed for revenge porn itself. To move beyond that requires more direct political action, online and/or offline.

Supportive and more explicitly political responses range widely, and may blur into the politicisation of the issue with friends, family, colleagues, the wider circle of acquaintances, and so on. They begin with taking the attack seriously. One short list of immediate advice for those experiencing cyberbullying more generally suggests the following:

- Don't engage. When the harassment is relatively mild, the old "I can't hear you" approach really can work. Block the person's social media profile or just stop replying...The troll *wants* you to get worked up. When you don't respond, he or she sometimes loses interest.
- Alert those in charge. Report abusive messages that include ad hominin attacks or vulgar language to someone who can make them stop–whether the police or an online forum's administrator …
- Talk to a professional. If online attacks are bad enough to make you seriously doubt your self-worth, consult a therapist. Cyberbullies are skilled at eliciting a very intense, instant reaction that may be unlike anything you have experienced. You most likely will need support to deal with it.

*(Svodoba, 2014, p. 51)*

These kinds of suggestions may help, and the question of social support is vital, but some parts of this advice, such as reporting to those in authority, are unlikely to be effective with web forums commemorated to and designed for expanding revenge porn. Also, the resort to therapy, as the lowest rung on the ladder of 'citizen participation' (Arnstein, 1969) may or may not be what is needed to change the more general political conditions, including seeing specific attacks as instances of a wide set of abusive phenomena. Also, and on the other hand, some postees respond by 'calling out' the poster, and/or breaking the taboo(s) of display in fighting back, perhaps parodying the very same posting previously put up by their attacker, as a more explicit political strategy and response.

Though not strictly revenge porn in the limited definition, when Caitlin Seida found to her horror that her photograph of her scantily dressed as Lara Croft of *Tomb Raider* had gone viral, along with a multitude of vicious comments, she responded with a deliberately staged 'boudoir photo shoot' in the Lara Croft outfit (*Daily Mail*, October 4, 2013). This was followed by an outreach campaign to fight such online attacks, with the website, ifeeldelicious.com, along with advising victims on what to do in such situations (Svodoba, 2014). Outreach and education are undoubtedly also very important parts of action against revenge porn. This, additionally, includes outreach, education and support for mental health advice and counselling, as well as for political community building, online.

Another example of direct fighting back was recently reported from Egypt (Baker, 2016, p. 1):

> One evening in 2009, Egyptian 18-year-old, Ghadeer Ahmed, spent an evening dancing with friends. She wore a dress, and didn't wear her hijab. A friend took a video of her dancing, which she then sent to her boyfriend.
>
> After their break-up, Ghadeer's ex-boyfriend posted the video online in an attempt to shame her, and in turn her whole family. "Our bodies are not our own: they belong to the male members of the family, and are the vessels in which the family's honour is carried," Ghadeer told the BBC, as part of their Shame Online series. "I was scared that the video would bring shame on my parents, that our friends and neighbours would condemn my father for failing to raise me as a 'good girl'."
>
> Ghadeer is a women-rights activist and heads a group called Girls' Revolution, which fights for women's place in Egyptian society. The group is active on social media, which of course attracts a lot of trolls. In 2014 one troll in particular hit a nerve when he posted the video of her dancing.
>
> As a response Ghadeer posted the video to her own Facebook page, with the caption: "Yesterday a group of men tried to shame me by sharing a private video of me dancing with friends. I am writing this to announce that, yes, it was me in the video, and no, I am not ashamed of my body. To whoever is trying to stigmatise me, as a feminist I've got over the social misconceptions about women's bodies that still dominate Eastern societies.

I don't feel ashamed because I was dancing happily, just as I did publicly at my sister's wedding, where I also wore a very short and revealing dress. Now, I want to ask you guys: what is it that really annoys you? Me being a slut, or me being a slut without sleeping with you? My body is not a source of shame. I have nothing to regret about this video."

Ghadeer's post, and the sharing of her story with the BBC, is a radical example of how women in patriarchal cultures are turning against the expectations and pressures placed on women. She hopes that other women in similar situations will be encouraged to turn to someone, saying, "Together, we can change the culture that makes us frightened and ashamed. Together, we can survive."

One 14-year-old victim has recently begun legal action against the Facebook corporation, claiming the social network is liable for the 'publication of a naked picture of the girl posted repeatedly on a "shame page" as an act of revenge' (Topping, 2016, p. 1). According to Topping, this legal action has spurred a number of other victims to seek advice about legal action against social media sites. Facebook claims the image was removed several times after being reported, but the girl argues that it was not permanently blocked, and so in due course re-emerged. The girl's legal team argues that this is a misuse of private information, negligence and breach of the Data Protection Act. Facebook argues that it is immune from liability for repeated posting of content since it followed current EU law, which only requires they react quickly to complaints.[5] A high court judge has rejected this claim, and the case will be heard in 2017. But whatever the outcome Topping (2016, p. 1) argues, quite accurately, 'It will take more than one high profile case to remove other barriers to victims of revenge pornography'.

One of the most useful short documents addressing ways to take a stand against revenge porn is that by Danica Johnson (2013, p. 1). She highlights: contact the photo hosting service; making revenge porn illegal; seek mental and emotional support; and remember: this is rape culture, not normality.

1    Contact the Photo Hosting Service
     First, get your photos taken down if you can.… Photo hosting websites like imgur are looking to avoid lawsuits. They are not as interested in protecting the creeps who post revenge pictures as they are of not being sued.
        Be firm, be forceful, and threaten legal action. This is the easiest way to get your photos removed from a public image hosting site.
        But what about sites like MyEx.com where the photos are hosted internally?
        We need to go further. We need to change the law.
2    Making Revenge Porn Illegal
3    Seek Mental and Emotional Support

4   Remember: This is Rape Culture, Not Normality
    … It's just one more battle in the war against rape culture, but it's one
    that we can all take part in by calling this exploitation out, educating
    people about why it's not okay, and working towards making it illegal.
    Claim your rights.

While some newspapers and other 'news' media have certainly exploited the
phenomenon of revenge porn, using it as a means of both advertising and out-
rageous indignation, others have actively campaigned against it (Penny, 2014,
p. 162). For example, *The Guardian*'s campaign project, 'the web we want', seeks
to counter online abuse, including abusive comments against journalists, with
ten of the most abused writers online, eight being women and two being black
men. More generally, national and international political leadership is needed.
In the United Kingdom a cross-party campaign of Labour, Conservative and
Liberal Democrat politicians was launched in July 2016 against online misogyny,
named Reclaim the Internet. The online consultation has called for contributions from individuals, organisations, employers, union members, victims, police
and companies (Laville, Wong, & Hunt, *The Guardian*, April 11, 2016).

There are now a whole range of feminist and feminist-led websites, campaigns
and organisations directed at fighting against revenge porn and online abuse more
generally. These include Crash Override network, Gadgette, Women, Action and
the Media (WAM), TrollBusters (see Alexander, *The Guardian*, 2016), End Revenge Porn, Cyber Civil Rights Initiative, Without My Consent, Army of She,
and Women Against Revenge Porn (Johnson, 2013), feministcurrent.com, every-
dayfeminism.com, Aufshcrei, Solidarityisforwhitewomen and many more. Much of
the information on them is itself online, and is necessarily changing and developing.

A good online example (Finch, 2015) of what is both a specific and a
wide-ranging feminist response to revenge porn is to be found at everyday-
feminism.com, beginning with a specific account of anti-revenge porn activism:

[Chrissy] Chambers, an American LGBTQIA+ activist and YouTube star,
is making history as the first person in the United Kingdom to bring both
civil and criminal charges against a former partner for posting revenge
porn.
   Chambers' story is horrifying, but not unfamiliar: After Chambers suggested to her then-boyfriend that they take a break from their relationship,
he suggested they meet up for drinks. After Chambers became extremely
intoxicated, her ex proceeded to sexually assault her and film it, all while
she was nearly unconscious and without her consent.
   Chambers says she has no memory of this night, let alone of any filming
taking place.
   After she broke things off, he posted the footage – *where it eventually
spread to 35 different porn websites* – including her full name and face, but
blurring out his own face.

Chambers' reported her ex to the Atlanta police for rape, but, unsurprisingly, they decided not to press charges …

That's when Chambers made the brave decision to seek out justice in the UK. Because her ex had posted the videos while in Britain, she could still bring charges against him as they related to the revenge pornography.…

As Chambers waits to hear if charges will be brought – *she was interviewed by police last April* – she is now using her voice and her platform on YouTube to call for an end to revenge porn, including petitioning the United States Congress to pass a bill that would criminalize revenge porn in the United States.

This account is a prelude to six statements and an extended discussion on revenge porn:

1   While anyone can be a victim of revenge porn, women are disproportionately the victims
2   Revenge porn is a form of sexual violence
3   It's an undeniable product of rape culture
4   The impact on victims is devastating and dangerous
5   People are exploiting victims to make more money
6   There are seldom (if ever) any legal ramifications for posting revenge porn

Finally, there are various forms of more direct and sometimes bodily resistance, online or offline. These include, perhaps most famously, the 'Free the nipple' campaign. Beginning in the United States, in part through the 2014 film of that name directed by Lina Esco and written by Hunter Richards, that aimed at the wider issue of societal taboos on public exposure of female breasts, it was reinvigorated in Iceland in 2015 as a feminist response to the online abuse directed at a young woman after she posted herself topless to promote gender equality. This led to various women supporting her and a 'Free nipples day' with various events in schools, colleges, the University of Iceland, swimming pools and outside the Houses of Parliament on 26 March 2015.

The day of protest was instigated as

> protest against shaming of women on the internet, when topless photographs of women are posted up on social media for shaming purposes. The movement wants to put the shame w[h]ere it belongs, to those who posted up the photographs for the purpose of shaming and began when women posted their own topless photographs on Twitter with the hashtag FreeTheNipple. The movement believes that women's nipples should not be sexualised, and that women should be able to go topless just as men do.

(Iceland Monitor, *2015, p. 1*)

At the subsequent June 13, 2016, public event, more than 1,100 people confirmed their attendance. Interestingly, photography and information on the campaign actions were incorporated in the National Museum of Iceland exhibition of women's history, 'A Woman's Place' which examines the working lives of Icelandic women from 1915 to 2015.

Such actions can be related to other feminist bodily attempts to oppose sexism, and other oppressions, through women's own use of their bodies, naked or not. In some ways, they can be related to other recent feminist protests such as Femen and Slut Walks. Together, these various bodily initiatives have led to significant debates, often online, including between feminists on the political pros and cons of baring the breast for political ends. These arguments include the feminist case for inverting the gaze of sexism, pornography and revenge porn; critiques thereof as reproducing the reduction of women to bodies and body parts; their effectiveness or lack of effectiveness for change; opposition to the use of the term, 'revenge pornography'; and the focus on what are said by some to be less important issues to the neglect of larger issues. For example, Gyða Margrét Pétursdóttir, Associate Professor in Gender Studies at the University of Iceland, was reported in commenting on the Icelandic campaign:

> And there's a question whether this will increase the power [women] have over their own bodies or whether it will strengthen the notion that the power is held by others and affirm the traditional ideas of women instead of revolutionizing them.
>
> *(Arnarsdóttir, 2015, p. 1)*

Annadís G. Rúdólfsdóttir and Ásta Jóhannsdóttir (forthcoming) have recently provided a much fuller description and analysis of the 2015 events in Iceland, and various, mainly feminist, interpretations of them across four phases of activity: 'The Revolution: Claiming the body back from Patriarchy'; 'Feminist reactions to #FreetheNipple: Is this a Revolution?'; 'Patriarchy strikes back'; and 'Defiance through solidarity against Patriarchy'. They locate their analysis within a broader discussion of young femininity and feminism in a post-feminist, digital age, including 'the intricate relationship between social media and mainstream media which mainstream media' in which 'many of the news items consisted entirely of selected texts from the social media network'.

There are many other examples, both historical and contemporary, of women's naked protests elsewhere, which may raise both similar and different issues, depending on context. For example, in South African universities, following the March 2015 Rhodes Must Fall movement,[6] the campaign under the hashtag NakedProtests has raised major historical questions around race, racism, imperialism and slavery:

> In choosing to be naked, these young women were harking back to historical protests across the African continent. In the late 1800s and early 1900s

African women sometimes used nudity to protest against colonial admin-
istrators. Baring their buttocks and breasts, they forced men with power to
look at them on their own terms.

*(Msimang, 2016, p. 1)*

Tigist Shewarega Hussen (forthcoming) has further analysed this movement
in South Africa, specifically the #RapeMustFall, #NakedProtest and
#RUReferenceList Movement, in terms of how ICTs and social media are em-
ployed for the claiming of public space and bodily space. Such protests disrupt the
positioning of women as carrying the burden of safety and responsibility from
rape culture and violent masculine behaviour more generally (see Rentschler,
2014).

Bringing this kind of angry protest into the realm of revenge porn may be
hard, for some, to imagine. However, it is in such ways that the ongoing and
complex politics of and against revenge porn are likely to develop, as women,
and perhaps some men and further genders, challenge virtual power with and
through their own bodies, and the exposure of their bodies. This is one part
and one example of the wider politics of gender, sexuality, feminism, bodies
and embodiments, not least in the recognition and disruption of the association
of women and bodies. These politics are being rethought and repracticed, especially in the light of the affordances made available by advanced technologies.
They entail the recognition of the power of bodies and embodiment, even as
virtual(ised) bodies, yet without conflating these with women or other gendered, sexual(ised) persons. In our final chapter, *Future directions*, we expand on
the issues raised in this chapter, and identify some further possible interventions
and responses.

## Notes

1 It should be noted that the following legal and governmental, and technological and
political responses were correct at the time of writing. However, we would like to
point out to readers that the landscape is constantly changing.
2 World Intellectual Property Organization, *Anti-Photo and Video Voyeurism Act of 2009*
(Republic Act No. 9995), www.wipo.int/edocs/lexdocs/laws/en/ph/ph137en.pdf.
3 House of Commons of Canada, Bill C-13.
4 'The "reasonable expectation of privacy" language is bracketed because of the benefits and drawbacks of including it. The benefit of including such language is to emphasise that the statute does not apply to images voluntarily created in commercial or
public settings. This point is already addressed in B(1) of the exceptions, but including it in the elements might helpfully underscore this aspect. The drawback of this
approach is twofold: 1. The term "reasonable expectation of privacy" might create
more ambiguity than it resolves, especially considering the doctrinal baggage of the
term from Fourth Amendment jurisprudence and 2. The term is an awkward fit for
cases involving sexual assaults in public or semi-public settings, as well as for hacking
scenarios. If privacy is included as an element, it would be prudent to address these
issues explicitly.'
5 On May 21, 2017, parts of the prescriptive manuals used by Facebook's 4,500 moderators, who check the platform's online content were published, as reportedly leaked

to *The Guardian*. The extract on revenge pornography is reproduced below (Hopkins, *The Guardian*, May 21, 2017):

## Revenge Porn (1)

CURRENT POLICY

**High-level:** Revenge porn is sharing nude/near-nude photos of someone publicly or to people that they didn't want to see them in order to shame or embarrass them.

**Abuse Standards:**

6. Attempting to exploit intimate images by any of the following:
- Sharing imagery as "revenge porn" if it fulfills all three conditions:
1. Image produced in a private setting. AND
2. Person in image is nude, near nude, or sexually active. AND
3. Lack of consent confirmed by:
- Vengeful context (e.g. caption, comments, or page title), OR
- Independent sources (e.g. media coverage, or LE record)

The following day, May 22, it was reported that in January 2017 Facebook assessed nearly 54,000 potential cases of revenge pornography and 'sextortion', leading to the disabling of over 14,000 accounts (Hopkins & Solon, *The Guardian*, May 22, 2017).

6  Rhodes Must Fall is a student-led campaign, under the hashtag #RhodesMustFall, begun in March 2015, initially for the removal of the Cecil John Rhodes statue on the University of Cape Town campus, but in turn leading to wider protests on other matters, such as student fees, and demands for democratising and decolonising the universities.

## References

Alexander, L. (2016). Online abuse: How women are fighting back. *The Guardian*. April 13. Retrieved September 1 from www.theguardian.com/technology/2016/apr/13/online-abuse-how-women-are-fighting-back.

Arnarsdóttir, E. S. (2015). 'Free the Nipple' Day's success disputed in Iceland. *Iceland Review Online*. Retrieved from http://icelandreview.com/news/2015/03/27/free-nipple-days-success-disputed-iceland.

Arnstein, S. R. (1969). A ladder of citizen participation. *Journal of the American Institute of planners, 35*(4), 216–224.

Baker, E. (2016). An Egyptian woman posted a video of her dancing to own her "shame": Ghadeer Ahmed's boyfriend tried to shame her by posting a video of her dancing online, but she wasn't going to let that happen. *The Pool*. October 27. Retrieved March 24, 2017 from www.the-pool.com/news-views/latest-news/2016/43/an-egyptian-woman-posted-a-video-of-her-dancing-to-own-her-shame.

Barrett, D. (2015). What is the law on revenge porn? *The Telegraph*. April 13. Retrieved September 1, 2016.

BBC. (2014). Is revenge porn already illegal in England? December 28. Retrieved April 10, 2015 from www.bbc.co.uk/news/uk-england-30308942.

Cooper, P. W. (2016). The right to be virtually clothed. *Washington Law Review, 91*, 817–846.

*Daily Mail*. (2013). 'Scrolling through the comments, my heart imploded': One woman's shock when an embarrassing photo of her went viral - and how she got back at hateful critics. October 4. Retrieved September 1, 2016 from www.dailymail.co.uk/femail/article-2444252/Caitlin-Seida-shock-embarrassing-photo-went-viral-got-critics.html.

Finch, S. D. (2015). 6 reasons Why revenge porn is really f*cked up (And how one woman is pushing back). 16 June. http://everydayfeminism.com/2015/06/6-reasons-why-revenge-porn-is-actually-really-fcked-up-and-how-one-woman-is-pushing-back.

Franks, M. A. (2016). Drafting an effective "revenge porn" law: A guide for legislators. *Cyber Civil Rights Initiative.* Retrieved March 19, 2017 from www.cybercivilrights.org/guide-to-legislation/.

Goldberg PLLC, C. A. (2015). States with revenge porn criminal laws. March 3. Retrieved April 3, 2015 from www.cagoldberglaw.com/states-with-revenge-porn-laws.

Hopkins, N. (2017). Facebook moderators: A quick guide to their job and its challenges. *The Guardian,* May 21. Retrieved May 21, 2017 from www.theguardian.com/news/2017/may/21/facebook-moderators-quick-guide-job-challenges.

Hopkins, N., & Solon, O. (2017). Facebook flooded with 'sextortion' and revenge porn, files reveal. *The Guardian.* May 22. Retrieved May 22, 2017 from https://www.theguardian.com/news/2017/may/22/facebook-flooded-with-sextortion-and-revenge-porn-files-reveal.

Hussen, T. S. (forthcoming). ICTs, social media and feminist activism: #RapeMustFall, #NakedProtest, and #RUReferenceList Movement in South Africa. In T. Shefer, J. Hearn, K. Ratele, & F. Boonzaier (Eds.), *Engaging youth in activist research and pedagogical praxis: Transnational and intersectional perspectives on gender, sex, and race.* New York: Routledge.

Hutchinson, E. (2014). Preventing revenge porn – why here? why now? *Scottish Women's Aid.* October 20. Retrieved April 8, 2015 from www.scottishwomensaid.org.uk/node/4592.

Hype Stat (2016). Myex.Com – Info. Retrieved September 1 from http://myex.com.hypestat.com.

*Iceland Monitor.* (2015). Women gather in the sunshine for #FreeTheNipple. 13 June. http://icelandmonitor.mbl.is/news/news/2015/06/13/women_gather_in_the_sunshine_for_freethenipple.

Is It Normal. (2015). Post naked pictures of my wife for guys to masturbate. Retrieved September 1, 2016 from http://isitnormal.com/story/post-naked-pictures-of-my-wife-for-guys-to-masturbate-141111.

Johnson, D. (2013). 4 ways to take a stand against revenge porn. Everydayfeminism.com. 3 December. Retrieved August 1 from http://everydayfeminism.com/2013/12/revenge-porn-and-internet-exploitation.

Kelsey, R. (2015). Revenge porn is being made a specific criminal offence. *BBC Newsbeat.* February 12. Retrieved April 8, 2015 from www.bbc.co.uk/newsbeat/31020831.

Laville, S., Wong, J. C., & Hunt, E. (2016). The women abandoned to their online abusers. *The Guardian.* April 11. Retrieved September 1 from www.theguardian.com/technology/2016/apr/11/women-online-abuse-threat-racist.

Lyons, K., Phillips, T., Walker, S., Henley, J., Farrell, P., & Carpentier, M. (2016). Online abuse: How different countries deal with it. *The Guardian.* April 12. Retrieved October 15 from www.theguardian.com/technology/2016/apr/12/online-abuse-how-harrassment-revenge-pornography-different-countries-deal-with-it?CMP=share_btn_link.

Matharu, H. (2015). First woman jailed for 'revenge porn' after posting sexually explicit photos of ex-girlfriend on Facebook. *The Independent.* November 26. Retrieved September 1, 2016 from www.independent.co.uk/news/uk/crime/first-woman-in-the-uk-jailed-for-revenge-porn-a6749941.html.

Msimang, S. (2016). South Africa's topless protesters are fighting shame on their own terms. *The Guardian.* Retrieved from www.theguardian.com/world/2016/may/05/south-africas-topless-protesters-are-fighting-shame-on-their-own-terms.

MyEx.com. (2015). MyEx.com! Naked Pics of Your Ex: FAQs. Retrieved from www.myex.com/faq/.

*Nottingham Post.* (2014). Revenge porn: Dad jailed for putting intimate photo of ex-lover on the internet. November 12. Retrieved April 3, 2015 from www.nottinghampost .com/Revenge-porn-Dad-jailed-putting-intimate-photo-ex/story-24527836-detail/story.html.

Parliament.UK. (2015). Criminal Justice and Courts Act 2015. Lords Amendments. November 12. Retrieved April 3, 2015 from www.publications.parliament.uk/pa/bills/cbill/2014-2015/0120/15120.pdf.

Penny, L. (2014). *Unspeakable things: Sex, lies and revolution.* London: Bloomsbury.

Rentschler, A. C. (2014). Rape culture and the feminist politics of social media. *Girlhood Studies,* 7(1), 65–82.

Ridley, L. (2015). Revenge porn victims are children as young as 11, new figures reveal. *Huffington Post.* September 30. Retrieved April 5, 2015 from www.huffingtonpost .co.uk/2014/09/30/revenge-porn-children_n_5905554.html.

Rúdólfsdóttir, A. G., & Jóhannedóttir, Á. (forthcoming). Fuck Patriarchy!: An analysis of digital mainstream media discussion of the #FreetheNipple activities in Iceland in March 2015. *Feminism and Psychology.*

Steinbaugh, A. (2014). Revenge porn site MyEx.com Sued for copyright infringement. March 7. Retrieved April 3, 2015 from http://adamsteinbaugh.com/2014/03/07/revenge-porn-site-myex-com-sued-for-copyright-infringement.

Svoboda, E. (2014). Virtual assault. *Scientific American Mind,* 25(6), 46–53.

Swedish National Council for Crime Prevention. (2015). The Swedish Crime Survey. Retrieved November 12, 2016 from www.bra.se/bra/bra-in-english/home/crime-and-statistics/swedish-crime-survey.html.

*The Guardian.* (2014). 'Revenge porn' laws must be clearer, say Lords. July 29. Retrieved August 12, 2014 from www.theguardian.com/law/2014/jul/29/revenge-porn-laws-must-be-clearer-say-lords.

*The Japan News.* (2015). Police flooded with queries over revenge porn. April 2. Retrieved April 3, 2015 from http://the-japan-news.com/news/article/0002054600.

Topping, A. (2016). Facebook revenge pornography trial 'could open floodgates'. *The Guardian.* October 9. Retrieved October 15 from www.theguardian.com/technology/2016/oct/09/facebook-revenge-pornography-case-could-open-floodgates?CMP=share_btn_link.

Tynan, D. (2016). Revenge porn: The industry profiting from online abuse: Sites charge $100 a year to access private photos and videos of non-porn stars in the nude, usually posted by spurned ex-lovers – but it doesn't end there. *The Guardian.* April 26. Retrieved September 1 from www.theguardian.com/technology/2016/apr/26/revenge-porn-nude-photos-online-abuse.

United Kingdom Intellectual Property Office. (2014). Copyright notice: Digital images, photographs and the internet: Copyright Notice Number: 1/2014. March. Retrieved April 7, 2015 from www.gov.uk/government/uploads/system/uploads/attachment_data/file/305165/c-notice-201401.pdf.

United States Copyright Office. (2011). Copyright law of the United States and related laws contained in title 17 of the United States code. Circular 92. Washington: Library of Congress. Retrieved April 7, 2015 from www.copyright.gov/title17/circ92.pdf.

Women against Revenge Porn. (2015). 3 ways to remove photos. Retrieved April 8, 2015 from www.womenagainstrevengeporn.com/#!photo-removal/c9fv.

Y Net News. (2014). Knesset outlaws revenge porn. January 6. Retrieved April 3, 2015 from www.ynetnews.com/articles/0,7340,L-4473849,00.html.

# 3

# SITUATING REVENGE PORN

## Introduction

Revenge porn can be understood from several different traditions and perspectives. This chapter looks at revenge porn as pornography, interpersonal revenge, violence and abuse, information and computer technologies (ICTs), publicisations and gender-sexual practices. Since the majority of victims of revenge porn are women, this phenomenon can be seen as yet another form of gender-based violence, and yet another example of the practices of men and masculinities that take place via ICTs. We begin by looking at how revenge porn can be seen as yet another form of pornography.

## Pornography

First, and most obviously, revenge porn can be seen as *pornography*. More precisely, it is a relatively new form or genre of pornography that importantly is publicly displayed. Revenge porn is another part of the explosion of (online) pornography (Dines, 2010; Hearn, 2006; Hughes, 2002; Jeffreys, 2013), and more general pornografication, pornographisation (Attwood, 2009) or 'mainstreamification' of pornography (Empel, 2011) in society. In this sense, it can be understood within a very long historical development of different elaborations of pornography, in part affected through different technological affordances (Rahman & Jackson, 2010). We can compare, for example, the move to video pornography, with the invention of that technology. This way of seeing revenge porn also resurfaces some very entrenched debates on such questions as the distinctions between pornography and erotica; the ethics of pornography; the effects of pornography on behaviour (cf. Itzin, 1993; Segal & McIntosh, 1993); its relation to prostitution and the sex trade more generally and the semiotics, and indeed textual conventions, of pornography (Boyle, 2010; Paasanen, 2011).

According to Hoff (1989, p. 17), the contemporary manifestation of pornography has 'come so quickly out of the shadows of antiquity into today's headline' we tend to presume that previous incarnations are mirrored in modern pornographies. Arguably, porn can be seen as part of the move from sex to a broader sense of sexuality and its institutionalisation with and through a proliferation of discourses, to sexuality as an identity. From public ritual to private personal relationships, women have tended to be positioned as submissive and men as dominant and powerful. Hoff (1989, p. 1) argues that liberalism in the form of freedom of speech and sexual liberation is one of the key factors in porn becoming mainstream – the pornografication, pornographisation (Attwood, 2009), mainstreamification of pornography (Empel, 2011) and the sexualisation of culture in Western societies (Dines, 2010; Durham, 2009; Levin & Kilbourne, 2009; Paasanen, Nikunen, & Saarenmaa, 2007).

What these terms refer to is the sense that Western societies are becoming different, sexually different, by virtue of the mass of sexual representations and discourses, with pornography increasingly influential and porous, permeating contemporary culture. The mainstreaming, and increasing visibility of sex, in modern Western societies can be seen in a number of forms. Attwood (2009, pp. xiii–xv) lists several of these, some of which include the following: porn stars now write books, advise lifestyle magazines and star in lad magazines; porn is now more visible in art, film, television and the press, as well as in music videos and advertising. There has been a significant growth of so-called gentlemen's clubs featuring pole and lap dancing; the popularity of sexual paraphernalia can be seen in the growth and more general public approval of lingerie, toys and erotica shops such as Ann Summers; there is an increasing trend to have Brazilian waxing and other forms of pubic hair removal and growing numbers of people are making, and circulating, homemade sexual images on mobile devices called 'sexting' (Hasinoff, 2015) and videos that can be uploaded onto specific pornography websites such as Cliphunter, Xvidoes and PornHub. Indeed, many of these activities have become 'respectabilised'. For example, pole dancing is now promoted as mainstream corporate entertainment or fitness activity (Ringrose, Gill, Livingston, & Harvey, 2012).

Pornography is both foregrounded and backgrounded in mainstream popular television entertainment:

> Pornography and related phenomena may become normalised as part of the background "visual wallpaper" of television and its viewing. This includes specifically its *intermittent* viewing. In this sense, the "design" of programmes as "meant" for a certain age group or for another real or imaginary viewing category is not necessarily the most significant issue. Pornographisation, as background or "wallpaper" can proceed even if it does not figure directly in those programmes that are designed for young people or even primarily viewed by them. Indeed perhaps this process operates even more powerfully by virtue of its incompleteness.
>
> *(Hearn & Jyrkinen, 2007, pp. 48–49)*

Scholars such as Attwood (2009), Empel (2011), Dines (2010), Durham (2009), Levin and Kilbourne (2009) and Paasanen et al. (2007) point out that the boundary between public and private is shifting from one of censorship to an 'informed' consumer culture. That is, the relationship between the two spheres is becoming more fluid and porous with sex often taking centre stage. While the use of technology for sexual purposes is as old as the printing press, what differentiates the modern world is the near universal availability of porn on the Internet and technological devices for accessing it, as well as the speed in which it can be accessed (Attwood, 2009). Gone are the days of the dominance of top shelf porn magazines and sex cinemas for consuming sex; consumption now tends to take place in the comfort of one's home. The ability to privately view and make porn both at home and in public, and the relative anonymity of doing so afforded by new technological developments has led to an explosion of online pornography (Dines, 2010; Hearn, 2006; Hughes, 2002).

Indeed, some scholars (Johansson & Hammarén, 2007; Weitzer, 2011) have recently argued that not all pornography is harmful, as long as both parties consent (Gordon-Messer, Bauermeister, Grodzinski, & Zimmerman, 2013), thus offering continuity with a long line of pro-pornography commentators whether within the sex industry or outside it (Segal & McIntosh, 1993). Arguably, in this explosion, new forms of pornography such as sexting, cybersex and revenge porn have emerged. While some forms of electronic pornography such as sexting may be considered consensual, Ringrose et al.'s (2012) interview and focus group study of sexting show it is often coercive and is often linked to peer-pressure, harassment, bullying and even violence. What they also found was that these phenomena predominantly affect girls and women who are often pressured into sending images of their naked bodies, and in time becoming the victims of revenge porn when relationships end.

Interestingly, some of the academic debate 'for' and 'against' pornography has to some extent been superseded by those researches that attend to the variable social uses and social practices of pornography, and its display and invocation, both directly and indirectly (Thomson, 1999). In this book, we situate revenge porn as a contemporary social problem and a contemporary social practice to intentionally inflict harm. One motivation for this is interpersonal revenge.

## Interpersonal revenge

One can clearly place revenge porn within the range of practices of revenge, specifically *interpersonal revenge*. Seen thus, revenge is not new. Previous interest by scholars has historically attempted to understand interpersonal revenge. More specifically, why do people want revenge, how do they express it and what happens after they act? Revenge has been seen as an extension of well-developed strategies and tactics for dealing with, and coping with, such emotions and social relations as disappointment, loss, punishment, shaming, conflict and antagonism (Yoshimura, 2007). Revenge can be material and/or symbolic.

It can be direct, involving getting one's presumed 'just' and material desserts, or extracting yet more than that, or it can be more tangential and symbolised in specific textual or representational acts. Practices of revenge, revenge practices, can of course lead on to counter-resistances, revenge to revenge: an eye for an eye, *ad infinitum*.

Some scholars (for example, Berkowitza & Cornell, 2005; Bies & Tripp, 1996) argue that revenge serves two purposes. First, revenge is often a 're-sponse to trauma and loss and is a fantasy of control' and, second, revenge acts as a '"safety-valve" that protects a victim against self-destructive impulses that accompany the act of being injured or insulted' (Berkowitza & Cornell, 2005, p. 316). In other words, the externalisation of harm helps to provide an inner sense of restored injured pride and justice. Yet seeking revenge through dis-playing explicit images of one's ex-partner may be perceived by others as purely vindictive (Johansson & Hammarén, 2007, p. 67), and, as such, the posters of revenge porn are compelled to provide an account of their action (Salter, 2013). That is, the posters seek to 'instrumentalise double standards in sexual mores to punish an ex-partner for leaving them', blaming the victim for their exposure (Salter, 2013, p. 1).

Similarities can be drawn here with Whisnant's (2010) analysis of men's con-sumption of online pornography. She points out that male consumers of porn are constantly reminded that no matter how violent their tastes are, or become, there is always somebody who has 'worse' tastes than them. In blaming the victim for their exposure, producers of revenge porn are able to take the moral high ground by implying that the victim's purported crime was worse, or at least equal to, the act of publicly displaying sexually explicit images of another person without consent. In addition, revenge porn perpetrators might also argue that their act 'only' embarrasses their victim at best, or that much worse happens to women by other men elsewhere on the web. The parallel with men's justifications for violence to known women, concretised in the use of the word 'just', is apparent (Hearn, 1998).

Consumers who in due course enjoy this material are able to displace re-sponsibility, since it is not they who hurt the woman. They are only looking at, or masturbating to, the images and perhaps also passing them on to others (Whisnant, 2010, p. 122). Given the wealth of data on MyEx.com both producers and consumers of this material might also point out that this practice is com-monplace as to diffuse responsibility. It is not they then who are the monsters, but other men who are posting these images or the women themselves for their purported crimes (Whisnant, 2010, p. 127). This 'quieter backstory' as Whisnant (2010, pp. 126–129) points out is about how men manage their identities as 'real' and still 'moral' men while engaging with the production and consumption of revenge porn. But regardless of whether the framing of this activity, because re-venge is being sought for a perceived prior misdemeanour, the seeker often tries to get revenge at a level more or equal to that which they feel they have been the victim. This often means violence and abuse are committed.

## Violence and abuse

Revenge porn can also be looked at as a form of *violence and abuse* and, in particular, by former intimate partners. Violence and abuse may be physical (hitting, shoving, kicking, biting or throwing things), emotional (yelling, controlling actions, making threats) or sexual (rape, sexual assault, non-consensual sexual acts, applying pressure to consent to do something sexual). The majority of intimate partner violence and abuse is of women. Recent figures from the World Health Organisation (WHO, 2014) show 35% of women experience either intimate partner violence or non-partner sexual violence at some point in their life. A third of women worldwide report experiencing sexual abuse by their partners and as many as 38% of murders of women worldwide are committed by an intimate partner. Given 90% of victims are women (Cyber Civil Rights Initiative, 2014; and EndRevengePorn.org, 2014; Franks, 2016), revenge porn can be understood as part of the huge range of gender-based violence, violence against women and men's/male violence against women (Hagemann-White et al., 2008; Hanmer & Itzin, 2000; Stark, 2009). The emphasis here is less on the motivation to equalise the felt wrong and more on the intention to harm itself. The emphasis, therefore, is on the power and control that is exerted and is reproduced in revenge porn. Revenge porn can then be understood as another form of gendered violence and abuse that ranges across femicide, rape, stalking and non-contact harassment (see Blumenstein & Jasinski, 2015, for more on intimate partner violence and femicide). It can also be encompassed within forms of violence and abuse that are not directly physical on the fleshy body, such as emotional violence, representational violence and non-contact bullying and sexual harassment, even though they are likely to have definite negative physical effects on the violated and the abused.[1]

## Information and computer technologies

While revenge porn may be the sharing of explicit images of another via cell phones within a specific locality or community, it is predominantly facilitated by *ICTs* accessing various online platforms. Seen thus, it is yet another part of the multifarious possibilities for virtual/online socialities, sexualities and violences, specifically cyberabuse – that is, intentional online behaviour to harm another, often repeatedly, where the victim is typically unable to defend himself or herself (Slonje, Smith, & Frisén, 2013). The crux of cyberabuse is the imbalance of power often facilitated by the perpetrator's ability to remain anonymous. It can take several forms such as cyberbullying, cyberstalking, online aggression, 'flaming', 'happy slapping', stalking and trolling (Hearn & Parkin, 2001). Revenge porn overlaps with and shares similarities with these forms of cyberabuses. Most obviously posting explicit images or videos along with offensive text carries the intention to harm or humiliate. The revenge porn can be accompanied by abusive emails, 'tag-team-style pile-ons' in Internet forums and personal attacks in blog and newspaper article comment sections (Svoboda, 2014, p. 48).

Revenge porn can also share similarities with other forms of cyberabuses. For example, intentional damage of someone's reputation by spreading malicious gossip, rumours or photos (these can be manipulated)[2]; cyberstalking – the intent to threaten or induce fear in the targeted person by circulating or sending repeated messages and photos (often via hyperlinks to revenge porn sites); outing and trickery – the sharing of or tricking someone into revealing aspects of their private live, with the intent to embarrass them; harassment – repeatedly sending offensive, rude and insulting messages or photos to the victim or people they know and happy slapping – videoing someone being swarmed by a group and then posting it online to platforms such as YouTube (Lacey, 2007).

ICTs have a number of distinctive features: time/space compression of distance and physical separation, instantaneousness in real time, asynchronicity, reproducibility of images, creation of virtual bodies, blurring of the 'real' and the 'representational'. More specifically, the affordances of computerised communication networks include broader bandwidth; wireless portability; globalised connectivity; personalisation (Wellman, 2001); and blurrings, even the abolition of the strict boundary between online and offline, and between codex and net (Gilbert, 2013). Revenge porn exploits those characteristics and elaborates them in all sorts of ways, with open-ended and undefined possibilities and effects. This raises more and more complex issues, for example, how revenge porn can be simultaneously embodied and virtual, is irreducible to one form or possibility, may be multimedial and may only be understandable in the context of the range of social practices beyond the visible and readable revenge porn text. For example, a particular revenge porn posting may reference, implicitly or explicitly, another earlier topic or social occasion offline and offscreen, positive or negative, for one, both or more parties, which would not be decipherable by an uninvolved party or viewer. Specific instances of revenge porn may also be part of a chain of events, occurrences, times and places beyond itself. Moreover, revenge porn can be seen in terms of the processual nature of the interactive web, in which 'produsers', 'prosumers' and other hybrids create the web interactively (see Whisnant, 2010, discussed below in relation to the production and consumption of pornography), as evidenced in do-it-yourself pornography, selfies, celebrity selfies, naked selfies, reality media, online lives, neknominate (drinking) challenges and the rest. Online revenge porn can also be understood as exemplars of novel and unfinished forms of online violences, violations, sexual violences and indeed sexualities.

More broadly still, revenge porn, as usually defined, can be compared with and related to the recent, or not so recent, phenomenon of 'autofiction', a term coined by the French writer, Serge Doubrovsky, in 1977, with some parallels to the genre of faction. In some examples of this genre, writers supposedly 'tell all' about their everyday lives, friends, partners, family and acquaintances, and sometimes call it a novel or some other composite production, sometimes with spectacular personal consequences. Perhaps the most famous protagonist here is Karl Ove Knausgård, the Norwegian author of six autobiographical autofictional novels. This form of writing can be a means of saying all without recourse to responsibility for others, at times as a form of revenge social porn.

## Publicisations

Another possible and related approach that might lead in other analytical and political directions is to focus on the recent high-profile *interest and concern for some mass media and governmental actors*, notably among national newspapers, government ministers and some activists in the United Kingdom, afforded to revenge porn. These publicisations (Brown, 1981) often also invoke demands for more legal or regulatory controls. In this perspective, the notion of 'moral panic' (Cohen, 1972) may be useful, without any playing down of the likely intentions to harm and violate and the likely associated experiences of harm of those victimised. Such mass media interest has been elaborated recently through the reporting of the hacking and online posting of naked photographs of female celebrities, such as the very high-profile film star of *Hunger Games* Jennifer Lawrence (Glenza, 2014).

This general perspective might also be seen as an example of a complex, unstable and rhizomic nexus of postings, violations, media interest, law and regulation, and further postings and violations, and so on. The elaboration of such governmentality may take different forms in different national and societal contexts, depending on wider framings of sexuality and violence. These networks of publicisations may broadly and in the longer run work to either promote or oppose revenge porn. At least 12 US states have laws that are expressly applicable to revenge porn. In the United Kingdom, government ministers, including the Prime Minister David Cameron, have committed themselves to more legal controls of revenge porn (Holehouse, 2014). The topic and contents of revenge porn circulate between and across these various forums in the public domain.

## Gender-sexual practices

Finally, but fundamentally, revenge porn can be seen as gender, gendered, sexual, gender-sexual practices. In these perspectives, revenge porn may be interpreted as structured action, resulting from the gender-sexual social order and social structures, sometimes called patriarchy, and/or as a way of doing gender, doing sexuality or doing gender/sexuality performatively. Either or both ways, it is part of the gender-sexual matrix, dominantly heterosexual, that (re)produces gender categorisations and places them into effect. The possible overlapping, and non-prioritisation, of gender over sexuality, and indeed *vice versa*, noted here is part of the actual and potential instability of the two categories: This is made explicit in some versions of queer theory or queer feminism, whether as theoretically inspired by Foucault or Butler or driven by direct subversive political action.

Having said that, as gendered, or intersectionally gendered, or gender-sexual practices, revenge porn appears to be most often and mainly a matter of the *practices of men and masculinities* (Connell, 1995) or similar concepts, such as *manhood acts* (Schwalbe, 2013). They thus can be instances of patriarchal, sexist, hegemonic and dominant forms, and complicit, subordinated, marginalised, ambivalent, resistant and counter-patriarchal forms. This is certainly not to stereotype such practices, but to see men's practices of revenge porn, and the discourses employed within and around them, as part of the diverse repertoires of men and masculinities, and in this sense perhaps less novel, less original, than they may appear to some or in some debates. In this view, revenge porn is less about the specific and rapidly changing affordances of ICTs, and more about gendered-sexual positions, positionings and possibilities within current gender-sexual orders.

There are no doubt other fertile approaches for examining this phenomenon, for example, as accounts of the psychological dynamics of shameful and shaming actions of self or others (Bradshaw, 1995; Kaufman, 1996), as conspicuous consumption of women (Hunter, 2011), as part of intimate or formerly intimate social relations (Delphy, 1976) and so on, but these six perspectives above suffice here for present purposes. Indeed, in this book we see revenge porn as both the combination of these perspectives – online gendered violent abusive pornographic revenge practices – while more specifically we focus in our analysis on the practices of men and women, and masculinities and femininities. We discuss these in more detail in our analytical Chapters 6 through 8, and in Chapter 9.

## Notes

1 Landrine and Klonoff (1997) suggest that it is the presence and exposure to oppressive (in their case, sexist) acts rather than the victims' subjective appraisals of such acts that better predict negative symptoms. Krieger and Sidney (1996) from a US survey of 4,000 black and white young adults report that blood pressure was highest for working-class black adults who accepted discrimination as 'a fact of life' or who denied they experienced discrimination, and lower for those who challenged unfair treatment. 'Accumulations of microaggressions' can affect self-confidence and self-respect of those targeted (Benokraitis, 1998, pp. 8–10).

2 Some of the 100 female A-listers involved in the so-called 'The Fappening' – leaked private naked photos – claimed that their images had been superimposed images of other people's naked bodies explicit images of sexual acts (Sanghani, 2014).

## References

Attwood, F. (Ed.). (2009). *Mainstreaming sex: The sexualization of Western sex*. London: I.B. Tauris.

Benokraitis, N. J. (1998). *Subtle sexism*. Thousand Oaks, CA: Sage.

Berkowitza, R., & Cornell, D. (2005). Parables of revenge and masculinity in Clint Eastwood's Mystic River. *Law, Culture and the Humanities, 1*(3), 316–332.

Bies, R. J., & Tripp, T. M. (1996). Beyond distrust: "Getting even" and the need for revenge. In R. M. Kramer & M. A. Neale. (Eds.), *Trust and organizations: Frontiers of theory and research* (pp. 203–219). Thousand Oaks, CA: Sage.

Blumenstein, L., & Jasinski, J. L. (2015). Intimate partner assault and structural-level correlates of crime: Exploring the relationship between contextual factors and intimate partner violence. *Criminal Justice Studies, 28*(2), 186–210.

Boyle, K. (Ed.). (2010). *Everyday pornography.* London: Routledge.

Bradshaw, J. (1995). *Family secrets.* London: Piatkus.

Brown, C. (1981). Mothers, fathers, and children: from private to public patriarchy. In L. Sargent (Ed.), *Women and revolution: The unhappy marriage of marxism and feminism* (pp. 239–267). New York/London: Maple/Pluto.

Cohen, S. (1972). *Folk devils and moral panics.* London: Paladin.

Connell, R. (1995). *Masculinities.* Cambridge: Polity.

Cyber Civil Rights Initiative. (2014). Victims' stories. January 27. Retrieved September 1, 2016 from www.cybercivilrights.org/page/5/?s=revenge+porn.

Delphy, C. (1976). Continuities and discontinuities in marriage and divorce. In D. Leonard Barker & S. Allen (Eds.), *Sexual divisions and society: Process and change* (pp. 76–89). London: Tavistock.

Dines, G. (2010). *Pornland: How porn has hijacked our sexuality.* Boston: Beacon.

Durham, M. G. (2009). *The lolita effect: The media sexualization of young girls and what we can do about it.* London and New York: Duckworth Overlook.

Empel, E. (2011). (XXX) potential impact: The future of the commercial sex industry in 2030. *Manoa: Journal for Fried and Half Fried Ideas (About the Future).* December. Retrieved 27 November, 2014 from www.friedjournal.com/xxxpotential-impact-the-future-of-the-commercial-sex-industry-in-2030.

Franks, M. A. (2016). Drafting an effective "revenge porn" law: A guide for legislators. *Cyber Civil Rights Initiative.* Retrieved March 19, 2017 from www.cybercivilrights.org/guide-to-legislation.

Gilbert, J. (2013). Materialities of text: Between the codex and the net. *New Formations: A Journal of Culture/Theory/Politics, 78*(1), 5–6.

Glenza, J. (2014). Jennifer Lawrence denounces nude photos hack as 'sex crime'. *The Guardian.* 7 October. Retrieved November 27, 2014 from www.theguardian.com/film/2014/oct/07/jennifer-lawrence-nude-photo-hack-sex-crime.

Gordon-Messer, D., Bauermeister, J. A., Grodzinski, A., & Zimmerman, M. (2013). Sexting among young adults. *Journal of Adolescent Health, 52*(3), 301–306.

Hagemann-White, C., et al. (2008). *Gendering human rights violations: The case of interpersonal violence.* Brussels: European Commission.

Hanmer, J., & Itzin, C. (Eds.). (2000). *Home truths about domestic violence: Feminist influences on policy and practice: A reader.* London: Routledge.

Hasinoff, A. A. (2015). *Sexting panic: Rethinking criminalization, privacy, and consent.* Champaign, IL: University of Illinois Press.

Hearn, J. (1998). *The violences of men.* London: Sage.

Hearn, J. (2006). The implications of information and communication technologies for sexualities and sexualized violences: Contradictions of sexual citizenships. *Political Geography, 25*(8), 944–963.

Hearn, J., & Jyrkinen, M. (2007). "I could be talking about a porn flick": Television-Internet Media Companies' Policies and Practices, Young People and Pornographisation. In *Unge, kjoenn og pornografi i Norden – Mediestudier [Young people, gender and pornography in the Nordic region – media studies]*, (pp. 11–155). Copenhagen: Nordic Council of Ministers. TemaNord 2006, 544. Retrieved from www.norden.org/da/publikationer/publikationer/2006-544.

Hearn, J., & Parkin, W. (2001). *Gender, sexuality and violence in organizations: The unspoken forces of organization violations.* London: Sage.

Hoff, J. (1989). Why is there no history of pornography? In S. Gubar and J. Hoff (Eds.), *For adult users only: The dilemma of violent pornography*, (pp. 17–46). Bloomington: Indiana University Press.

Holehouse, M. (2014). Cameron backs curbs on revenge pornography. *The Daily Telegraph*. 14 July. Retrieved 27 November, 2014 from www.telegraph.co.uk/news/politics/david-cameron/10956790/David-Cameron-backs-crackdown-on-revenge-pornography.html.

Hughes, D. (2002). The use of new communication and information technologies for the sexual exploitation of women and children. *Hastings Women's Law Journal*, *13*(1), 127–146.

Hunter, M. (2011). Shake it baby, shake it: Consumption and the new gender relation in hip-hop. *Sociological Perspectives*, *54*(1), 15–36.

Itzin, C. (Ed.) (1993). *Pornography: Women, violence and civil liberties: A radical new view*. Oxford: Oxford University Press.

Jeffreys, S. (2013). The 'agency' of men: Male buyers in the global sex industry. In J. Hearn, M. Blagojević, & K. Harrison (Eds.), *Rethinking transnational men: Beyond, between and within nations* (pp. 59–75). New York: Routledge.

Johansson, T., & Hammarén, N. (2007). Hegemonic masculinity and pornography: Young people's attitudes toward and relations to pornography. *Journal of Men's Studies*, *15*(1), 57–71.

Kaufman, G. (1996). *The psychology of shame* (2nd ed.). New York: Springer.

Lacey, B. (2007). Social aggression: A study of internet harassment. Unpublished Doctoral Dissertation, Long Island University.

Levin, D. E., & Kilbourne, J. (2009). *So sexy so soon: The new sexualized childhood and what parents can do to protect their kids*. New York: Ballantine Books.

Paasanen, S. (2011). *Carnal resonance: Affect and online pornography*. Cambridge, MA: MIT Press.

Paasanen, S., Nikunen, K., & Saarenmaa, L. (Eds.). (2007). *Pornification: Sex and sexuality in media culture*. Oxford and New York: Berg.

Rahman, M., & Jackson, S. (2010). *Gender & sexuality: Sociological approaches*. Cambridge: Polity.

Ringrose, J., Gill, R., Livingston, S., & Harvey, L. (2012). A qualitative study of children, young people and sexting. *NSPCC*. Retrieved April 26, 2015 from www.nspcc.org.uk/globalassets/documents/research-reports/qualitative-study-children-young-people-sexting-report.pdf.

Salter, M. (2013) 'Responding to revenge porn: Gender, justice and online legal impunity'. Paper delivered at: Whose justice? Conflicted approaches to crime and conflict, University of Western Sydney, Sydney, September 27.

Sanghani, R. (2014). Jennifer Lawrence photo leak: Let's stop calling this hacking 'the fappening'. *The Telegraph*. September 2. Retrieved August 13, 2015 from www.telegraph.co.uk/women/womens-life/11069829/Jennifer-Lawrence-photo-leak-Lets-stop-calling-this-hacking-The-Fappening.html.

Schwalbe, M. (2013). *Manhood acts*. Boulder, CO: Paradigm.

Segal, L., & McIntosh, M. (1993). *Sex exposed: Sexuality and the pornography debate*. New Brunswick, NJ: Rutgers University Press.

Slonje, R., Smith, P. K., & Frisén, A. (2013). The nature of cyberbullying, and strategies for prevention. *Computers in Human Behavior*, *29*(1), 26–32.

Stark, E. (2009). *Coercive control: How men entrap women in personal life*. New York: Oxford University Press.

Svoboda, E. (2014). Virtual assault. *Scientific American Mind, 25*(6), 46–53.

Thomson, R. (1999). 'It was the way we were watching it': Young men negotiate pornography. In J. Hearn & S. Roseneil (Eds.), *Consuming cultures: Power and resistance.* (pp. 178–198). London: Palgrave Macmillan.

Weitzer, R. (2011). Review essay: Pornography's effects: The need for solid evidence: A review essay of everyday pornography, edited by K. Boyle (New York: Routledge, 2010) and Pornland: How porn has Hijacked our sexuality, by G. Dines (Boston: Beacon, 2010). *Violence Against Women, 17*(5), 666–675.

Wellman, B. (2001). Physical space and cyberspace: the rise of personalized networking. *International Journal of Urban and Regional Research, 25*(2), 227–252.

Whisnant, R. (2010). From Jekyll to Hyde: The grooming of male pornography consumers. In K. Boyle (Ed.), *Everyday pornography* (pp. 114–133). London: Routledge.

World Health Organisation. (2014). Violence against women: Intimate partner and sexual violence against women. November. Retrieved August 11, 2015 from www.who.int/mediacentre/factsheets/fs239/en.

Yoshimura, S. (2007). Goals and emotional outcomes of revenge activities in interpersonal relationships. *Journal of Social and Personal Relationships, 24*, 87–98.

# 4

# ONLINE INTERACTIONS

## Internet usage

The growth, popularity and speed of worldwide interconnections between individual networks operated by government, industry, academia and private parties, or rather the Internet, is quite remarkable. Its growth since 2000 has been a staggering 900.4%, and it is regularly used by 49.2% of the world's population, or more than 3 and a half billion people worldwide (Internet World Stats, 2016, June 30: www.internetworldstats.com/stats.htm). Unsurprisingly, many of those users live in the more developed regions of Europe, North America and Oceania, but also on the rise are those in the Middle East and Latin America where more than half of the population regularly go online (ibid.).

The Internet provides almost instantaneous and near universal access with 3G mobile broadband, with superfast broadband and 4G on the increase (OFCOM, 2016), providing faster online access to various online resources. The Internet is used for a multitude of purposes. Popular usage varies from sending emails, information searches, banking, watching movies, social networking, news reading, shopping, booking holidays and listening to music. According to the Office of Communications' (OFCOM, 2016, p. 197) *The Communications Market Report: United Kingdom,*

> adult users in the UK currently spend an average of one day per week (25 hours) online; 42% say they go online or check apps more than 10 times a day, while around one in 10 (11%) access the internet more than 50 times daily.

While the majority of users fall into the 16–24 age bracket, more than half of those ages 55 and above in the more developed regions of the word also use the Internet on a regular basis (ibid.). The portability of devices to access the Internet – smartphones, laptops, tablets – means the Internet can be accessed almost anywhere and at any time of day.

## Types of interaction in cyberspace

Laurillard (2002) examined the various ways Internet platforms are designed to interact with viewers. She identified five levels of viewer interaction with electronic media. The most basic form of interaction is the 'narrative' level in which the viewer is a passive receiver of information. Examples of this are some news websites and watching videos. The second level is 'interactive', which allows the viewer to actively explore the website and decide what to view. The viewer however, cannot change the online content. Visitors to revenge porn websites can explore the images, videos and accompanying text of the numerous victims, view adverts and visit external websites via hyperlinks. The next level is 'communicative'. This level includes online media that allows viewers to participate in discussions or interact with the material they encounter. For example, people can engage with each other in Internet forums and with each other through comments to news articles, videos, revenge porn material and so on. This is a common facility on revenge porn websites and is often used as a means for viewers to anonymously abuse and insult the victim, the perpetrator and other specified and non-specified others. The fourth is the 'adaptive' level, and includes media that allows the viewer to communicate with the moderator. Until fairly recently MyEx.com's moderator 'Casey' was the first to provide commentary on the victim presumably to encourage viewers to respond and thus maximise the impact of revenge act. While skewed toward the victim, the perpetrator is not immune, especially if the victim is deemed visually pleasing and sexually desirable. The final level is that of the cognitive level, 'productive'. This includes media that allow viewers to demonstrate their understanding of the information provided and may include writing stories or creating a garment. This final and highest level is not yet, and unlikely to be, available on revenge porn sites.

## Communicating in cyberspace

Given the vast array of ways people can engage with online sources and each other via computer-mediated forms of communication, it should not be surprising to learn that these have impacted on identities (Tyler & Feldman, 2005) – that is, how people present themselves to others when surfing the web. These have important implications for the study of revenge pornography since it allows us to see who commits revenge porn – genuine ex-partners or hoaxers – and what motivates them, for example, purely motivated by revenge or for entertainment, excitement and so on. Focusing on the construction of online identities, we look at self-presentation, identity deception and the co-construction of the online self.

## Self-presentation

According to Goffman (1959, p. 9) 'When an individual plays a part, he [sic] implicitly requests his observers take seriously the impression that is fostered before them.' What Goffman was saying, was that people manage their own self-image in their everyday interactions, which is akin to a performance. Performances are aimed at creating a definitive impression to an audience at a given time in a specific context. As such, performances are dependent on the occasion in which they are taking place. So for example, one may wish to create the appearance of frivolity and sexual appeal while partying with friends yet present oneself as a high achiever, exacting and as an individual and team player while at a job interview. Such performances consist of both verbal and non-verbal cues. Verbal cues might include intonations, pauses, openings, greetings, insertion repairs and so on (Wilkinson & Weatherall, 2011), while non-verbal cues could range from basic facial expressions like smiles and frowns or body movements, posture, dress sense and hairstyles to more subtle cues such as eye tracks, smells, twitches and so on (Goffman, 1959).

Communication in cyberspace environments is, in part, different since many of these cues are absent. For example, a simple non-photographic or location status update on Facebook is devoid of visual and verbal cues. 'Facebook friends' are instead left to gain additional details from the content of the post; from word selection, grammar, word capitalisation, vernaculars, emoticons, positioning and orientations. This means that spatial characteristics of virtual environments are often considerably different to those of physical environments (see Bargh & McKenna, 2004; McKenna & Bargh, 2000 for reviews). For instance, in a discussion forum one can remain anonymous with a tag, avatar or pseudonym, which may not bear any resemblance to the offline self. An additional way of maintaining anonymity is communicating in the Deep Web. Web users can surf anonymously using The Onion Router (TOR). TOR is a network of virtual tunnels that allows people to avoid being tracked by other websites and their identity revealed through 'traffic analysis' – that is, identifying users from their data payload and their header. As a consequence, anonymity in online communication has the potential to facilitate deceptive (and criminal) behaviour or allow individuals to reveal or construct an aspect of a real or desired identity which may be deemed taboo or difficult in their offline life such as the sexual desires and preferences of those with disabilities (Shildrick, 2007; Tyler & Feldman, 2005). Yet, the presentation of the self in an online setting is often infused with what we want to reveal and that which we might not. As Turkle (2013, p. 154) points out:

> When part of your life is lived in virtual places – it can be Second Life, a computer game, a social networking site – a vexed relationship develops between what is true and what is 'true here', true in simulation. In games where we expect to play an avatar, we end up being ourselves in the most revealing ways; on social-networking sites such as Facebook, we think we

will be presenting our-selves, but our profile ends up as somebody else – often the fantasy of who we want to be.

So what are the contexts in which people choose to be (un)intentionally deceptive or create fantasy selves, or simply reveal their 'true' or 'real' offline identities?

## Online deception

Many police forces across the globe now have specific Internet units that solely target cybercrimes such as identity, copyright and financial theft, hacking, stalking, bullying and child and adult sexual abuse. Headlines such as *Girl groomed online 'had gut feeling it was wrong'* (BBC, August 19, 2016) seem all too common as are headlines about fraudsters, hackers, 'cyberbullies' and 'trolls': *Vile internet trolls brand Glaswegian 'trans' woman as 'that' and 'man in a dress' after she posts photo online of prom outfit for sale* (Stewart, *The Daily Record*, September 7, 2016). Sadly, such forms of illegal deception may have fatal consequences. For example, the Latvia-based social network site *Ask.fm* – platform for users to ask each other questions – in recent years has come under strong criticism after anonymous bullying led to death in at least seven teenager suicides (NoBullying.com, 2016).

Legal and more mundane levels of deception have been reported in various Internet computer-mediated communication channels such as résumé sites like LinkedIn (Guillory & Hancock, 2012) and online dating sites. The growth of online dating has been exponential. It is an industry worth $2 billion worldwide with some companies such as Lovestruck experiencing a growth rate of 2,658% (Gibbs, *The Guardian*, November 17, 2013). Members create a profile of themselves (photos are optional) including indicating partner preferences, which the dating website then sends to suitable matches based on the information provided. Members then review others' profiles and decide whether to make contact through the dating website. If communication is reciprocated, offline communication may follow. However, research suggests that some users of these present unrealistic or deceptive images of themselves (Epstein, 2007; Gibbs, Ellison, & Heino, 2006; Schmitt, 2002; Toma, Hancock, & Ellison, 2008; Wiszniewski & Coyne, 2002). Epstein (2007) and Wiszniewski and Coyne (2002) argue that online identities are unreliable, since there is a greater potential for creating a 'mask' (Wiszniewski & Coyne, 2002). Individuals and groups are able to do this because they are in a position to control the flow of information that others receive (Hollingshead, 2001). The granting or denying of access to 'real' information means that online identities can be wholly manufactured as in the world of gaming or a combination of 'real', exaggerated, fantasy and intentionally deceptive. These identity constructions have been reported not only in online dating, but also in social media, professional, curriculum vitae and any other Internet site that requires the user to construct a visible identity profile (McKenna, Green, & Gleason, 2002).

Revenge porn websites also offer the potential for online deception. A US woman, who claimed to be a victim of revenge porn, filed a lawsuit against the social media organisation Facebook for $123 million (Mazza, 2014). She claims a former ex-partner set up a fake Facebook page in her name and posted explicit images of someone else's body but with her face. According to the defendant, she asked Facebook to take it down, but the social network failed to act. Facebook has since clarified its guidelines, providing more details about the removal of posts such as those threatening to harm people physically, online bullying, shaming and degradation, anything that discusses self-harm such as suicide or eating disorders and so on (Elise, 2015).

This example shows how easy it is for perpetrators to undertake revenge porn anonymously, even though the victim may not have allowed explicit images to be taken. One could remain anonymous with a tag, avatar or pseudonym, which may not bear any resemblance to the offline self on any revenge porn website, pornography website, social media or any other website that allows for the uploading of explicit images. As we noted earlier, this can be facilitated by communicating in the Deep Web via platforms such as The Onion Router (TOR), Anonymouse, ProxFree, HideMe and so on. However, that is not to say that every person who posts explicit images of someone else for revenge posts anonymously because the person pictured, their family, friends, work colleagues and acquaintances may know who has committed the act even hiding behind a tag, avatar or pseudonym. The victim is likely to know (if they are aware of the images) who took them and who is likely to have posted them, especially if the accompanying text claims for example, 'This is my ex'. Of course this does not guarantee the person posting them is an ex-partner since, as we noted in Chapter 1, some revenge porn is committed by hackers.

### Revealing oneself

According to McKenna, Green and Gleason (2002, p. 30),

> individuals use [the Internet] as a means not only of maintaining ties with existing family and friends but also of forming close and meaningful new relationships in a relatively nonthreatening environment. The Internet may also be helpful for those who have difficulty forging relationships in face-to-face situations because of shyness, social anxiety or a lack of social skills [our emphasis].

A relatively nonthreatening environment is important then for the development of various types of communities, especially ones in which membership is a social taboo, such as a cult or sexual fantasy group. It may simply be someone wanting to discuss a socially or personally delicate topic such as sex, sexuality, illness, disability, political and religious persuasion to name just a few. Such epistemic, associational or communities of practice and persuasion tend to be reinforced and facilitated by a shared language of experience (Greer, 2012; Hall, Grogan, & Gough, 2015; Thelwall & Vaughn, 2004; Wenger, 1998). Greenfield and Subrahmanyam (2003) and Coyle and MacWhannell (2002) suggest that this language of experience is identifiable when examining how such communities go about constructing their group identity. Online shared experiences rely on the same references to spaces, embodiment, time and emotional and social bonds. Many of these features have been identified in health-related forums for depression, anxiety, obesity, cancer (Tanis, 2010), those affected by suicide (Horne & Wiggins, 2009), eating disorders (Winzelburg, 1997) and sexual abuse (Moursand, 1997). These communities were seen to be disclosing shared experiences and stories, knowledge, meanings and social positions with those who have membership entitlement within the same electronic space. While the majority of responses to revenge porn are sexual and image based abuses aimed at the pictured person, some people also disclose shared meanings, stories, experiences, etc.

Online communities can provide a variety of benefits to members, which can help to develop stronger and deeper relationships with other members (McKenna et al., 2002). Greer (2012) and Ba (2001) suggest that members benefit from increased self-esteem, respect and community status. For example, those who post revenge porn often boast about the sexual acts they claim to have done to the victim. We show some of these in our analytical chapters later in the book. Support can take the form of instrumental, informational and emotional, although instrumental support is likely to be sparse given its physicality. However, informational can be incredibly important in sharing practical information about legal issues related to revenge porn, contact details of people posted, other revenge porn websites and so on. As Tanis (2010) points out, this type of knowledge-based support allows others to gain additional control over their current situation, reducing uncertainty and facilitating decision making. Emotional support on the other hand involves shared understanding of feelings displaying through empathy, compassion, comforting and commitment. This can often take the form of simply talking about the issue and knowing that someone is willing to listen without passing judgement. While both of these forms of social support can be beneficial in reducing anxieties and stress, exposing one's vulnerabilities may also have its setbacks. That is, the wrong advice and information, however well intended, could have serious consequences. Indeed, as we pointed out earlier, trolls take pleasure in deliberately upsetting others (Stewart, *The Daily Record*, September 7, 2016) and revenge porn viewers may also post responses intended to upset the poster.

## The co-construction of identity

We argue in the following chapter that during conversation, interactants may orientate to a particular identity or identities depending on who the other interactants are, the context of the interaction and what the interactants are trying to achieve. So for example, in a conversation with one's line manager one may be attempting to construct an identity of a loyal, hard-working employee who is committed to the organisation with the objective of seeking better working conditions and a pay raise, whereas the line manager might be attempting to work up an identity of the employer who is strapped for cash and so unable to grant the requests. In a different context one may try to work up an identity of someone who is too busy to stop, or that already donates to several charities on a regular basis, when being addressed by a street fundraiser. One may also wish to disidentify with others but not feel comfortable enough to do so publicly because social taboos exist for this identity. Of particular interest for this book is how revenge porn posters' identities and their bounded-activities and characteristics are managed, specifically, how this identity co-constructed during interactions between poster and the presumed viewers. These social 'facts' as we show in our analytical chapters can be observed and studied through available data on talk and action. With the advent of the Internet this includes online electronic forms of communication.

## Online privacy

Given the negative aspects of some online communications it might not be surprising to learn that a significant number of people report being concerned about their online privacy (Jiang, Heng, & Choi, 2013; Madden & Smith, 2010). Buchanan, Paine, Joinson and Reips (2007) note several multidimensional definitions of privacy. *Informational privacy* relates to a person's right to determine how, when and to what extent their information is released to others. *Accessibility privacy* relates to a person's right to determine how, when and to what extent their information is accessible to others. This overlaps *informational privacy* where the acquisition or attempted acquisition of information involves gaining access to that person. It overlaps also with the *physical dimension of privacy*. The *physical dimension of privacy* is the degree to which a person is physically accessible to others. Thus, *accessibility privacy* overlaps with this where physical access is at stake (intrusions by spam mail, computer viruses, accessing personal information). The final dimension of privacy is *expressive privacy*. This provides a person with the opportunity to continue or to modify identity-related behaviours from interferences, pressure and coercion from others, for example, trolls. Of course, central to these dimensions is the person's ability to control the information that others can access and use. Thus, the level of privacy depends on the individual based on the individual's personal values.

Clearly, revenge porn breaches the victim's privacy on all four levels. The posting of explicit images of another without his or her consent infringes the victim's right to determine who sees his or her body. Revenge porn images are often accompanied by the victim's personal information such as full name, home, work and email addresses; details of family, friends and colleagues and the social media sites the victim uses, the objective being to humiliate the victim to as many people who they come into contact with as possible. Making private information public can often lead people to recognise the victim in public, to come to their home address and to contact him or her by phone, text messages, emails and through Facebook (BBC *Newsbeat*, 2014). Victims therefore also lose the opportunity to continue or to modify identity-related behaviours.

What is clear is that the perpetrator is able to determine his or her own levels of online privacy. Having the means to post anonymously and via online privacy platforms such as TOR, perpetrators are able to determine what information about themselves they provide to others. They are also able to determine how their information is accessible to others, if at all (disclosure to those who know the victim, police forces). Given that revenge porn is illegal in some countries, perpetrators thus walk a fine line between providing enough information so that the victims know who is responsible but not incriminating themselves. Some of this information is visible in the study of perpetrators' online texts. In the following chapter we detail a discursive approach to analysing online texts.

## References

Ba, S. (2001). Establishing online trust through a community responsibility system. *Decision Support Systems*, *31*(3), 323–336.

Bargh, J. A., & McKenna, K. Y. A. (2004). The internet and social life. *Annual Review Psychology*, *55*, 573–590.

BBC. (2014). Revenge porn victim: I trusted him, now I'm on 200 sites. *Newsbeat*. April 3. Retrieved April 2, 2015, from www.bbc.co.uk/newsbeat/26852254.

BBC. (2016). Girl groomed online 'had gut feeling it was wrong'. August 19. Retrieved September 12 from www.bbc.co.uk/news/uk-wales-37120572.

Buchanan, T., Paine, C., Joinson, A. N., & Reips, U. D. (2007). Development of measures of online privacy concern and protection for use on the Internet. *Journal of the American Society for Information Science and Technology*, *58*(2), 157–165.

Coyle, J., & MacWhannell, D. (2002). The importance of 'morality' in the social construction of suicide in Scottish newspapers. *Sociology of Health & Illness*, *24*(6), 689–713.

Elise, A. (2015). Facebook clarifies rules on cyberbullying, revenge porn, nudity and more. *International Business Times*. March 16. Retrieved September 13, 2016 from www.ibtimes.com/facebook-clarifies-rules-cyberbullying-revenge-porn-nudity-more-1848210.

Epstein, R. (2007). The truth about online dating. *Scientific American Mind*. Retrieved June 19, 2010 from http://drrobertepstein.com/pdf/Epstein-TheTruthAboutOnlineDating-2-07.pdf.

Gibbs, J. L., Ellison, N. B., & Heino, R. D. (2006). Self-presentation in online personals: The role of anticipated future interaction, self-disclosure, and perceived success in Internet dating. *Communication Research*, *33*(2), 152–176.

Gibbs, S. (2013). Growth of 3,000%? Meet Britain's top tech startups. *The Guardian*. November 17. Retrieved January 13, 2016 from: http://www.theguardian.com/technology/2013/nov/17/britain-top-10-tech-startups.

Goffman, E. (1959). *The presentation of self in everyday life*. Garden City, NY: Doubleday.

Greenfield, P. M., & Subrahmanyam, K. (2003). Online discourse in a teen chatroom: New codes and new modes of coherence in a visual medium. *Applied Developmental Psychology*, *24*(6), 713–738.

Greer, G. (2012). *Online communities of practice: Current information systems research*. Create Space Independent Publishing Platform.

Guadagno, E. R., Okdie, B. M., & Kruse, S. A. (2012). Dating deception: Gender, online dating, and exaggerated self-presentation. *Computers in Human Behavior, 28*(2), 642–647.

Guillory, J., & Hancock, J. T. (2012). The effect of Linkedin on deception in resumes. *Cyberpsychology, Behavior, and Social Networking, 15*(3), 135–140.

Hall, M., Grogan, S., & Gough, B. (2015). Bodybuilders' accounts of synthol use: The construction of lay expertise. *The Journal of Health Psychology, 21*(9), 1939–1948.

Hollingshead, A. B. (2001). Communication technologies, the internet and group research. In M. A. Hogg & R. S. Tindale (Eds.), *Blackwell handbook of social psychology: Group processes* (pp. 221–235). London: Sage Publications.

Horne, J. & Wiggins, S. (2009). Doing being 'on the edge': Managing the dilemma of being authentically suicidal in an online forum. *Sociology of Health & Illness, 31*(2), 170–184.

Internet World Stats. (2016). Internet usage statistics. *Miniwatts Marketing Group.* June 20. Retrieved September 12 from www.internetworldstats.com/stats.htm.

Jiang, Z., Heng, C. S., & Choi, B. C. (2013). Research note—Privacy concerns and privacy-protective behavior in synchronous online social interactions. *Information Systems Research, 24*(3), 579–595.

Laurillard, D. (2002). *Rethinking university teaching: A conversational framework for the effective use of learning technologies.* New York: Routledge Falmer.

Madden, M., & Smith, A. (2010). Reputation management and social media. Retrieved 3 August 2017 from http://www.pewinternet.org/2010/05/26/reputation-management-and-social-media/.

Mazza, E. (2014). Facebook sued for $123 million over 'revenge porn'. *The Huffington Post.* July 30. Retrieved September 13, 2016 from www.huffingtonpost.com/2014/07/30/facebook-sued-over-revenge-porn_n_5632865.html.

McKenna, K. Y. A., & Bargh, J. A. (2000). Plan 9 from cyberspace: The implications of the internet for the personality and social psychology. *Personality and Social Psychology Review, 4*, 57–75.

McKenna, K. Y. A., Green, A. S., & Gleason, M. E. J. (2002). Relationship formation on the Internet: What's the big attraction? *Journal of Social Issues, 58*(1), 9–31.

Moursand, J. (1997). Sanctuary: Social support on the Internet. In J. E. Behar (Ed.), *Mapping cyber-space: Social research on the electronic frontier* (pp. 121–123). Oakdale, NY: Dowling College Press.

NoBullying.com. (2016). Stories of 7 teen suicides because of Ask.fm bullying. August 14. Retrieved September 12 from https://nobullying.com/stories-of-7-teen-suicides-because-of-ask-fm-bullying.

Office of Communications. (2016). The communications market report: United Kingdom. August 4. Retrieved September 12 from: http://stakeholders.ofcom.org.uk/binaries/research/cmr/cmr16/uk/CMR_UK_2016.pdf.

Schmitt, D. P. (2002). A meta-analysis of sex differences in romantic attraction: Do rating contexts moderate tactic effectiveness judgments? *British Journal of Social Psychology, 41*(3), 387–402.

Shildrick, M. (2007). Dangerous discourses: Anxiety, desire, and disability. *Studies in Gender & Sexuality, 8*(3), 221–244.

Stewart, K. (2016). Vile internet trolls brand Glaswegian 'trans' woman as 'that' and 'man in a dress' after she posts photo online of prom outfit for sale. *The Daily Record.* September 7. Retrieved September 12 from www.dailyrecord.co.uk/news/scottish-news/vile-internet-trolls-brand-glaswegian-8785355.

Tanis, M. (2010). Online social support groups. In A. Joinson, K. McKenna, T. Posters, & U. Reips (Eds.), *The Oxford handbook of internet psychology* (pp. 139–154). Oxford: Oxford University Press.

Thelwall, M., & Vaughn, L. (2004). Webometrics. *Journal of the Association for Information Science and Technology, 55*(14), 1213–1215.

Toma, C. L., Hancock, J. T., & Ellison, N. B. (2008). Separating fact from fiction: An examination of deceptive self-presentation in online dating profiles. *Personality & Social Psychology Bulletin, 34*(8), 1023–1036.

Turkle, S. (2013). *Alone together: Why we expect more from technology and less from each other.* New York: Basic Books.

Tyler, J. M., & Feldman, R. S. (2005). Deflecting threat to one's image: Dissembling personal information as a self-presentation strategy. *Basic & Applied Social Psychology, 27*(4), 371–378.

Wenger, E. (1998). *Communities of practice: Learning, meaning, and identity.* Cambridge: Cambridge University Press.

Wilkinson, S., & Weatherall, A. (2011). Insertion repair. *Research on Language & Social Interaction, 44*(1), 65–91.

Winzelburg, A. (1997). The analysis of an electronic support group for individuals with eating disorders. *Computers in Human Behaviour, 13*(3), 393–407.

Wiszniewski, D., & Coyne, R. (2002). Mask and identity: The hermeneutics of self construction in the information age. In K. A. Renninger & W. Shumar (Eds.), *Building virtual communities* (pp. 191–214). New York: Cambridge Press.

# 5

# A DISCURSIVE APPROACH TO REVENGE PORN

## Ethnomethodology

Since the focus in this book is the electronic text accompanying perpetrators' postings of sexually explicit material, this chapter examines this phenomenon through the lens of discourse analysis. In particular, we draw upon Jonathan Potter's (1996) approach set out in *Representing Reality: Discourse, Rhetoric and Social Construction*. This approach, deployed in Chapters 6, 7 and 8, derives from Harold Garfinkel's (1967) *Studies in Ethnomethodology*. Garfinkel's primary aim was to develop a methodology for studying the social orders people use in making sense of their everyday interactions. His work was informed by the constitutive phenomenological ideas of Edmund Husserl.

Phenomenology appears to have developed in four phases from Husserl's early realist phenomenological search for universal essences of human actions in order to develop constitutive phenomenology and its reflections of phenomenological methodology. A third phase of existential phenomenology was developed by Heidegger, Sartre and Merleau-Ponty and considered specific actions, conflict, desire, finitude, oppression and death. The latter phase of hermeneutical phenomenology began in the 1960s and looked at textual interpretations, as well as issues such as ecology, ethnicity and gender.

Broadly speaking, phenomenology disengages with philosophical concerns with the nature of reality, our existence, knowledge, values and ethics instead focusing on understanding how people collectively construct meaning from their experiences of their everyday lives and interactions. These are the collective meanings people co-create. So, for example, gender and notions of appropriate conduct in intimate relations as well as participating in sexually explicit images and videos are meanings created collectively by people and subject to change and location. Such meanings are intersubjective because they are co-created from people's interactions with each other. People vary their interactions depending on who they are talking to, what they are talking about, when they are talking and where they are talking. We might discuss our work on revenge porn differently with colleagues than we would with the media or an activist. Meanings are rooted in people's actions and words. From a phenomenological perspective, words do things such as describing, ordering, accounting and so rather than acting as neutral vehicles in which meaning in an internal attribute of those who speak them.

People's experiences of the social world are also perceived as orderly and intelligible through their correspondence with the activities of other people. People are therefore, not passive receivers of their experiences, but rather, the interpreters of their world in which they live and act upon. While there is a multiplicity of ways of interpreting social phenomenon, people are still able to understand how others are defining the world from what they do. Essentially, people read the behaviour of others for what it tells them about how others understand a situation and act according to their readings. On account of this, people are able to produce orderliness out of their own and others' actions.

Schütz's (1967) interest was to rework conventional forms of positivist social research that attempted to emulate the research on the natural sciences. Particular characteristics that Schütz challenged were the researcher's ability to enjoy separateness from the object of study. Instead, he argued that the ontological status of the social researcher is one of being part of the social world that is being examined and interpreted. The social researcher who focuses on aspects of the social world, such as social interaction, should therefore, develop consistent, adequate and meaningful interpretations that relate to the common-sense understandings people use to experience the social world. Schutz (1967) argued that the methods people use are the ones, which social researchers should relate their interpretations to since they are created through a process of continual typification. That is, the everyday social actions, interactions and behaviours that people experience are identified, classified and assigned by them to a specific type or category of action or interaction. It was Schutz's work that had the greatest influence on Garfinkel's work.

Garfinkel's (1967) research set out in his book *Studies in Ethnomethodology* developed a methodological apparatus for understanding the social processes and social actions that are routinely produced from the orderly and intelligible interactions of people. For example, in the 1960s Agnes, a 19-year-old male-to-female transsexual presented herself at the Gender Identity Clinic, University of California, Los Angeles, as a physically and socially feminine woman but with male genitals. Agnes wanted genital reassignment surgery in order to have a vagina. Although raised as a boy, Agnes claimed she began to be feminised during puberty and was comfortable with that identity. Doctors at the clinic categorised Agnes as an intersex person with rare testicular feminisation syndrome. The co-construction as Agnes as a woman requiring genital surgery by clinical staff, and by Agnes herself, during interviews and assessments served as powerful example for Garfinkel to show how gender and sexual norms become collaboratively worked up and maintained during interaction. The existence of such norms meant that Agnes' accomplishment of gender required (1967, p. 134)

> securing and guaranteeing for herself the ascribed rights and obligations of an adult female by the acquisition and use of skills and capacities, the efficacious display of female appearances and performances, and the mobilising of appropriate feelings and purposes.

Garfinkel's aim in studying Agnes was to identify the features that 'normal' sexed people take for granted. Thus, he wanted to understand how people achieve sex category membership in various circumstances and contexts, while their actions appear as objective, factual and trans-situational, in other words, the management or 'passing' for being a woman or man. Ergo, Garfinkel was able to produce a list of the properties that constituted people as 'natural, normally sexed persons' (Garfinkel, 1967, p. 122). In brief, Garfinkel argued:

1    Society is populated by only two sexes – fe/male.
2    This dichotomisation is motivated on compliance.
3    Each person routinely enforces either fe/male on themselves.
4    Fe/male are the only *bona fide* members.
5    Insignia such as a vagina or penis are essential in the identifying process whereas qualities, actions, relationships etc. are transparent and temporary.
6    Other people recognise each other as fe/male pre-, peri-, post-life.
7    The presence of only two sexes is seen the natural state of affairs.

Accordingly, he was able to develop a methodology that allows for the observation of, '*how* normal sexuality is accomplished through witnessable displays of talk and conduct' (1967, p. 180). Ethnomethodological enquiry therefore reports on the 'apparent concreteness' of social phenomena as it is understood by members of society, which is then drawn upon to maintain a sense of meaning and existence in social life even though 'concreteness' does not actually exist in itself (Garfinkel, 1991, pp. 10–19). These social 'facts' Garfinkel argued can be observed and studied through available data on talk and action. We show in our analytical chapters that posters deploy gender and sexuality norms in accounting for their normative action (revenge) for another's non-normative actions. For example, these might include challenging someone's gender based on genital size or questioning a person's sexuality based on his or her sexual preferences and desires. We show how these and others are invoked in posted online electronic talk in action in our analytical chapters focused on heterosexual men and women, and gay men and lesbians.

Of course, Garfinkel's work has been subject to much criticism (Bologh, 1992; Denzin, 1990; Goldthorpe, 1973). For example, ethnomethodology cannot tell us anything very important about many large political and social issues, as its main concern is with how we constitute this world, rather than what we constitute it as being. In this respect, it is argued that although people's interactions produce a social reality, some outcomes of the interaction may not be intended for some of the participants, and some of the interactional content will remain independent of the actors that created it. Goldthorpe (1973, p. 456) argues that 'a law, a regulation, a customary practice, a point of etiquette is an "intelligible" even when it is in no one's mind'. Therefore, as objective content exists outside of people's interactions, even though it originated through people's interactions, they are still valid and of some interest for social researchers to study. Furthermore, Goldthorpe (1973, p. 457) argues that the physical world and objective content continue to interact and influence the intersubjective world that people co-create in their interaction. Goldthorpe and others therefore call for the continuation of ontological pluralism in social research. The argument is a compelling one, but is unable to dismiss the usefulness of a methodology of social action that provides an understanding of the social processes and social actions that are routinely produced from the orderly and intelligible interactions of people. It is this latter point that has kept ethnomethodology influential in psychological enquiry (Kessler & McKenna, 1978; West & Zimmerman, 2009).

There are several discursive traditions that focus on language, which include conversation analysis, critical discourse analysis, discursive psychology, ethnography of communication, Foucauldian research, membership categorisation analysis to name only a few. Logically, which method is chosen depends largely on one's data and analytical focus. For example, if one is looking at macro social issues, then conversation analysis (Jefferson, 1984, 1991; Sacks, 1967, 1972a, 1972b, 1979, 1992; Schegloff, 1997, 1998, 2007) or its relative discursive psychology (Edwards & Potter, 1992) would be inappropriate since their epistemology means they cannot comment on macro issues unless participants make it relevant during their conversational interactions. Critical discourse analysis (Fairclough, 2001) or Foucauldian analysis (Foucault, 1978, 1980) might be more appropriate for this. On the flip side, if one were aiming to focus on the micro details of social interaction, one might choose conversation analysis, discourse analysis, discursive psychology or membership categorisation analysis. While these approaches have similar epistemological standpoints, the appropriate method would depend largely on one's focus and the quality of one's data. Conversation analysis and discursive psychology rely on being able to transcribe the micro verbal and on-verbal details in naturally occurring data (not elicited by the researcher), in either casual or institutional conversation using Jefferson's (1991) transcription notations. If the data are devoid of details such as timeable pauses, in-and out-breaths, conversational repairs and overlaps and so on, as is perpetrators electronic texts, then discourse analysis (Potter, 1996) is more appropriate. While we do draw on tenets, of other methods such as membership categorisation analysis when focusing on posters' accounts, the majority of our analysis follows Potter's discourse analytical approach (DA hereafter), as set out in *Representing Reality: Discourse, Rhetoric and Social Construction*.

## Discourse analysis

Discourse analysts aim to explore how 'versions of world, of society, events and inner psychological worlds are produced in discourse', and so there is 'a concern with participants' constructions and how they are accomplished and undermined' (Potter, 1996, p. 146). In other words, versions of the world are worked up during conversational interaction – including online electronic talk. The relevant version(s) of the world depend on the topic of conversation (for example, revenge), who one is conversing with (for example, [un]known others), the context (for example, cheated on), location (for example, social media) and time (for example, current trend). Versions of the world are presented as factually stable, mirroring some aspect of the world to which they refer. However, these versions are always contestable. Some are perhaps more easily undermined than others. For example, an account by a police officer in a court of law is probably less questionable than the accused's account. In the construction of these descriptions, accounts and blaming each person must bolster their own position while minimising others undermining their claims. One way of understanding this is by the 'dilemma of stake' (Edwards & Potter, 1992). That is,

> [t]he dilemma is anything that a person (or group) says or does may be discounted as a product of stake or interest. The referencing of such as stake is one principle way of discounting the significant of an action, or reworking its nature.
>
> *(Potter, 1996, p. 110)*

Thus, the police officer's blaming of the accused might be discounted as simply needing to secure a conviction regardless of who committed the crime. One might recall the convictions of the Birmingham Six found guilty and sentenced to life imprisonment for the pub bombings at Lancaster Crown Court in 1975. While in custody the Six were deprived of food, sleep and sustained long periods of interrogation without break to elicit a confession regardless of guilt. They were finally acquitted in 1991 (Blom-Cooper, 1997). Ergo, people treat each other's descriptions, accounts and so as self-serving and so are open to dispute.

There are a vast number of ways one can construct an account to bolster what one is claiming to minimise potential challenges from others. Central to these constructions is the categorisation of the object or event being talked about. Categorisations tend to have specific properties (Potter, 1996, p. 111). The object or event can then be presented positively or negatively and supported by recourse to social norms. Such norms included categories' characteristics and associated activities (Sacks, 1996). For example, in Western societies heterosexual relationships are presumed normative for most wo/men. Thus, categorising someone as gay/lesbian can be a term of abuse. These are the (un)spoken rules of social conduct in everyday interactions, which also include conversational norms such as turn taking and providing reasons for decisions such as posting sexually explicit material of another person in a public place. These common features of talk are evident in analysis. In order to see such features, analysts collect naturally occurring conversation by audio-recording casual or institutional talk, and this can be both on- or offline. Offline audio recordings are transcribed, and depending on what one wants to focus on, for example, identities or repair construction, determines the detail of the transcription set out by Jefferson (1984).

Analyzing the text in this way does not mean analysts are searching for the 'truth', or someone's true motivations, but rather how participants have worked their accounts up and what they are designed to achieve. What this means is that a search for 'truth' would lead to an over-analysis of the text because the analysts would be drawing on their own knowledge of social norms and expectations as well as psychologising each participant's intentions. Edwards and Potter (1992) argue therefore, that to avoid analyst-led interpretations of real-world phenomena, analysts should instead read the interactions, that is only what is made relevant, by the participants involved. This later point is one of the major differences with DA and other discursive methodologies such as critical discourse analysis (Fairclough, 2001) and Foucauldian analysis (Foucault, 1978, 1980). Where discursive methodologies such as these also become interpretative commentaries is when they attempt to make links between what emerges from the micro-analysis and macro-issues such as the operation of power, ideology and persuasion. What discourse analysis (Potter, 1996) argues is that macro-structures (and truth claims) can only be commented on if the participants in the interaction make it relevant. If not, then it is simply analyst commentary. It is these features of DA that we use in the examination of the data in the analytical chapters.

## Membership categorisation analysis

Similarly to discourse analysis, Membership Categorisation Analysis (1967, 1972a, 1972b, 1979, 1992 and subsequently extended by Hester & Eglin, 1997; Jayyusi, 1984; Sharrock, 1974; Schegloff, 1997, 1998, 2007 and many others) also has an ethnomethodological underpinning as its focus is on how meaning is co-created during people's interactions with each other. In particular, it is able to show how identity category meanings are worked up, deployed and negotiated during people's talk. Membership categorisation analysis specifically focuses on 'the organization of common-sense knowledge in terms of the categories members employ in accomplishing their activities in and through talk' (Francis & Hester, 2004, p. 21). Put simply, identity categories such as 'slut', 'Whore', 'Domestic Abuser', 'prick', 'dude', 'father' etc. are 'inference rich', carrying large amounts of culturally rich common-sense social knowledge. These categories are able to tell us something about the identity of the categorised. For example, 'father' references a male, typically over 18, who has a biological or adopted child, or indeed is a church leader and considers his congregation his children.

Such social knowledge is not only available from the category itself, but also observable in how people go about identifying others, their realities, social orders, their social relationships with others and how they judge (Jayyusi, 1984). Being able to see these aspects in talk means that talk can be treated as 'culture-in-action' (Hester & Eglin, 1997). Sacks pointed out that there are rules and procedures regarding categories. For example, categories are classifications or social types that may be used to describe people (husband/wife), their actions (providing love and support) and characteristics (caring and sharing). Categories are organisable into membership categorisation devices (Hester & Elgin, 1997; Jayyusi, 1984; McHoul & Watson, 1984). Membership categorisation devices (MCDs) are

> any collection of membership categories, containing at least a category, which may be applied to some population containing at least a member, so as to provide, by use of some rules of application, for pairing of at least a population member and a categorization device member.
>
> *(Sacks, 1974, p. 218)*

MCDs comprise two parts. The first part, is that one or more categories form a collection. Collections of categories (MCD) are ones that go-together and have some meaning in which they all relate. So, for example, husband, wife, child(ren) all go together because they are related and form part of the collection 'nuclear family'. The second feature of MCDs is that the categories within them contain certain 'rules of application'. These rules are applicable to both category and non-category members (Sacks, 1992, p. 238). For example, the 'economy rule' means that a single category suffices to refer to some member of a population, even though multiple other categories could be used to describe that person; we could be referred to 'authors', 'scholars', 'lecturers', 'speakers' and so on. Yet only one of these categories is required to provide meaning for others. Of course, the relevant category selected is dependent on the context in which the person is being referred to. Categories can also be 'duplicatively organised' to produce complete units, for example in relation to universities, such as researchers, lecturers, students, administration and support staff and so on (Sacks, 1992, p. 240). Categories can also form 'standardised relational pairs' (for example, husband/wife) each having their own rights, obligations, responsibilities and duties to the other (for example, care and support) (Jayyusi, 1984). Categories can often be hierarchically organised, where a lecturer (based on knowledge and academic skills) might be considered higher than a student in a university context.

The final rule Sacks identified was the 'consistency rule'. This means that if one category is used for some given population (for example, husband/wife) then all other members of that population can be categorised the same, as they are presumed to have the same attributes (love and support) (Sacks, 1992, pp. 238–239). Sacks suggested that this latter rule contains two 'hearer's maxims'. He demonstrated this in his well-cited example from a children's storybook – 'The baby cried. The mommy picked it up' (Sacks, 1992, p. 236). Sacks argued that we hear the baby as the baby of the mother, even though this is not explicitly stated. This occurs because, 'If there are two categories used, which can be found to be part of the same collection, hear them as part of the same collection – which is how you hear them' (Sacks, 1992, p. 239). However, the baby/mother relationship also contains a second 'hearer's maxim'. This links specific activities and predicates to a specific category of incumbents. Such that,

> If a category-bound activity is asserted to have been done by a member of some category where, if that category is ambiguous (i.e. is a member of at least two different devices) but where, at least for one of those devices, the asserted activity is category bound to the given category, then hear that at least the category from the device to which it is bound is being asserted to hold.
>
> *(Sacks, 1974, p. 224)*

In other words, categories and incumbents are presumed to be doers of particular actions 'category-bound activities' and have specific characteristics 'natural predicates'. For example, the social convention is for babies to cry and mothers to pick them up. Sharrock (1974, p. 49) explains the importance of category-bound activities and predicates:

> The assignment of a name to a corpus sets up the way in which further description is to be done. The name is not, then, merely descriptive in that once it has been assigned it becomes a device-for-describing: that is, the name is not to be revised in light of events but is, rather, to be invoked in the description of whatever events occur.

What Sharrock is saying therefore, is that once a category has specific attributes assigned to it, these attributes don't change but rather, become invoked in the category's deployment (for example, babies crying and mothers picking them up). These category-bound activities and predicates are also important for members in making sense of the everyday social world because this allows for people to make value assessments of other's actions (Wowk, 1984, p. 76) This assessment of morality is important since, 'standards, criteria, judgments, implications, etc. – are bound up with various other practical matters – categorisations, descriptions inferences etc.' (Jayyusi, 1984, p. 181). These moral values tend to become embedded over time through continuity of use, and because they appear 'natural', these moral values help influence members' actions. That is, they constitute normative behaviour in which to judge the actions and characteristics of other people in the same or another category. When norms are breached a disjuncture occurs. This leads to other category members passing moral judgments on the transgression with accusations of the person being 'an exception', 'different' or even 'defective' (Schegloff, 2007, p. 469). Ultimately this would lead to the person either halting the transgressive behaviour or being re-categorised (Speer, 2005, pp. 119–120).

We draw on these characteristics of identity categories and the tools of discourse analysis in our analysis of revenge porn perpetrators' electronic text accompanying the posting of explicit images of their ex-partners.

## MyEx.com

Founded in 2013, the MyEx.com service and website owned by Web Solutions B.V, Netherlands, provides people across national boundaries with a facility to anonymously upload and share images, videos and text of ex-partners and other people they know for the apparent purpose of getting revenge or entertainment. Similar to other porn-related sites there are links to other hardcore porn sites (for example, 'Slut Roulette', 'Better Than Tinder', 'Reality Kings'), sex-dating sites (for example, 'Craigslist', 'Fuckbook', 'Instabang'), sexual versions of well-known gaming (for example, 'Call of Booty', 'Ms PacWhore' and 'Grand Fuck Auto') and live sex links.

Unlike other online revenge porn sites, MyEx.com provides both posters and viewers with the ability to engage with the material they encounter through the computer-mediated communication channel, namely, comments and, specific search facilities. The front page provides visitors with the ability to either post images, search for specific categories of posts such as wo/men, watch live sex, meet other people for sex or find other pornography-related websites via 'The Porn Dude' (TPD). Once one clicks on a specific person the viewer is then taken to the person-specific page on which the videos and images can be viewed. Viewers can then either respond to the poster's accompanying text or each other's posts, or comment on the explicit images of the person they see. Other features of this page included links to specific pornographic videos, 'What's hot' and other people posted on the website by 'Most rated' or 'Most viewed'.

Although people can post explicit images, videos and text of others anonymously, MyEx.com does claim to moderate and remove content perceived to be illegal, such posts containing minors or physical abuse. Ironically, given what we know about the impact of revenge porn on victims, its user content guide states that it does not allow any inappropriate conduct:

> As a condition of your use of the Website:
> - You will not use the Website to submit, publish, display, disseminate, or otherwise communicate any defamatory, inaccurate, abusive, harmful, threatening, obscene, offensive, hateful, discriminatory, or illegal material to any other user of this Website;
> - You will not use the Website to harass or otherwise invade the privacy of another person (including the dissemination of personal information);
> - You will not "stalk" or otherwise harass anyone on the Website.

The site also states elsewhere that users should not engage in 'any activity that is harmful, threatening, abusive, harassing, tortious, invasive of another's privacy or otherwise objectionable to any third party or in any way violates a third party's (or the Company's) rights' (MyEx.com, 2014, August 8, www.myex.com/terms-of-use/). Posts are reported to be removed after 48 hours of receiving a complaint or request to remove material. This 48-hour window might be sufficient for others to begin copying and posting on other web pages. A victim reported being posted on 200 websites in a relatively short period of time (BBC, 2014). However, to remove images, MyEx.com asks for the person to 'Send us the copyright registration number that you received from the copy right office after you registered the photos. If you do not have a copy right registration number, we will ignore your emails.' Being able to remove images is an unlikely scenario for most victims since copyright law states that the photographer who takes the image or video is the owner of the original copyright (Gov.UK, 2014). Thus, within this organisational frame, one might see revenge porn as not just abuse, but controlled, organised or even constrained abuse.

## Data and analysis

MyEx.com's database expands daily and currently contains explicit images, videos and texts of thousands of people and contains posts by male-to-female, female-to-male, female-to-female and male-to-male. We conducted our analysis on March 28, 2016: 10,587 posts (90%) are of women and 1,173 of men (10%). Although images are posted anonymously the gender of the poster can be see through gender orientation and indexing (see Antaki & Widdicombe, 1998). For example, male indexing occurred through male references ('blokes', 'dude', 'guys', 'boys'), positioning in relation to female partners ('wife', 'missus', 'girl-friend') and invoking typical heterosexual masculine markers ('your wife dude') and homosexual masculine markers ('he does take it up the arse I know I've done him'). Female indexing occurred through female references ('girls', 'slut', 'whore', 'women') positioning themselves in relation to the men being displayed ('my ex-husband', 'fucks other girls', 'my ex-boyfriend') and invoking typical heterosexual feminine markers ('got me pregnant'); and lesbian feminine markers ('she's what we call in the lesbian community a pretesbian'). These are treatable as 'fe/male' heterosexual/gay/lesbian even without these identities being 'named out aloud' (Antaki & Widdicombe, 1998, p. 4).

The general aim of our data collection process was to identify, for microtextual discourse analysis, the different ways in which gender and sexuality were invoked by the poster in their accounting for publicly displaying sexually explicit images, movies and text of their ex-partner in revenge seeking. Given this context, we employed the following framework and reviewed the posts according to the following stages:

1   *Identifying relevant texts* by examining title and accompanying text;
2   *Selecting text* according to explicit inclusion and exclusion criteria; and
3   *Discursively analysing the data* following Baker's (1997) three-step process (Chapters 6, 7 and 8).

**TABLE 5.1** Gender inclusion/exclusion criteria matrix

| Inclusion/exclusion criteria | Number of posts | Male | Female |
|---|---|---|---|
| Written in English[a] | 10,813 | 9,731 | 1,082 |
| Non-consensual posts[b] | 10,272 | 9,245 | 1,026 |
| About a former intimate partner | 4,930 | 4,437 | 493 |
| Other[c] | 5,342 | 4,808 | 534 |
| Heterosexual | 4,903 | 4,418 | 529 |
| Same-sex | 24 | 19 | 5 |

a  Approximation only based on aggregating the number of posts in the United States 9,285; United Kingdom 796; Canada 496; Australia 214; and New Zealand 22.
b  Includes, for example, rate my wife/partner, swingers, porn stars.
c  Includes, for example, hacker, a friend, a former ex but not for revenge, sexting, a casual acquaintance, not non-revenge bragging, recognition, rejection.

The inclusion and exclusion criteria were

a    those written in English;
b    posts that were non-consensual;
c    posts claiming to be about a former intimate partner who had cheated on them; and
d    posts by those orientating to heterosexual/gay/lesbian (Table 5.1).

We coded the remaining 4,437 texts by men and 493 texts by women explicitly revenge seeking with NVivo. We created a list of key words and phrases depicting the various types of gender violences and abuses (see GOV.UK, 2013), such as

- physical (e.g. force resulting in pain, discomfort or injury; hitting, pinching, hair-pulling, arm-twisting, strangling, burning, stabbing, punching, pushing, slapping, beating, shoving, kicking, choking, biting);
- sexual (e.g. rape, forcing sexual acts that may be degrading or painful; making unwelcome sexual comments; withholding sexual affection; denial of a person's sexuality or privacy; humiliating, criticising or trying to control a person's sexuality; forced prostitution; unproven allegations of promiscuity and/or infidelity; deliberately exposing a person to a sexually transmitted infection or HIV);
- emotional (e.g. name calling; using silent treatment; denying contact with family and friends; jealousy; humiliating or making fun of the person);
- psychological (e.g. threats of violence; threats of abandonment; stalking/harassment; inappropriately controlling the person's activities);
- spiritual (e.g. not allowing the person to follow her or his preferred spiritual or religious tradition; belittling or making fun of a person's spiritual or religious tradition, beliefs or practices);
- cultural (e.g. committing 'honour' or other crimes where the person may be physically harmed, shunned, maimed or killed);

- verbal (e.g. recalling a person's past mistakes; expressing distrust; yelling; lying; insulting);
- financial (e.g. illegally or improperly using a person's money, assets or property; acts of fraud; pulling off a scam against a person; misusing funds through lies, trickery, controlling or withholding money); and
- neglectful (e.g. failing to meet the needs of a person who is unable to meet those needs alone; not remaining with a person who needs help).

In addition to this we developed codes around the different traditions and perspectives we discussed in Chapter 3: revenge as pornography, interpersonal revenge, violence and abuse, information and computer technologies, publicisations and gender-sexual practices. Numbers of codes were collated into the Table 5.2.

Clearly, many posts contained several, and often competing, discourses. Since we are unable to present all posts here, we then randomly selected exemplars where each of these discourses was drawn on by the poster (not necessarily all in the same post). For these we aimed to examine how posters constructed accounts, gave descriptions, managed their stake in revenge porn and so on, for what they can tell us about their motives. That is, the text is analysed for its individual parts as well as a sequential whole. There are numerous elements of talk that are

**TABLE 5.2** Central discourses

| Central discourses | Heterosexual men | Heterosexual women | Gay | Lesbian |
|---|---|---|---|---|
| Physical assault | 0 | 37 | 0 | 0 |
| Relationship control | 17 | 201 | 0 | 2 |
| Sexual objectification | 1,220 | 83 | 1 | 0 |
| Infidelity[a] | 4,417 | 477 | 19 | 5 |
| Prostitution | 554 | 35 | 0 | 1 |
| Sexuality[b] | 611 | 99 | 4 | 3 |
| Sexual practices[c] | 378 | 104 | 6 | 0 |
| Money[d] | 217 | 110 | 0 | 0 |
| Parenthood[e] | 58 | 64 | 0 | 0 |
| Sexting | 90 | 49 | 1 | 0 |
| Hygiene[f] | 2,573 | 149 | 0 | 1 |

a  This is a metadiscourse and so we only use as an exemplar when the poster refers to their own infidelity as a motivation such as on p. 85.
b  Heterosexual and same-sex post where the victim's sexuality is questioned.
c  Posts in which the victim is portrayed as interested in non-vanilla sexual practices.
d  Posts in which the perpetrator reports either themselves or the victim as having pilfered money, for example, child maintenance or stolen goods and sold them.
e  Where the perpetrator reports themselves or the victim as a poor parent, for example, loss of access to the child(ren) or missed maintenance payments.
f  Refers to people reported to have a sexually transmitted disease or poor bodily hygiene practices. We do not include those that are reported to have had multiple unsafe sexual partners even though this might by some be considered unclean. These we considered were more appropriately categorised as sexual infidelity.

traceable in participants' talk. These are discussed individually where participants have made them relevant and orientated to them. Some of these include letter capitalisation, which is a form of electronic shouting (Robb, 2014), listing and in particular, three-part lists to help bolster claims (Jefferson, 1991), the use of extreme-case formulations (Pomerantz, 1986), as well as non-extreme generalisations to legitimise and support allegations (Edwards, 2000), and the construction of identities and bounded activities and predicates (Sacks, 1992).

## Ethical considerations

Online research can pose a host of specific ethical considerations not necessarily mirrored in offline settings. As the British Psychological Society (2013, p. 1) states,

> Internet-mediated research (IMR) can raise particular, sometimes non-obvious, challenges in adhering to existing ethics principles...These include: the public-private domain distinction; confidentiality and security of online data; procedures for obtaining valid consent; procedures for ensuring withdrawal rights and debriefing; levels of researcher control; and implications for scientific value and potential harm

Given these considerations, ethical approval was sought and received from a former university of the lead author.

Collecting data from the Internet typically presents ethical challenges around what is deemed a 'public' or 'private' space (Hookway, 2008; Rodham & Gavin, 2006; Walther & Boyd, 2002). One obvious issue is whether informed consent can be gained. Scholars (Hookway, 2008; Rodham & Gavin, 2006; Walther & Boyd, 2002) argue that every effort should be made to obtain consent even in open-access online websites. Given that the images, text and video are posted anonymously, gaining consent from each poster would be almost impossible without substantial detective work, as would be consent from victims. Yet privacy issues are still applicable for those whose images are posted on MyEx.com and similar sites. We therefore only draw on the text, and, in line with British Psychological Society (2013) guidelines, we have anonymised the dataset as far as possible (for example, omitting biographical data and replacing names with [identifier omitted etc.] and removing any in-text personal details, vernaculars or references). Certain personal information has also been removed for legal reasons. We have anonymised any visual material used for reference as we do not want to further compromise the dignity of those pictured, even though that restricts some kinds of analysis and interpretation. The question of anonymisation takes on extra importance, as part of the power and practice of revenge pornography is the use of images and text without consent, and in view of the process of damage, sometimes very extended over time, that follows for particular non-anonymised people.

# References

Antaki, C., & Widdicombe, S. (Eds.). (1998). *Identities in talk*. London: Sage.

Baker, C. (1997). Membership categorization and interview accounts. In D. Silverman (Ed.), *Qualitative research: Theory, method and practice*. London: Sage.

BBC. (2014). Bang goes the theory: Big data. *Series 8*. March 24. Retrieved March 24 from www.bbc.co.uk/programmes/b03zjwqw

Blom-Cooper, L. (1997). *The Birmingham Six and other cases: Victims of circumstance*. London: Duckworth.

Bologh, R. W. (1992). The promise and failure of ethnomethodology from a feminist perspective: Comment on Rogers. *Gender & Society*, 6(2), 199–206.

British Psychological Society. (2013). Guidelines for Internet-mediated research. Retrieved December 13, 2013 from www.bps.org.uk/system/files/Public%20files/inf206-guidelines-for-internet-mediated-research.pdf

Denzin, N. K. (1990). Harold and agnes: A feminist narrative undoing. *Sociological Theory*, 8, 198–216.

Edwards, D. (2000). Extreme case formulations: Softeners, investment, and doing non-literal. *Research on Language & Social Interaction*, 33(4), 347–373.

Edwards, D., & Potter, J. (1992). *Discursive psychology: Inquiries in social construction*. London: Sage.

Fairclough, N. (2001). The discourse of new labour: Critical discourse analysis. In M. Wetherell, S. Taylor, & S. Yates. (Eds.), *Discourse as data: A guide for analysis*. London: Sage.

Foucault, M. (1978). *The history of sexuality, Volume 1: An introduction*. Trans. R. Hurley. New York: Vintage Books.

Foucault, M. (1980). *Power/knowledge*. Brighton: Harvester.

Francis, D., & Hester, S. (2004). *An invitation to ethnomethodology*. London: Sage.

Garfinkel, H. (1967). *Studies in ethnomethodology*. Cambridge: Polity Press.

Goldthorpe, J. H. (1973). Book review: A revolution in sociology? *Sociology*, 3, 449–462.

GOV.UK. (2013). Domestic and violent abuse. March 26. Retrieved April 18, 2016 from www.gov.uk/guidance/domestic-violence-and-abuse.

GOV.UK. (2014). Copyright notice: Digital images, photographs and the internet. Retrieved November 26, 2015 from www.gov.uk/government/publications/copyright-notice-digital-images-photographs-and-the-internet.

Hester, S., & Eglin, P. (Eds.). (1997). *Culture and action: Studies in membership categorization analysis*. Washington: University Press of America.

Hookway, N. (2008). Entering the blogosphere. Some strategies for using blogs in social research. *Qualitative Research*, 8(1), 91.

Jayyusi, L. (1984). *Categorization and the moral order*. Boston: Routledge & Kegan.

Jefferson, G. (1984). Transcription notation. In J. Atkinson & J. Heritage (Eds.), *Structures of social interaction*. New York: Cambridge University Press.

Jefferson, G. (1991). List construction as a task and a resource. In G. Psathas (Ed.), *Interactional competence*. New York: Irvington Publications.

Kessler, S. J., & McKenna, W. (1978). *Gender: An ethnomethodological approach*. London: University of Chicago Press.

McHoul, A., & Watson, D. R. (1984). Two axes for the analyses of 'commonsense' and 'formal' geographical knowledge in classroom talk. *The British Journal of the Sociology of Education*, 5(3), 281–302.

MyEx.com. (2014). Terms of use. Retrieved August 8 from www.myex.com/terms-of-use.

Pomerantz, A. (1986). Extreme case formulations: A way of legitimizing claims. *Human Studies, 9,* 219–229.

Potter, J. (1996). *Representing reality: Discourse, rhetoric and social construction.* London: Sage.

Robb, A. (2014). How capital letters became internet code for yelling. *New Republic.* April 17. Retrieved August 3, 2017 from: https://newrepublic.com/article/117390/netiquette-capitalization-how-caps-became-code-yelling.

Rodham, K., & Gavin, J. (2006). The ethics of using the Internet to collect qualitative research data. *Research Ethics Review, 2*(3), 92–97.

Sacks, H. (1967). The search for help: No one to turn to. In E. S. Shneidman (Ed.), *Essays in self-destruction* (pp. 203–223). New York: Science House.

Sacks, H. (1972a). An initial investigation of the usability of conversational data for doing sociology. In D. Sudnow (Ed.), *Studies in social interaction* (pp. 31–74). New York: Free Press.

Sacks, H. (1972b). On the analyzability of stories by children. In J. J. Gumperz & D. Hymes (Ed.), *Directions in sociolinguistics: The ethnography of communication* (pp. 325–345). New York: Rinehart & Winston.

Sacks, H. (1974). On the analysability of stories by children. In R. Turner (Ed.), *Ethnomethodology.* Middlesex: Penguin.

Sacks, H. (1979). Hotrodder: A revolutionary category'. In G. Psathas (Ed.), *Everyday language: Studies in ethnomethodology* (pp. 7–14). New York: Irvington.

Sacks, H. (1992). *Lectures on conversation.* Oxford: Blackwell.

Schegloff, E. A. (1997). Whose text? Whose context? *Discourse & Society, 8*(2), 165–187.

Schegloff, E. A. (1998). Reflections on studying prosody in talk-in-interaction. *Language & Speech, 41,* 235–263.

Schegloff, E. A. (2007). A tutorial on membership categorization. *Journal of Pragmatics, 39,* 462–482.

Schütz, A. (1967). *The phenomenology of the social world.* Evanston: Northwestern University Press.

Sharrock, W. W. (1974). On owning knowledge. In R. Turner (Ed.), *Ethnomethodology* (pp. 45–53). Harmondsworth: Penguin.

Speer, S. (2005). *Gender talk: Feminism, discourse and conversation analysis.* Hove: Routledge.

Walther, J. B., & Boyd, S. (2002). Attraction to computer-mediated social support. In C. Lin & D. Atkin (Eds.), *Communication technology and society. Audience adoption and uses* (pp. 153–188). Cresskill, NJ: Hampton Press.

West, C., & Zimmerman, D. H. (2009). Accounting for doing gender. *Gender & Society, 23*(1), 112–122.

Wowk, M. T. (1984). Blame allocation, sex and gender in a murder interrogation. *Women's Studies International Forum, 7*(1), 75–82.

# 6

## 'SHE TOOK MY KIDS, RUINED MY LIFE'

### Heterosexual men's accounts

## Introduction

This chapter focuses on how heterosexual men discursively account for making public sexually explicit material of an intimate (typically former) partner; we show the complex ways in which masculinities, manhood acts, femininities and sexualities are invoked by men to account for their practices. Around 90% of the images and videos in MyEx.com's database are of women who have been posted by male ex-partners. Although posters can remain anonymous, it was clear from our dataset that many contributors were male through indexing. Male indexing was visible through positioning themselves in relation to the women and other men ('my ex-wife', 'She took my kids', 'I'm sharing her with you guys', 'Her fella plays for my football team'). These are treatable as 'male' even without this identity being 'named out aloud' (Antaki & Widdicombe, 1998, p. 4).

Posts that clearly indexed heterosexual men were initially coded according to response type, yielding the following examples of accounting:

- *apathy*: 'just went in different directions but thought I would submit these anyway';
- *bragging*: 'The Best Shag I have ever had, dirty, will do anything x';
- *cheated on*: 'She cheated on me several times';
- *conned*: 'this woman stole thousands of pounds from me';
- *exposing*: 'not an ex, just someone I know':
- *immorality*: 'She took my kids, ruined my life';
- *promotion*: 'naughty girl who loves for you to look at her massive tits';
- *rating*: 'Tell me what you guys think of her';
- *recognition*: 'An old friend of mine';
- *regret*: 'dunno what to say what a mistake';

- *rejection*: 'Met her in a chatroom, we chatted, sent some photos then she blocked me. Mistake';
- *reminiscing*: 'Would love to sleep with her again';
- *service provision*: 'Her friends all wanted to see these';
- *sharing*: 'I'm sharing her with you guys, but please don't tell her about this post';
- *trolling*: 'Another Silly Model using her Real Name on her profile!';
- *trophy*: 'Her fella plays for my football team and she is constantly on my dick';
- *uncovered*: 'caught out cheating on her bloke while he was in prison'; and
- *warning*: 'Warning She has an STD'.

Given our focus is on masculinities and manhood acts and their relationship to intimate partner abuses, we focus on negative and apparent non-consensual posts – not non-revenge bragging, recognition, rejection and trolling (Anderson & Umberson, 2001) – that is, we examine those posts where men appear to be seeking revenge for a partner's cheating but where other discourse are evident. Further coding the remaining texts produced the following loosely classified emergent discourses: relationship control (including power over other men), sexuality, sexual objectification, infidelity, prostitution, sexual practices, money and parenthood. By far the most popular masculine discourse we encountered was women's heterosexual promiscuity which was cited as the cause of the intimate relationship breakdown. In this context women were depicted derogatively as 'sluts' (see Schulz, 1975 and Stokoe, 2003 on the semantic derogation of women). Unsurprisingly, lesbian infidelity was portrayed positively if it coincided with the posters own sexual desires. We begin our analysis by looking at relationship control in an extract posted in 2013 not long after MyEx.com had been founded:

### Relationship control

A1
"My Ex"
Anonymous says:
Recently broke up because I was too controlling apparently, well I wouldn't check her phone or tell her to close her fb[1] if she didn't flirt with every guy!!! As she is now done with me, no point keeping these to myself.

It is clear that A1 claims his ex-partner ended their relationship because he was 'too controlling'. Although A1 disbelieves this accusation 'apparently' we get a sense with his use of 'too' that A1 sees some level of control was acceptable. This notion fits with work by Dutton (2007), and Franklin and Menaker (2014) on gender power in intimate relationships. What they point to is the mirroring and reproducing of patriarchal power in society in intimate relationships (Stark, 2009), 'so that men are charged with decision-making and authority' (Franklin & Menaker, 2014, p. 2). Ergo, this implies that some men (and women) may find some forms of intimate relationship control as inevitable and normative. This is further cemented in this extract by A1 checking her 'phone or tell her to close her fb', which is accounted for by accusing her of flirting 'with every guy!!!' As Anderson and Umberson (2001, p. 359) point out, some men attempt to control women who don't meet their 'unspoken physical, sexual or emotional needs' – including being friendly with other men.

What is also interesting is that although A1 positions his partner as the one in control since she is the one who ended their relationship 'As she is now done with me', he does not use this as the reason for posting the explicit photos. This may indicate that A1 sees the possibility of some viewers' seeing posting pictures of his ex-partner as vindictive, so undermining his suggestion that he is the victim rather than the perpetrator (Edwards & Potter, 1992, p. 158). What he does instead is work up an account where privacy is only applicable within the confines of an intimate relationship; once the relationship has ended he has the 'right' to make public for others to consume what he consumed in person and private. This commodification or her body works to mask the violence of posting non-consensual images by establishing this as an acceptable form of revenge and homosocial exchange between men (Whisnant, 2010).

In the following extract, intimate relationship control is perceived as undertaken by his ex-partner, but this is critiqued as gender non-normative:

A2

"4/10"

Anonymous says:

Stuck up, frigid, boring bitch who knew nothing about sex and tried to control every aspect of my life. I couldn't even go out with my friends because she was so needy and clingy that she made me spend all of my time with her. I wanted to break up with her after not even a year but didn't until like 2 and a half years later. She'd search through my Facebook, my texts, etc. Seriously annoying and childish. Small, low hanging boobs, massive nose and attitude problems. Thinks she is a LOT prettier than she is. Couldn't do anything in the bedroom and would never spice things up in the slightest.

The first thing to notice in this extract is A2 begins by scoring his ex-partner '4/10'. Sacks (1992) pointed out that there was some procedural rule for greetings and introductions. That is, the person who speaks or addresses first chooses the form of address others follow. Thus, by beginning with a title in which the pictured has received a low score sets up the context in which the remainder of the post is to be read by others – that is, based on her personality and sexual performance. We can see this is the initial three-part list of character-related critiques 'stuck up', 'frigid' and 'boring' who is purported to know 'nothing about sex'. Jefferson (1991) showed that the presence of three items on a list adds clarity and weight to arguments.

What is also noticeable in this extract is that A2 claims he was the one who ended the relationship 'I wanted to break up with her after not even a year but didn't until like 2 and a half years later'. In doing so A2 is obliged to provide an account for this since he is the one posting sexually explicit images of his ex-partner. Similarities can be seen between A1's account of her as controlling and sexually promiscuous and A2's account of the relationship breakup as 'her' poor sexual performance 'knew nothing about sex' and apparent attempt to 'control every aspect of my life'. Both posters can be seen to work up an account in which their 'physical, sexual or emotional needs' have not been met (Anderson & Umberson, 2001). Thus, in both posts the women are presented as not fulfilling their normative gendered and sexuality roles in which he can experience the control over them that he is entitled to (Whisnant, 2010, p. 127). Indeed, this is further observable in A2's additional three-part list of critiques of her body 'Small, low hanging boobs, massive nose', which fits with previous scholars' research in which some men expect subordination of the use of women's bodies and their appearance (Connell & Messerschmidt, 2005; Johansson & Hammarén, 2007). Given pornography tends to be viewed predominantly by men (Weitzer, 2011), A2's account can be read as being constructed not only in masculine terms for a predominantly male audience but like A1, violence is masked and a homosocial exchange between men is established.

Similarly to A2, the following extract works up notions of gender and sexuality expectations, albeit differently:

### Sexual objectification

> A3
> "(identifier omitted) the Hoe"
> Anonymous says:
> This waist [sic.] of Oxygen is my ex of 15 years. She has been cocked more times than John Wayne's Gun. She has been shot over more times than Bagdad. She has seen more loads than your Mums Washing Machine. Enter at your own Risk!

This text is simultaneously readable as boastful talk of sexual activity but also talk about an ex-partner's sexual infidelity. The latter is immediately readable from the disparaging term applied to her in the title 'Hoe' but also in the warning to others 'Enter at your own Risk!' Schulz's (1975) historical analysis of derogative terms applied to women and girls shows that 'Hoe' (whore) is a term typically applied to heterosexually promiscuous women (see also Winkler Reid, 2014, on the construction of women as 'slags'). Combined with the warning 'Enter at your own Risk!' which is readable as heterosexual 'Enter', suggests A3 is male and is speaking to a male audience.

A3 presents as 'fact' a three-part list (Jefferson, 1991) of sexual activities that have been done to the woman 'she has been cocked', 'she has been shot over' and 'she has seen more loads'. This works to raise his masculine status by suggesting that 'he' is the one that has done these things to her. However, given that this post is also a warning, his masculine status might be challenged without him providing a reason for the breakdown of their '15 years' relationship since other readers might interpret these sexual acts as done by other(s). What A3 does to try and avoid this interpretation is construct his account as 'humorous': 'cocked more times than John Wayne's Gun', 'shot over more times than Bagdad' and 'seen more loads than your Mums Washing Machine' (see Benwell, 2004 for more on how men use humour as a deflection strategy). In other words, the sexual humour works to position him as the 'doer' of these sexual acts because it portrays him as less emotively invested. A3's deployment of 'jokey' humour also works to present him as one of the lads (albeit a more mature one since his age is referenced with his knowledge of John Wayne) and so his responsibility for any harm caused to the woman by posting explicit images of her is diffused. That is, this is normative behaviour for men whether they produce or consume this type of material, and so he is not to blame (Whisnant, 2010, p. 122).

In the following extract heterosexual men's promiscuity is normalised with the addition of point-scoring against another man. This can also be seen in men's violence against women (Hearn, 1998).

> A4
> "Your wife dude"
> Anonymous says:
> I had an affair with this lady for over two years. But her sneaky husband kept following us around, trying to take photos of us together. He threatened to expose our relationship. In the end I got so annoyed I ended it. So here you are dude your wife and the photos you never got to take. She had never given a full blowjob before she met me her husband was super uptight I left her as a cock sucking anal queen.

It is immediately clear from the title that A4 has had some form of relationship with another man's 'wife'. In A4's description of his affair two aspects are marked out. The first aspect is that the woman he had an affair with was a 'lady'. The selection of a category carries important implications for how the text is read. Edwards (1998, p. 25) argues that these categories carry 'potentially useful conventional associations with age, marital status, and potential sexual availability' such that 'lady' infers she is respectable (Stokoe, 2003, p. 331). It could also convey literally, ironically or sarcastically that she is smart, sensible or selective, or specifically not these. Second, his marker of time 'over two years' suggests that this was not purely sexual but that they were perhaps also emotionally involved. In working up this position A4 is able to position himself as the victim of 'her sneaky husband' who 'threatened to expose' them, which suggests A4 was also cheating on someone. Threatening to expose them positions the 'sneaky husband' in a position of power and indeed the outcome was that the affair was 'ended'. A4's posting explicit images of his ex-partner is readable as a way to re-empower himself, and this can be seen in the sexual acts he claims she has done 'given a full blowjob' 'anal queen' with him and not with her husband. The graphic detail of the sexual acts also works to position him as sexually powerful (and her weak) vis-à-vis her husband since he was able to get her to do things she might not have done with her husband; visible in his downgrading of her from a 'lady' to a 'cock sucking anal queen'. While the selection 'lady' infers respectability and modesty, 'cock sucking anal queen' infers 'frivolity' and 'sleaziness' (Stokoe, 2003, p. 331). This 'category, predicate and task' (Hester & Eglin, 1997) in switching from 'lady' to 'cock sucking anal queen' functions to downgrade the overall victory of her husband in keeping his wife, while claiming victory over her husband in the sexual acts he had with his wife, a theme of cuckolding familiar to Shakespeare.

In the following post A5 turns his ex-partner's same-sex cheating as positive. In doing so, we see a different dimension to heterosexual masculinity.

### Sexuality

> A5
> "Bisexual"
> Anonymous says:
> I found my girlfriend masturbating over these pics. When she left her iPhone lying about I downloaded them all. This blonde was trying to get my girl into bed. I had no idea my girl was bisexual. So all being well she is going to set up a FFM for me with a younger playgirl to join us. But I was annoyed that this older lady was sending my girl photos of herself. If you send pics into cyber space you have no idea where they may end up.

What is interesting in this post about cheating is that the victim is not the poster's 'girlfriend' but rather, an 'older lady' who is reported to have sexually aroused his partner: 'I found my girlfriend masturbating over these pics'. He positions the victim as a lesbian predator: 'This blonde was trying to get my girl into bed' by 'sending my girl photos of herself' in order to account for his actions. What is also evident is that it is his taste in women, age and sexual preference that are key: 'set up a FFM for me with a younger playgirl to join us' (FFM: female, female, male sexual encounter). As such, lesbian infidelity is presented as acceptable as long as the victim concurs with the perpetrator's choice of partner, which fits with previous research showing some heterosexual men tending to have a 'more positive prejudice' toward lesbians in sexual contexts (Herek, 2000, p. 262; Pichastor, Manuel, & Gabriel, 2009). Given the popularity of lesbian pornography for some heterosexual male consumers (Webber, 2013), one might suspect that this post also serves to raise A5's homosocial status with male viewers providing him with a 'real man' affirmation (Whisnant, 2010).

We suspected women's sex and sexuality would feature highly given the focus of the website, but we were somewhat surprised how openly some men were discussing their own sexual promiscuity.

## Men's infidelity

> A6
> "nasty girl"
> Anonymous says:
> After 6 year relationship I started cheating on her, when she found out cause massive problems with me and friends. I'm sure she gave me an STD, stay away and be happy.

A6's title clearly shows his disapproval or dislike of his former partner. Interestingly he begins by discussing his own extra-relationship affair(s). It is interesting to note that A5 makes the time of his relationship relevant, 'After 6 years', which indexes how the rest of the text is to be understood (Antaki & Widdicombe, 1998). That is, by deduction, he was faithful for 6 years before he 'started cheating on her'. We can only speculate as to his reasons, but what the marker of time does is minimise the impact of his action, a relativising strategy used in men's accounts of physical violence to women (Hearn, 1998). In other words, cheating after six years is perhaps not as bad as after one year. When people provide accounts for their actions, they must select, construct and manage for 'stake' (i.e. their personal interest). As Edwards and Potter (1992, p. 158) point out:

> Anyone who produces a version of something that happened in the past, or who develops a stretch of talk that places blame … does so at the risk of having their claims discounted … participants should be thought of as caught in a dilemma of stake or interest: how to produce accounts which attend to interests without being undermined as interested.

What is interesting is that he does not provide an account of why he started 'cheating on her' only that it was 'After 6 years'. In doing so A6 normalises his action. That is, sexual promiscuity is represented as normative for men (see Murnen, Wright, & Kaluzny, 2002 for more on gender, social norms and sexuality). Additionally, he makes relevant the consequences when she found out 'cause massive problems with me and friends'. His use of 'massive' suggests he thought her reaction was perhaps excessive. Interestingly, A6 culminates his post by accusing his ex-partner of being unfaithful and giving him a sexually transmitted disease: 'I'm sure she gave me an STD, stay away and be happy'. This acts as a part-account for his own cheating by implying that she was promiscuous, but also that like A3 that his ex-partner is frivolous. This might also suggest both that he is generous, and that he does not value her.

In the following post, sexual competitiveness is linked to finance and status.

## Prostitution

> A7
> "[identifier omitted] Mistress"
> Anonymous says:
> [identifier omitted] was a kept girl by a [identifier omitted] businessman.
> He bought her a sports car; put her up in a fancy apartment. She had to be
> on call for him every Monday. He wanted her to get a vajazzle and do all
> the kinky stuff he basically paid her for. She saw me on the side, but in the
> end chose the cash and the lifestyle. Guess that's the way it goes, but she
> was a great fuck.

Unlike A4, A7 isn't claiming victory 'in the end she chose the cash and the lifestyle' in his competition for the 'Mistress'. A7 categorises (Sacks, 1992) the other man as a 'businessman', which invokes notions of money and power since he is able to purchase expensive items for the 'Mistress' 'bought her a sports car; put her up in a fancy apartment'. One might suspect that his lost 'battle' with the businessman challenges and demotes A7's homosocial status. However, in avoiding this A7 presents himself as not emotionally invested with the woman, worked up by presenting her as a sexual commodity – a prostitute. In return for the businessman's gifts, he claims she 'had to be on call for him every Monday. He wanted her to get a vajazzle[2] and do all the kinky stuff'. Notice the use of the extreme-case formulations 'every', 'all', 'he basically'. Downgrades 'he basically' and upgrades 'every', 'all' (extreme-case formulations) are ways of referring to events and objects by invoking minimal or maximal properties (Pomerantz, 1986). What this does is reduce the basis for others to search for an account. Pomerantz's (1986, pp. 219–220) work shows that people use extreme-case formulations in adversarial situations and when they anticipate others undermining their claims or to propose that some behaviour is not right (or wrong) especially if it can be regarded as frequently occurring 'every Monday'. Or, as Potter (1996, p. 61) points out, accounts are often provided for dis-preferred actions, so that if an action is not the preferred action of the actor then a reason for such action may be required. Therefore, we see that A7's use of these extreme-case formulations proposes that she 'should not' have chosen the businessman over him. However, A7 does anticipate that some viewers may still need an account, and so provides a justification with a three-part list (Jefferson, 1991) for his claim that she is a prostitute 'on call', 'get a vajazzle' and 'do... kinky stuff'. A7's downgrading of her serves to minimise the businessman's hollow victory and the relevance of money, but also that he is not/was not emotionally involved with her 'Guess that's the way it goes', again emotionally distancing himself from her.

While A7 presents himself as blasé, A8 other the other hand is quite open about the emotional impact of the relationship.

## Money

> A8
>
> "nasty woman!!!"
>
> Anonymous says:
>
> This woman is a nasty lying piece of work, she led me on to bleed me dry of money then put me into a false sense of security then abandoned me when I was ill, I now have panic disorder and anxiety from what she put me through.

A8 claims he is seeking revenge because she attempted to con him, 'bleed me dry of money', and eventually rejected him, 'abandoned me'. We see that her reported intention 'she led me on [in order] to bleed me dry' was unsuccessful because as Edwards (2008, p. 177) points out, intentions are 'tied to circumstances in which the intended actions are in some way balked, unfulfilled, or a departure from expectation'. Since A8 implies she was not successful in conning him he is required to provide an account of his action to post onMyEx.com (Potter, 1996). He does this by positioning himself as vulnerable 'I was ill' and detailing the impact this has had on him: 'I now have panic disorder and anxiety from what she put me through'. What is interesting is that by laying bare his vulnerabilities he is able to portray her as heartless while simultaneously maintaining his financial status.

The last extract we present draws on fatherhood as justification for blaming the victim.

## Parenthood

> A9
>
> "My Slut ex who has ruined my life!"
>
> Anonymous says:
>
> She took my kids, ruined my life and now bitches about me to everyone since the divorce.

What is immediately noticeable in A9's post is that his ex is categorised as a 'Slut' (see Stokoe, 2003 for more on the construction of the 'slut' in discourse). This category is associated with the category predicate of 'being sexually promiscuous' and as such acts to provide an account of why he is posting in MyEx .com (Hester & Eglin, 1997). Indeed, *being* posted at all on such a site might in itself suggest such to a male audience or be intended to do so. A9 provides an additional justification for his actions with a three-part list of her reported misdemeanours: 'took my kids', 'ruined life!' and 'bitches about me'. What's implied here is that both his private and public life have been 'ruined' since he has lost living with the 'kids' and she 'bitches' to 'everyone' (Pomerantz, 1986). This was a fairly common example that implied the poster's masculine identity had been challenged by the loss of living with their children. Like many of the extracts that we have read and presented, here the posters position themselves as the victims rather than the persons who have had explicit pictures of them posted in cyberspace. Thus, he is able to take the moral high ground while also presenting his activity as normative masculine behaviour and also while establishing a homosocial exchange with other men: any undermining of his sense of a masculine self can be reclaimed by presenting himself as a 'real man' (Whisnant, 2010).

While A9 focused on his own reported lost fatherhood as a legitimate justification for revenge seeking, A10's accounts while centring on the woman's personal hygiene also invoke social moralistic discourse on disability, legitimate benefit claims, honesty, her infidelity, prostitution and her educational attainment level.

### Hygiene

> A10
> "Worthless Whore"
> Anonymous says:
> This woman, who's (identifier omitted) is a 2 cent whore. She will lie directly to your face to get what she wants. Her pussy is so worn out because she shat out (identifier omitted) kids (identifier omitted). She is so dumb, she dropped out of (identifier omitted), and that was in (identifier omitted) nonetheless! Now, she's posting on (identifier omitted) trying to get money for that stinky, nasty twat. Avoid this woman at all cost. She has diseases that even condoms can't protect you!

Clearly A10 does not hold any regard for the postee: 'Worthless Whore'. Although A10 does not explicitly state he has had an intimate relationship with the woman, he does provide intimate details (and photos) of her 'who's (identifier omitted)', 'She will lie', 'Her pussy is', 'she dropped out of school', 'Now, she's posting', which suggests he is likely to have had an affair with the postee since she is reported to be in a relationship with another man '(identifier omitted)'. There are two reasons A10 may not have explicitly admitted to a relationship with the woman. First, she is reported to be in a relationship with another man, and other viewers might be known to both him and, the woman and her husband. Second, he constructs her as unhygienic, 'stinky, nasty twat', 'She has diseases that even condoms can't protect you!' To claim to have had a sexual relationship with this woman and then claim she is unhygienic invites readers to question the authenticity of his claims.

Drawing on negative social and moralistic discourses about personal hygiene ('stinky, nasty twat'), current status ('who's [identifier omitted]'), honesty ('She will lie'), legitimacy of current status ('who's [identifier omitted]'), her infidelity and prostitution ('she's posting on [identifier omitted] trying to get money'), and her educational attainment level ('She is so dumb, she dropped out of [identifier omitted], and that was in [identifier omitted] nonetheless!'), work to construct her as a 'chav' (UK term; Tyler, 2008), or perhaps in US terminology 'white trash' or 'redneck' (Newitz & Wray, 2013). Constructing her in this way draws on contemporary class and gender discourses, and representations, about young working-class mothers: 'mums who choose to get pregnant as a career option' (Tyler, 2008, p. 17). Tyler (2008) argues that the construction of young mothers in this way is aimed at producing disgust reactions, which A10 reinforces with notions of personal hygiene with the aim of deterring others 'Avoid this woman at all cost'.

What is interesting is that while her reported infidelity is problematised, his is not. That is, she is the one in the wrong for having an extra-marital affair. This perspective mirrors that of A4 in which men who have multiple sexual partners (both in or outside an intimate relationship) are positioned as normative (Connell, 2014). That is, a high value is placed on men's 'success' with women, whereas women's sexual agency is problematised. In doing so, he is implicitly able to take the moral high ground in presenting his infidelity with a married woman as typical masculine behaviour, which helps to establish a homosocial exchange with other male viewers (Whisnant, 2010). What is different about this post, compared to others we have read and presented, is that the poster only implicitly positions himself as the victim, presumably from her ending the relationship.

## Discussion

The analysis in this chapter has focused on how men accounted for – and justified – posting explicit images of women (mostly ex-partners). The accounts presented can be situated in the different perspectives for understanding revenge porn set out in Chapter 3: pornographic traditions; online pornography and technologies; interpersonal revenge; gender violence and abuse; mass media interest; and gendered practices of men and masculinities. Most men in the dataset claimed the women deserved being posted because they were reported to have controlled the relationship, committed infidelity, passed on an STD and deemed unclean more generally, stolen money or committed sexual acts in return for money, and stolen 'his' children, thus constructing online pornography as, in their own terms, a legitimate form of interpersonal revenge. In some cases, men could be seen to position themselves as the wronged victims in seeking revenge: in other words, positioning the ex-partner as the perpetrator of a form of gender violence and abuse. We showed also that many of these reported or alleged misdemeanours are linked, even tied, to and invested in masculinised, hierarchical, heterosexual, intimate relationships, fatherhood and financial contexts. Indeed, it is arguable that the loss of personal power in the men's relationship was a means of felt emasculation. Overall, revenge was reported positively by at least some men posters as a supposedly equalising action downplaying any culpability.

The analysis also has similarities with studies of gender violences in (online) pornography (Dines, 2010; Hearn, 2006; Hughes, 2002; Jeffreys, 2013), in which women are sexually commodified and degraded. Thus, the structuring of revenge pornography fits with studies that examine the multifarious computer-mediated communication possibilities for virtual/online socialities, sexualities and violences (Hearn & Parkin, 2001). What is often common across these perspectives is the relative invisibility of the perpetrator – that is, violences can be committed without the identity of the perpetrator being revealed.

This relative invisibility is complicated by the fact that the victim is known but at a distance and not seen, so the impact and consequences of action are not immediate. Interestingly, there is also some evidence of greater propensity and power to insult and abuse, when there is less facial or eye contact (Lapidot-Lefler & Barak, 2012). In such ways one might characterise some revenge porn as cowardly violence and abuse, with unpredictable outcomes discontinuous in time and space. In addition, the revenge porn may be directed to various possible audiences: the women in question, their intimates or associates, to the man's own friends, an undefined viewing 'public'. In some cases, the revenge porn may be part of the enactment of homosocial relations between men rather than action that is primarily directed to the woman or women (Whisnant, 2010).

Revenge porn has unfortunately become a fact of life in the digital age and is yet another part of the multifarious possibilities for virtual/online cyberabuses that intend to harm another, often repeatedly, where the victim is typically unable to defend himself or herself (Slonje, Smith, & Frisén, 2013). The predominant feature of this cyberabuse is the imbalance of power often facilitated by the perpetrator's ability to remain anonymous. Yet as was clear from the extracts, the victim knows the perpetrator in revenge porn, and the perpetrator desires the victim to know his or her identity in order for the revenge to carry meaning. Yet knowing the identity of the perpetrator does not seem to be enough to secure a conviction, and conviction rates currently remain low. Given the posting of explicit (pornographic or similar) images by others is fraught with unknown psycho-social outcomes for the victims (mostly women), and more could, and should, be done. Notions of control and dignity also featured high in men's accounts of posting images and videos of other men – that is men's intimate relations with other men. In the next chapter we examine heterosexual women's accounts for posting pornographic images and videos of male ex-partners.

## Notes

1  Fb refers to Facebook.
2  Vajazzle is a form of genital decoration by the application of crystal ornaments on the shaved pubic region.

# References

Anderson, K. L., & Umberson, D. (2001). Gendering violence: Masculinity and power in men's accounts of domestic abuse. *Gender & Society, 15*(3), 358–380.

Antaki, C., & Widdicombe, S. (Eds.). (1998). *Identities in talk*. London: Sage.

Benwell, B. (2004). Ironic discourse: Evasive masculinity in British men's lifestyle magazines. *Men and Masculinities, 7*(1), 3–21.

Connell, R. (2014). *Gender and power: Society, the person and sexual politics*. New York: John Wiley & Sons.

Connell, R., & Messerschmidt, J. W. (2005). Hegemonic masculinity: Rethinking the concept. *Gender & Society, 19*(60), 829–859.

Dines, G. (2010). *Pornland: How porn has hijacked our sexuality*. Boston, MA: Beacon.

Dutton, D. G. (2007). *The abusive personality: Violence and control in intimate relationships* (2nd ed.). New York: Guilford Press.

Edwards, D. (1998). The relevant thing about her: Social identity categories in use. In C. Antaki & S. Widdicombe (Eds.), *Identities in talk*. London: Sage.

Edwards, D. (2008). Intentionality and *mens rea* in police interrogations: The production of actions as crimes. *Intercultural Pragmatics, 5*(2), 177–199.

Edwards, D., & Potter, J. (1992). *Discursive psychology: Inquiries in social construction*. London: Sage.

Franklin, C. A., & Menaker, T. A. (2014). Feminism, status inconsistency, and women's intimate partner victimization in heterosexual relationships. *Violence Against Women*, Online July, *16*, 1–21.

Hearn, J. (1998). *The violences of men: How men talk about and how agencies respond to men's violence to women*. London: Sage.

Hearn, J. (2006). The implications of information and communication technologies for sexualities and sexualized violences: Contradictions of sexual citizenships. *Political Geography, 25*(8), 944–963.

Hearn, J., & Parkin, W. (2001). *Gender, sexuality and violence in organizations: The unspoken forces of organization violations*. London: Sage.

Herek, G. M. (2000). Sexual prejudice and gender: Do heterosexuals' attitudes toward lesbians and gay men differ? *Journal of Social Issues, 56*(2), 251–266.

Hester, S., & Eglin, P. (Eds.). (1997). *Culture and action: Studies in membership categorization analysis*. Washington, DC: University Press of America.

Hughes, D. (2002). The use of new communication and information technologies for the sexual exploitation of women and children. *Hastings Women's Law Journal, 13*(1), 127–146.

Jefferson, G. (1991). List construction as a task and a resource. In G. Psathas (Ed.), *Interactional competence*. New York: Irvington Publications.

Jeffreys, S. (2013). The 'agency' of men: Male buyers in the global sex industry. In J. Hearn, M. Blagojević, & K. Harrison (Eds.), *Rethinking transnational men: Beyond, between and within nations* (pp. 59–75). New York: Routledge.

Johansson, T., & Hammarén, N. (2007). Hegemonic masculinity and pornography: Young people's attitudes toward and relations to pornography. *Journal of Men's Studies, 15*(1), 57–71.

Lapidot-Lefler, N., & Barak, A. (2012). Effects of anonymity, invisibility, and lack of eye-contact on toxic online disinhibition. *Computers in Human Behavior, 28*, 434–443.

Murnen, S. K., Wright, C., & Kaluzny, G. (2002). If "boys will be boys," then girls will be victims? A meta-analytic review of the research that relates masculine ideology to sexual aggression. *Sex Roles, 46*(11–12), 359–375.

Newitz, A., & Wray, M. (2013). *White trash: Race and class in America*. Abingdon: Routledge.

Pichastor, F., Manuel, M., & Gabriel, M. (2009). "I'm not gay... I'm a real man!": Plague of revenge porn. *Journal of Mass Media Ethics: Exploring Questions of Media Morality*, *9*, 168–183.

Pomerantz, A. (1986). Extreme case formulations: A way of legitimizing claims. *Human Studies*, *9*, 219–229.

Potter, J. (1996). *Representing reality: Discourse, rhetoric and social construction*. London: Sage.

Sacks, H. (1992). *Lectures on conversation*. Oxford: Blackwell.

Schulz, M. (1975). The semantic derogation of women. *Language and Sex: Difference and Dominance*, *64*(75), 134–147.

Slonje, R., Smith, P. K., & Frisén, A. (2013). The nature of cyberbullying, and strategies for prevention. *Computers in Human Behavior*, *29*(1), 26–32.

Stark, E. (2009). *Coercive control: How men entrap women in personal life*. New York: Oxford University Press.

Stokoe, E. H. (2003). Mothers, single women and sluts: Gender, morality and membership categorization in neighbour disputes. *Feminism & Psychology*, *13*(3), 317–344.

Tyler, I. (2008). "Chav mum, chav scum" Class disgust in contemporary Britain. *Feminist Media Studies*, *8*(1), 17–34.

Webber, V. (2013). Shades of gay: Performance of girl-on-girl pornography and mobile authenticities. *Sexualities*, *16*(1–2), 217–235.

Weitzer, R. (2011). Review essay: Pornography's effects: The need for solid evidence: A review essay of everyday pornography, edited by K. Boyle (New York: Routledge, 2010) and Pornland: How porn has hijacked our sexuality, by G. Dines (Boston: Beacon, 2010). *Violence Against Women*, *17*(5), 666–675.

Whisnant, R. (2010). From Jekyll to Hyde: The grooming of male pornography consumers. In K. Boyle (Ed.), *Everyday pornography* (pp. 114–133). London: Routledge.

Winkler Reid, S. (2014). 'She's not a slag because she only had sex once': Sexual ethics in a London secondary school. *Journal of Moral Education*, *43*(2), 183–197.

# 7
# 'JUST WANTS TO USE YOU FOR SEX'

## Heterosexual women's accounts

## Introduction

The previous chapter showed how heterosexual men accounted for revenge pornography. In this chapter, we follow a similar analytic process but instead focus on heterosexual women's posts, highlighting how each poster accounts for their actions. Around 15% of posts on MyEx.com are of men who have been posted by female ex-partners. Although posters tend to remain anonymous (although identities are often deducible by the claims made), it was clear from our dataset that some contributors were female. Similarly, to men, heterosexual women's indexing occurred through positioning themselves relation to the men being displayed ('my ex-husband', 'fucks other girls', 'my ex-boyfriend', 'got me pregnant') (Antaki & Widdicombe, 1998, p. 4).

Those posts which were clearly heterosexual women were followed with a similar initial coding process to heterosexual men. The response types were

- *apathy*: 'Just an ex thought I'd show his small dick to the world!';
- *bragging*: 'Used him from the start, but that's what type of treatment this guy needs';
- *cheated on*: 'Cheated on me with some slut rewind my life';
- *conned*: 'This guy is slimy piece of shit that uses girls for their money';
- *exposing*: 'Exposing his dirty little cross-dressing secret';
- *immorality*: 'He got me pregnant and left me';
- *jealousy*: 'I went to school with this guy, and he was very quiet. I admit I have the hots for him. Too bad he is married to a Mexican and likes Mexican pussy...';
- *liar:* 'I met this guy and he said he would look after me and my kids. BIG FAT LIE this guy only wants pussy and anal';

- *provoked*: 'I deleted him off Facebook, blocked him I'm still getting abuse off his boyfriends so here's one back';
- *rating*: 'my hubby's small dick what do you ladies think';
- *regret*: 'The sex was awful, I was able to pleasure myself more with a cocktail sausage';
- *reminiscing*: 'He is amazing in bed he is the best I've ever fucked but he couldn't handle me fucking lots of other guys';
- *retribution*: 'He went to prison for attacking me, cracking my head open, and fracturing a rib';
- *romantic intentions*: 'Pretends he cares but fucks women on pof[1] all the time';
- *scorned*: 'Doesn't want to settle down!';
- *sharing*: 'This guy asked me out loads and tried to tempt me with these pics and video, seriously it's so small doubt anyone could feel it';
- *uncovered*: 'This guy cheated on his girlfriend so many times when she was pregnant and never stopped'; and
- *warning*: 'grooms girls asking them to visit him at his flat where he plies them with alcohol until they are very drunk then rapes them'.

Given our focus is on femininities and womanhood acts and their relationship to intimate partner abuses we focus on negative and apparent non-consensual posts (Anderson & Umberson, 2001). That is, we examine those posts where women appear to be seeking revenge for a partner's cheating but where other discourse is evident. Further coding the remaining texts produced the following loosely classified emergent discourses: physical assault, parenthood, sexual objectification, sexual promiscuity, sexting, sexual practices and sexuality. By far the most popular discourse we encountered was men's heterosexual promiscuity, which was cited as the cause of the intimate relationship breakdown. We begin our analysis with a poster reporting her ex-partner as violent:

### Physical assault

A1

"Violent and Psychological Domestic Abuser"

Anonymous says:

He (identifier omitted) attacking me, cracking my head open, and fracturing a rib. He lies constantly, is manipulative. Is trying to get me to lie for him (identifier omitted) right now, because he stole my car, to drive it work. He has no license, he lied to the police claiming to be his brother as his brother has a license. His brother doesn't have fully comp insurance though, so he expects me and his brother to take 6/8 points and a fine. Just found out he cheated on me too. It's amazing what you put up with when someone has battered your confidence so badly. Please avoid for your own safety and sanity!

Drawing on Hester and Eglin's (1997) 'category, predicate and task' A1 categorises her ex-partner as a violent criminal with a list of category-bound activities and predicates 'attacking me, cracking my head open, and fracturing a rib', '(identifier omitted)', 'Is trying to get me to lie for him (identifier omitted)', 'he lied to the police'. In doing so A1 is able to work up a warning to others 'Please avoid for your own safety and sanity!'. What this also does is provide a justification for seeking retribution through distributing explicit images of her ex-partner, which works as a deflection strategy to avoid others raising questions about the legitimacy of her actions, in other words, avoiding being held morally accountable (Jayyusi, 1984). Yet despite the defensibility of an account it always remains contestable. Thus, people report social phenomenon as factual, 'He lies', 'he stole', 'He has'. Speakers present social phenomenon as factual where they anticipate 'others' undermining their claims (Potter, 1996, p. 61). A1 also deploys a three-part list to bolster her claims 'attacking me, cracking my head open, and fracturing a rib'. As noted in the preceding chapter, Jefferson's (1991) work on lists shows they serve two key purposes: they add clarity and weight to arguments and act as an 'orientated-to-procedure' (Jefferson, 1991, p. 68) such that speakers/hearers/readers are provided with a means to discursively position themselves in relation to the items on the list. Here we can see A1 is positioning herself as the 'victim' since he is reported 'attacking me' and '(identifier omitted)'. Positioning herself as 'victim' and her ex-partner as 'perpetrator' also works to deflect readers' attention from him being seen as the 'victim' and her as the 'perpetrator' for posting explicit images of him in an online public space. What A1 also does is anchor her claims in legal discourse '(identifier omitted)', '(identifier omitted)', 'to police', 'fine'. Foley and Faircloth (2003) show that some discourses (medical, legal) enjoy a higher social status and so are an excellent way in which to build legitimacy in claims.

A1's revenge seeking in this way can be viewed as a well-developed strategy and tactic for dealing with, and coping with, emotions and intimate relations associated with a violent ex-partner (Yoshimura, 2007) and presented positively as a means of empowerment (see Wolf, 2013 for more on contemporary forms of women's empowerment by fighting fire with fire). A1's empowerment can also be seen in her categorisation of him as a violent criminal prone to assault women. Although the categorisation of criminal might elevate his masculine status with some viewers (see Heidensohn & Gelsthorpe, 2012 for more on masculinities' and criminal behaviour) he can also be held morally accountable for these violent physical assaults on her as a woman (Jayyusi, 1984). Stokoe's (2010) discursive study of men charged with assaulting women showed that most men deny violence against women as it is viewed as less masculine.

Similarly, A2 challenges her ex-partner's masculine status by claiming he avoids his parental responsibilities and in particular, financially supporting their child.

## Parenthood

> A2
>
> "scumbag small prick loser thinks he\'s good in bed"
>
> Anonymous says:
>
> I met this prick 8 yrs ago and was foolish enough to be drunk and go to bed with him, by the way he is crap in bed left me with a baby who told me to GET RID OF IT. THIS LOSER HAS NOT PAID A SINGLE PENNY TO MY CHILD SINCE AND HE HAS LOADS OF WOMEN WITH HIS KIDS WARNING LADIES DO NOT GIVE THIS LOSER MONEY OR TIME, HE DOES NOT WANT CONTACT WITH HIS CHILD,THE CURRENT GIRLFRIEND WHO BY THE WAY YOU HAVE MY TOTAL SYMPATHY AS HE GAVE ME CRABS TOO,HERE IS SOME FREE ADVICE DO NOT HAVE HIS KIDS AS HE WILL NOT PAY FOR THEM WHEN YOU HAVE HAD THEM AND [identifier omitted] YOU SHOULD BE ASHAMED OF YOURSELF KNOWINGLY WHAT HE IS DOING WITH OTHER WOMEN AND NOT PAYING FOR HIS KIDS BUT WILL PAY FOR YOURS INSTEAD WHAT A LOW LIFES YOU BOTH ARE.....IM VERY SURPRISED HE DOES NOT HAVE HIV OR WORSE.

It is immediately obvious that there is an in-text transition from small-case letter words to capitalisation. Barrett's (2012) study of online chat showed that capitalisation represents shouting in the absence of verbal interaction and is readable as a marker of anger. The transition point to capitalisation occurs when A2 reports her ex-partner as telling her to terminate her pregnancy 'GET RID OF IT'. This works to signal to readers her anger at his suggestion. What this also does is help to downgrade the importance of the previous text. That is, her being 'drunk and go to bed with him', which some readers might view as means to hold her accountable for being left 'with a baby'. This fits with scholarly work that shows that while both women and men report being in favour of equal responsibility for contraception, in practice, the onus tends to be on women (Brown, 2012; Brunner Huber & Ersek, 2011). Indeed, this sexual double standard (Lefkowitz, Shearer, Gillen, & Espinosa-Hernandez, 2014) often means that women are held more accountable for unwanted pregnancies. Stokoe's (2003) work on the 'types' of women indicates getting 'drunk and go to bed with him' might be viewed by some less favourably. Indeed, what is noticeable is that although A2 holds herself, in part, accountable 'I...was foolish enough to be drunk and go to bed with him'. This works to distract the attention from her actions to his.

Given this distraction A2 is compelled to work up an account in which the focus is on his actions and not hers. She does this in four ways. First, she works up an account of him as a poor father 'THIS LOSER HAS NOT PAID A SINGLE PENNY TO MY CHILD', 'HE DOES NOT WANT CONTACT WITH HIS CHILD' to her child 'MY CHILD'. Second, she works up an account of him as sexual promiscuity, perhaps also a sexual predator, 'HE HAS LOADS OF WOMEN WITH HIS KIDS'. Third, he is reported to be a thief 'WARNING LADIES DO NOT GIVE THIS LOSER MONEY OR TIME'. Last, he is positioned as someone who is likely to have a sexually transmitted disease: 'HIV OR WORSE'. These warnings work in two ways. First, they work as deterrents to potential women suiters but also as a warning to his current partner: 'CURRENT GIRLFRIEND WHO BY THE WAY YOU HAVE MY TOTAL SYMPATHY', 'HERE IS SOME FREE ADVICE DO NOT HAVE HIS KIDS'. This would suggest that both her ex-partner and his new partner are aware of A2's actions. We noted in Chapter 1 that the impact of revenge porn was amplified if the victim's family, friends, work colleagues and acquaintances were made aware. What is also noticeable is that while A2 warns her ex-partner's new partner, his new partner is also abused: 'WHAT A LOW LIFES YOU BOTH ARE'. This would suggest that her ex-partner's new partner is implicated in the relationship breakdown. However, the advice given to the new partner 'HERE IS SOME FREE ADVICE DO NOT HAVE HIS KIDS' suggests that A2 also views her, in part, as a victim of her ex-partner's sexual promiscuity.

Working up an account of her ex-partner in this way also challenges his manhood. Manhood in Europe and North America tends to be tied to notions of fatherhood and responsibility, sexual performance and hygiene and cleanliness (see Zaider, Manne, Nelson, Mulhall, & Kissane, 2012). Pejoratively talking about men's sexual performance, preferences and genitals was a common feature of women's posts. In the following post, the poster challenges the victim's manhood with disparaging comments about his genital size and sexual performance.

### Sexual objectification

A3
"So small you have to look twice, to see it!"
Anonymous says:
This guy promised he had a big, long, thick dick, but boy was I in for a surprise! I was with this guy for a year, we didn't have sex until the last few months of our relationship. When I first laid eyes on his dick, I couldn't believe how small it was. I tried my best to stay with him because I really liked him. To be honest the sex was terrible, the only thing he did well was eating me out. That wasn't enough and I decided to end things with him after a year long relationship. I couldn't even feel it when I tried putting it in my mouth. Size really does matter, no matter what you hear!!!

Given the context of revenge porn A3's title is immediately readable (see Sacks, 1992, for more on the hearer's maxims) as related to the victim's penis size. Disparaging comments about the man's penis size or aesthetics (see A4 below) was common in our dataset. This is not surprising given that a 'big, long, thick dick' 'in many cultures it has come to symbolise attributes such as largeness, strength, endurance, ability, courage, intelligence, knowledge, dominance over men, possession of women; a symbol of loving and being loved' and fertility (Hall, 2015; Wylie &Eardley, 2007, p. 1449). A3's account centers on his deceitfulness: 'This guy promised' her a large penis and her desire for sexual satisfaction; 'To be honest the sex was terrible'. Yet an account which centers, in part, on her own sexual satisfaction related to his penis size might be viewed by some as shallow and derisory. Indeed, some viewers might not see penis size as key to sexual satisfaction. A3 preempts such views by suggesting that they practiced cunnilingus 'the only thing he did well was eating me out' and fellatio 'I tried putting it in my mouth' yet arguing that 'Size really does matter, no matter what you hear!!!' A3 also attempts to ward off potential criticisms by working up an account of herself in which she is positioned as considerate: 'we didn't have sex until the last few months of our relationship', 'I was with this guy for a year', 'I tried my best'. In other words, 'I tried my best' but she is the victim of his deceit and thus justified in seeking revenge.

In the following post the man's penis is mocked for its aesthetics as a result of his reported sexual promiscuity.

## Sexual promiscuity

A4
"JUST WANTS TO USE YOU FOR SEX"
Anonymous says:
This guy goes through women like there is no tomorrow they all must wanna feel what a square cock feel like. Then they find out he's a kinky guy into all sorts of toy play. He loves himself so much its time share the love, so here is his square cock. Plus to show how kinky he is a vid of him showing you how he uses toy on himself. He said it never makes him cum but I think he was contracting on that dildo I let you decide if does or not

A4 describes her (ex)partner as sexually promiscuous, 'goes through women like there is no tomorrow', which is followed by speculation on his appeal to other women, 'must wanna feel' his 'square cock'. Ridiculing the shape of his penis serves two purposes. First, it challenges his manhood. As we noted in our analysis of A3's text, penis size and aesthetics are important for masculine status (Wylie & Eardley, 2007). Second, in conjunction with the extreme-case formulation 'all' (Pomerantz, 1986) in 'they all must wanna feel what a square cock feel like' positions him as a sexual novelty. On the flip side, of course, multiple sexual partners and desirability potentially raise his masculine status (see Dickerson, 2000; Miller, 2008; Nylund, 2007 for more on typical masculine attributes). Thus, A4 proceeds to work up an account of her ex-partner as having non-typical sexual desires: 'a kinky guy into all sorts of toy play'. What's interesting is the supplementary information to his 'kinkiness'. Given that unusual sexual behaviour might not be deemed problematic A4 proceeds to frame his 'kinkiness' as related to homosexual practice: 'he uses toy on himself. He said it never makes him cum but I think he was contracting on that dildo'. In addition to providing her with a justification for revenge seeking, it might also work to diminish his masculine status with some viewers (see Edwards, 2006 for more on masculinities and homosexuality).

The following postee is also reported to have committed infidelity with A5 and his wife.

## Infidelity

> A5
> "Married lying scumbag"
> Anonymous says:
> [anonymised] aka [anonymised] or [anonymised] or [anonymised] is married 28 year old. He tells girls he's single and when they find out he's married he starts lies about not sleeping with his wife and going through divorce procedure. He borrows money and doesn't return it. Sleeps around and has STI

A5 immediately produces a three-part list (Jefferson, 1991) of identity categories 'Married', 'lying', 'scumbag' which have logical sequential relationship. Identity categories have 'hearer's maxims' (Sacks, 1992, pp. 238–239). That is, people hear them as having certain characteristics. 'Married' in Western cultures is associated with monogamy (MacDonald, 2002). Thus, categorising the postee as 'Married' followed by 'lying' is hearable as, he lied about his marital status to A5, and so she has recategorised him as a 'scumbag'.

Producing a list (Jefferson, 1991) of the man's names and pseudonyms works to strengthen her claims that he is deceitful but also acts as a warning to other women. Pluralising 'girls' strengths A5's account of his infidelity by positioning herself as one of many victims of his deceitfulness 'He tells girls he is single'. What this implies is that A5 is aware of his infidelity with other women, since she knows 'they find out he's married', thus suggesting she may know some of them personally. Given this context others might not agree with her account. Indeed, what is implied by 'lies about not sleeping with his wife and going through divorce procedure' is that she was aware that he was married but not that the postee was not still in an intimate relationship with wife. Given A5 claims to be aware of his infidelity with other women and that he was married some readers might view A5 as naïve. Thus, A5 bolsters her claims by adding to 'scumbag' the additional category-bound activities (Sacks, 1992): 'He borrows money and doesn't return it. Sleeps around and has STI'.

Categorising the postee as a criminal was noticeable in several posts by heterosexual women, usually in the form of stealing as reported by A5 and A1.

However, what was less noticeable was the ex-partner categorised as a drug user. This A6 does in the following post.

> A6
> "My 18 year old, coke loving, (identifier omitted) ex boyfriend"
> Anonymous says:
> Yes he's only (identifier omitted) years old and he already has a high paying job (identifier omitted), pretty cool Not really when you learn that he's a cheating, coke sniffing arsehole. Although we wasn't official, I was under the impression that we were exclusive, clearly he didn't think the same. He thinks he's a smooth playboy but really he's just a horny coke head. Below are some pics he sent me showing off his body, and the picture that caught him out, my friend took the picture of him kissing another girl in a nightclub. CUNT

What is interesting about this post is that her title A6 anticipates viewer's reactions: 'Yes he's only (identifier omitted) years old and he already has a high paying job (identifier omitted), pretty cool'. In other words, she anticipates that some readers might consider her foolish for ending their relationship given his age and employment status. Indeed, biological-based discourses abound which presume women have a preference for men physically fit and financially secure as partners (for example, Larson, Haselton, Gildersleeve, & Pillsworth, 2013). Given his reported employment and financial status, she is thus, compelled to provide an account for her revenge seeking, especially since she highlights some uncertainty over whether they were in an intimate relationship 'My... ex boyfriend', 'Although we wasn't official'. What this suggests is that she perceived them to be in a relationship but this was perhaps not public knowledge. Thus, inviting challenges by some viewers (perhaps known to either poster/postee), which would undermine her account of his reported infidelity: 'he's a cheating', 'I was under the impression that we were exclusive', 'him kissing another girl'. Given the potential for her account to be undermined A6 does two things. First, she constructs him as leading her on for sex, 'I was under the impression that we were exclusive, clearly he didn't think the same. He thinks he's a smooth playboy but really he's just a horny coke head'. What this does is position him as immoral and deceitful. Second, she also positions him as a criminal 'coke loving', 'coke sniffing', 'coke head'.[2] Sacks (1992, p. 238) argued that a single identity category is sufficient to refer to some member of a population, in order to provide meaning for others. All members of that identity category are presumed to have the same attributes. Thus, deploying the identity category 'coke head', readers will hear the postee as having specific identity-bound characteristics (perhaps selfish and self-centered, orientated to getting high) and doing specific identity-bound activities (perhaps orientated to scoring cocaine, involved in criminal behavior). Sharrock (1974, p. 49) explains the importance of these category-bound activities and predicates:

> The assignment of a name to a corpus sets up the way in which further description is to be done. The name is not, then, merely descriptive in that

once it has been assigned it becomes a device-for-describing: that is, the name is not to be revised in light of events but is, rather, to be invoked in the description of whatever events occur.

In other words, category-bound activities and predicates are important for when making sense of the everyday social world because this allows for people to make value assessments of other's actions. This assessment of morality is important since, 'standards, criteria, judgments, implications, etc. – are bound up with various other practical matters – categorisations, descriptions inferences etc.' (Jayyusi, 1984, p. 181). Drug users tend to be viewed as socially undesirable in Western societies and are often marginalised (Nettleton, Neale, & Pickering, 2013). A6's account of him as a cocaine user can be read as an attempt to marginalise her ex-partner.

Attempting to marginalise an ex-partner was a common feature in our dataset. While the previous poster's account centered on sexual promiscuity and criminality, the following poster relates her account to online sexual practices and sexuality.

## Sexting

A7

"Lying little cunt"

Anonymous says:

Met this prick on pof, such a liar! he played the innocent inexperienced guy and slowly talked me into swapping pics claiming he had never done it before, he told me he had never met a person he felt understood him like I did but then he slipped up and I found out he's a slut and a player and now I've found out he's been known to get with guys too! fucking asshole

A simple gloss of this post is revenge by someone who was perhaps tricked into exchanging, presumably sexually explicit photos 'talked me into swapping pics' via the online dating site Plenty of Fish 'pof'. Since images are reported to have been exchanged this might be retaliation for him posting images of her. We have noted throughout our analysis hitherto, that the person seeking revenge is compelled to provide an account to avoid changes of vindictiveness (Johansson & Hammarén, 2007). Indeed, as we noted in Chapter 1, swapping explicit images invites charges of her own culpability since swapping might be considered consensual (Citron & Franks, 2014). Thus, to deter such charges she works an account of him as a 'player' – that is, someone who is pathological 'Lying little cunt', calculating 'slowly talked me into' and deceitful 'told me he had never met a person he felt understood him like I did'. In other words, she implies she was coerced and thus not accountable (Ringrose et al., 2012). Similarly, to A4, A6 questions his sexuality 'been known to get with guys too!' which works to challenge his masculine status (Edwards, 2006).

Like many perpetrator's accounts A7's post acts as an implicit warning to others. That is, this person is someone to be avoided. In the following extract A8's account is an explicit warning which suggests that the victim might be known by some readers.

## Sexual practices

A8

"A delivery man with a tiny package"

Anonymous says:

Ladies, be careful of this man! He is a driver delivery man and he is only out for one thing... Sex! Do not trust him with yourself or any female member of your family. He is not safe. He is a pervert. I can't name the company he works for because it's not their fault but please, if you see his face, don't trust him. He is scum. Report him if he is inappropriate or is abusive.

A8's title combines the man's employment 'delivery man' with an employment-related colloquialism for small genitals 'a tiny package' in the title. This works in two ways. First, like A3 and A4, claiming he has small genitals works to challenge his manhood (Wylie & Eardley, 2007). Second, it is readable as humour (Benwell, 2004). While this may have the additional benefit of catching readers' attention it potentially undermines the warning that follows: 'Ladies, be careful of this man!'.

The invocation of the addressee's identity category 'Ladies' does an interesting piece of rhetorical work. Membership categorisation devices (MCDs) are collections of categories that go together and have some meaning in which they all relate (Sacks, 1992). For example, the MCD 'gender' contains the categories wo/men and boys/girls and so on. The selection of one category over another within the device 'gender' (or any other) is not arbitrary; it is selected to serve a purpose because the social knowledge associated with categories carries important implications for how the text is read (or talk is heard). Edwards (1998, p. 25) argues that gender categories carry 'potentially useful conventional associations with age, marital status, and potential sexual availability'. Stokoe (2003, p. 331) suggests that when the category 'lady' is invoked it infers maturity, likely partnered and sexually unavailable, whereas a deploying a term such as 'girl' would imply 'frivolity, a lack of authority and purpose'. The invocation of 'Ladies' in the context of this warning helps to construct this man as heterosexual sex predator 'only out for one thing... Sex!' with women presumed to be uninterested in casual sex.

What is also noticeable is that the warning extends beyond the viewer: 'Do not trust him with yourself or any female member of your family'. This suggests two things. First, that viewers should pass the warning on and second, it also carries the implication female family members might be underage further qualified by 'He is not safe. He is a pervert'. Given the ethical, moral and legalistic dimension of this claim it is interesting that she frames this as protecting the organisation he works for 'I can't name the company he works for because it's not their fault'. What this suggests is that she is only reporting hearsay and not her own first-hand experience. Indeed, A8 concludes her post by inviting others to report him: 'Report him if he is inappropriate or is abusive'.

Accusations of inappropriate sexual conduct were common in our dataset. In the following post, this centers on transvestism:

> A9
> "He's a sissy"
> Anonymous says:
> He's a sad little sissy boy, loved wearing my clothes. Would rather look at porn and masturbate than have sex with me.

A9's title 'He's a sissy' provides the initial backdrop for her subsequent critique. Sacks (1992) pointed out people categorise themselves and others in particular contexts depending on who they are interacting with (for example, as a lecturer in university but father or husband at home). Sacks also pointed out that these identity categories carry common-sense social knowledge such as associated characteristics (predicates) and actions (activities). We can see this in A9's post in which she categories him as a 'sissy' qualified by the associated predicates and activities of 'wearing my clothes' and 'rather look at porn and masturbate than have sex with me'. This 'category, predicate and task' (Hester & Eglin, 1997) serves two purposes. Claiming he wears her clothes emasculates him by positioning him as 'effeminate'. In doing so, this also helps to detract from her being viewed by some readers as the reason he masturbates to porn. That is, she might not sexually satisfy him.

Categorising someone as effeminate or gay in developed nations might invite accusations of homophobia. A10 seems aware of this in the extract below by opening her post with the title "Ok to be gay, but not to be a liar"

### Sexuality

> A10
> "Ok to be gay, but not to be a liar"
> Anonymous says:
> This is my ex-boyfriend. We were engaged, but I have found out that he is gay. I found these nude pics of him on his note book and other pics showing him sucking cocks. Please help me to punish him. He promised me so much. I would like to have his life destroyed. It is ok to be gay! But it is not ok to be a liar. Please punish him! Expose him! Ruin his life.

Non-normative categories such as 'gay' are often seen as delicate categories because they contravene the common-sense knowledge, or what is known about a masculine category, in a predominantly heteronormative society with perceived gender distinctions. 'Gay' is seen as 'exception', 'different' or even a disjunctive category by virtue of its member's sexual orientations (Schegloff, 2007, p. 469). Although 'gay' is typically non-normative, categorising someone as 'gay' as a means to chastise risks accusations of homophobia. Thus, anyone doing so must design, select and manage their interest in their discursive action (Silverman, 1998, p. 132). A10's 'stake inoculation' (protecting her own interests) (see Edwards & Potter, 1992) presents as an attempt to protect herself from such charges by explicitly stating 'Ok to be gay' and reaffirming this later in the text. Managing her stake (Edwards & Potter, 1992) in this 'delicate' topic (Silverman & Peräkylä, 2008) is achieved by discursively positioning her 'ex-boyfriend' as a 'liar' regarding his sexuality. By categorising her ex-boyfriend as untruthful she is then required to provide evidence for doing so. A10 does this by stating that he ex-boyfriend 'found these nude pics of him' and 'pics showing him sucking cocks'. Yet to do so still risks inviting charges of homophobia and so A10 marks the extent of her ex's deceit with the time they were together 'We were engaged' and claimed unfulfilled commitments: 'He promised me so much'. Combining the length of his claimed infidelity and deceitfulness with a three-part list (Jefferson, 1991) of desired outcomes 'Please punish him! Expose him! Ruin his life' presents as attempting to co-opt others in her revenge seeking. In doing so, she minimises her culpability.

## Discussion

Our analysis focused on how women accounted for, and justified, posting explicit images of men (mostly ex-partners). Unsurprisingly, the women claimed the men deserved being posted because they were reported to have been violent, a poor father, sexual predator (both online and offline), homosexual, effeminate, liar and not fulfilling their intimate partner sexual duties. We showed also that many of these reported or alleged misdemeanors are linked, even tied, to and invested in notions of gender and sexual interactions. Thus, overall, revenge was reported positively by women posters as a supposedly equalising action, while downplaying their culpability.

There are similarities between women and men's motivations and accounts for revenge porn. Both draw on control within the relationship, committing infidelity, sexual performance, parenting and sexual health, thus constructing revenge pornography as, in their own terms, a legitimate form of interpersonal revenge. However, there are importance differences. Some women, such as A1, reported physical assaults by men, but we found no examples of men reporting assaults by women. This might be due to difficulties men find in reporting such assaults, which might be viewed as a sign of weakness, or emasculation (Migliaccio, 2001). There was an important difference in parenthood too. Men argued that women denied them access to their children, thus, denying them the right to fatherhood. That is, denying access to children as a means of revenge (Chesler, 2011). Women on the other hand, such as A2, argued these men avoided their parental responsibilities, in particular, the provision of finance. This contrasted with some men's semantic derogation of women as 'gold diggers' (see Schulz, 1975 for a historical analysis of derogative terms for women).

Women could be seen to challenge men's manhood and masculine status with claims of inadequate genital size and shape, sexual performance, sexual preferences and sexuality. Men, on the other hand, reported women as not fulfilling their sexual entitlements, viewed women as sexual objects, or where women were reported displaying sexual agency, this was sometimes linked to prostitution. But despite these differences in the way women and men talked about their former partner's sex practices and preferences, both indicated a nuanced understanding of how these can be deployed to abuse. Indeed, this also suggests they were aware that the impact of revenge porn is amplified, if, seen by a known viewing public, such as the victim, their current partner and others known to the victim. In the next chapter we look at posts by self-identifying as gay or lesbian.

## Notes

1 Plenty of Fish (POF) claims to be the largest online dating agency with more than 3 million daily users in Brazil, France, Germany, Spain and the United States (www.pof.com/).
2 Slang terms for cocaine users.

## References

Anderson, K. L., & Umberson, D. (2001). Gendering violence: Masculinity and power in men's accounts of domestic violence. *Gender & Society, 15*(3), 358–380.

Antaki, C., & Widdicombe, S. (Eds.). (1998). *Identities in talk*. London: Sage.

Barrett, M. (2012). The efficacy of interviewing young drug users through online chat. *Drug and Alcohol Review, 31*(4), 566–572.

Benwell, B. (2004). Ironic discourse: Evasive masculinity in British men's lifestyle magazines. *Men & Masculinities, 7*(1), 3–21.

Brown, S. (2012). Young men, sexual health and responsibility for contraception: A qualitative pilot study. *Journal of Family Planning & Reproductive Healthcare, 38*(1), 44–47.

Brunner Huber, L. R., & Ersek, J. L. (2011). Perceptions of contraceptive responsibility among female college students: An exploratory study. *Annals of Epidemiology, 21*(3), 197.

Chesler, P. (2011). *Mothers on trial: The battle for children and custody*. Chicago: Chicago Review Press.

Citron, D. K., & Franks, M. A. (2014). Criminalising revenge porn. *Wake Forest Law Review, 49*, 345–391.

Dickerson, P. (2000). "But I"m different to them": Constructing contrasts between self and others in talk-in-interaction. *British Journal of Social Psychology, 39*(3), 381–398.

Edwards, D. (1998). The relevant thing about her: Social identity categories in use. In C. Antaki & S. Widdicombe (Eds.), *Identities in talk*. London: Sage.

Edwards, T. (2006). *Cultures of masculinity*. London: Routledge.

Edwards, D., & Potter, J. (1992). *Discursive psychology: Inquiries in social construction*. London: Sage.

Foley, L., & Faircloth, C. A. (2003). Medicine as discursive resource: Legitimation in the work narratives of midwives. *Sociology of Health & Illness*, 25(2), 165–184.

Hall, M. (2015). 'When there's no underbrush the tree looks taller': A discourse analytical examination of how men account for genital grooming. *Sexualities*, 18(8), 997–1017.

Heidensohn, F., & Gelsthorpe, L. (2012). *Gender and crime*. Oxford: Oxford University Press.

Hester, S., & Eglin, P. (Eds.). (1997). *Culture and action: Studies in membership categorization analysis*. Washington: University Press of America.

Jayyusi, L. (1984). *Categorization and the moral order*. Boston: Routledge & Kegan Paul.

Jefferson, G. (1991). List construction as a task and a resource. In G. Psathas (Ed.), *Interactional competence*. New York: Irvington Publications.

Johansson, T., & Hammarén, N. (2007). Hegemonic masculinity and pornography: Young people's attitudes toward and relations to pornography. *Journal of Men's Studies*, 15(1), 57–71.

Larson, C. M., Haselton, M. G., Gildersleeve, K. A., & Pillsworth, E. G. (2013). Changes in women's feelings about their romantic relationships across the ovulatory cycle. *Hormones and Behavior*, 63(1), 128–135.

Lefkowitz, E. S., Shearer, C. L., Gillen, M. M., & Espinosa-Hernandez, G. (2014). How gendered attitudes relate to women's and men's sexual behaviors and beliefs. *Sexuality & Culture*, 18(4), 833–846.

MacDonald, K. (2002). What makes Western culture unique? *The Occidental Quarterly*, 2(2), 8–38.

Migliaccio, T. A. (2001). Marginalizing the battered male. *Journal of Men's Studies*, 9(2), 205–226.

Miller, K. (2008). Wired: Energy drinks, jock identity, masculine norms, and risk taking. *Journal of American College Health*, 56(5), 481–490.

Nettleton, S., Neale, J., & Pickering, L. (2013). 'I just want to be normal': An analysis of discourses of normality among recovering heroin users. *Health*, 17(2), 174–190.

Nylund, D. (2007). *Beer, babes, and balls: Masculinity and sports talk radio*. Albany: State University Press New York.

Pomerantz, A. (1986). Extreme case formulations: A way of legitimizing claims. *Human Studies*, 9, 219–229.

Potter, J. (1996). *Representing reality: Discourse, rhetoric and social construction*. London: Sage.

Ringrose, J., Gill, R., Livingstone, S., & Harvey, L. (2012). *A qualitative study of children, young people and sexting*. London: NSPCC.

Sacks, H. (1992). *Lectures on conversation*. Oxford: Blackwell.

Salter, M. (2013). Responding to revenge porn: Gender, justice and online legal impunity. Paper delivered at: *Whose justice? Conflicted approaches to crime and conflict*, University of Western Sydney, Sydney, 27 September.

Schegloff, E. A. (2007). A tutorial on membership categorization. *Journal of Pragmatics*, 39, 462–482.

Schulz, M. R. (1975). The semantic derogation of woman. In B. Thorne & N. Henley (Eds.), *Language and sex: Difference and dominance* (pp. 64–75). Rowley: Newbury House Publishers Inc.

Sharrock, W. W. (1974). On owning knowledge. In R. Turner (Ed.), *Ethnomethodology* (pp. 45–53). Harmondsworth: Penguin.

Silverman, D. (1998). *Harvey sacks: Social science and conversation analysis*. Cambridge: Polity Press.

Silverman, D., & Peräkylä, A. (2008). AIDS counselling: The interactional organisation of talk about 'delicate' issues. *Sociology of Health & Illness*, *12*(3), 293–318.

Stokoe, E. (2010). 'I'm not gonna hit a lady': Conversation analysis, membership categorization and men's denials of violence towards women. *Discourse & Society*, *21*(1), 59–82.

Stokoe, E. H. (2003). Mothers, single women and sluts: Gender, morality and membership categorization in neighbour disputes. *Feminism & Psychology*, *13*(3), 317–344.

Wolf, N. (2013). *Fire with fire: New female power and how it will change the twenty-first century.* London: Random House.

Wylie, R. R., & Eardley, I. (2007). Penile size and the 'small penis syndrome'. *BJU International*, *99*(6), 1449–1455.

Yoshimura, S. (2007). Goals and emotional outcomes of revenge activities in interpersonal relationships. *Journal of Social and Personal Relationships*, *24*(1), 87–98.

Zaider, T., Manne, S., Nelson, C., Mulhall, J., & Kissane, D. (2012). Loss of masculine identity, marital affection, and sexual bother in men with localized prostate cancer. *Journal of Sexual Medicine*, *9*(10), 2724–2732.

# 8

# '...CHEATER! LIAR! THIEF!'

## Gay and lesbian accounts

### Male-to-male accounts

Despite revenge porn being predominantly carried out by male heterosexuals we wondered how people in former same-sex relationships accounted for revenge porn and what (dis)similarities there were in their accounts. We noted in previous chapters that around 90% of the posts on MyEx.com and other revenge porn sites were posted by men. Less than 1% of all revenge porn posts were by those in former same-sex relationships (September, 2016). There are likely to be two explanations for this. First, posting as self-identified gay or lesbian, or orientating to a same-sex relationship, reveals one's sexuality to an unknown or known public. In effect 'outing' oneself. Even with the West arguably becoming more tolerant and accepting of non-heterosexual relationships, Anderson (2009) argues, for some, making public their relationship may still be problematic (Chan, 2016). Second, we only counted those posts in which we could be sure of the poster's sexuality; we discuss this below. Thus, there may have many more same-sex former relationship posts, but we could not be certain of this.

Having collected more than 1,000 texts (March, 2016) accompanying explicit images of men on MyEx.com's section 'Just Guys', we examined the texts for orientations and indexing of same-sex male relationships. We discounted posts where terms for same-sex relationship seemed to be used as terms of abuse, for example, 'Fucking faggot!', 'Think he prefers men over women', 'he's gay', 'he hooks up with any boys he can meet when he is travelling. I wondered why he always wanted Anal sex, not my ass his!!!' We selected texts where same-sex relationship orientation and indexing was clear ('He was my first gay relationship', 'we met on a gay site', 'his new bf') and invoking same-sex markers ('he does take it up the arse I know I've done him'), and by reference to well-known gay dating sites such as 'Grindr'.[1] This resulted in a total of 19 potentially eligible male-to-male posts. These posts were initially coded by response type:

- *cheated on*: 'Cheating cunt!!';
- *genital size:* 'Guy with baby dick';
- *payback:* 'Payback to a closetted gay cocksucker who posted me';
- *rejection*: 'Cunt only wants you when he does';
- *sexual promiscuity:* 'he was a typical whore type gay guy'; and
- *unsafe sex*: 'likes nothing more than to meet as many guys as possible from (identifier omitted) and other apps usually asking for Bareback sex'.

We further coded the texts, producing the following loosely classified emergent discourses: sexual promiscuity, warnings and risky sex, and sexual control and sexuality. We analyse five posts as exemplars covering these discourses. We begin with sexual promiscuity:

### Sexual promiscuity

A1

"Cheating ex-boyfriend exposed and totally humiliated"

Anonymous says:

This is my cheating ex-boyfriend in all his glory. I found out he was cheating, so I didn't say I knew. I just spent weeks making loads of humiliating sex snaps and vids of him! So I could expose him and get revenge after dumping him. This is what the cheating slut deserves!! I've got loads of him sucking dick, balls, licking ass, spreading his legs and being the slut he always is. I've no doubt that his new bf doesn't have any idea what he's really like, so maybe he'll come across these photos and realise. Have fun jacking off guys, and if you reblog or repost these pics please let me know so I can get a kick out of seeing them spread

A1's account for revenge seeking centers his ex-partner's reported infidelity: 'cheating ex-boyfriend', 'I found out he was cheating', 'cheating slut', 'the slut he always is'. In doing so, infidelity is presented as a 'just' reason for revenge. Any poster who believes that his or her ex-partner has committed infidelity or terminated the relationship is likely to be in a position of disempowerment since he or she was not the one to end it. One of the tactics for dealing with, and sometimes coping with, disempowerment is to do something to regain control – seek revenge (Berkowitza & Cornell, 2005). A1 does this in two ways. First, he claims that he was the one who ended the relationship "after dumping him" and second, he believes that what he set out to achieve has been achieved: 'Cheating ex-boyfriend exposed and totally humiliated'. Although this suggests some level of re-empowerment, it is likely to have had less of an impact if A1's ex-partner was not aware of the act. A1 implies that his ex-partner is likely to be aware of him posting these images by suggesting he knows his ex-partner's experiences 'totally humiliated'.

A1 presents as 'fact' 'I've no doubt' that his ex-partners 'new bf' remains unaware of his actions: 'doesn't have any idea what he's really like'. This suggests that A1 might know his ex-partner's new partner or that A1 has been informed that the new partner is not aware of the images, and his ex-partner's reported sexual activities, thus indicating that A1 has the ability to escalate the impact of the images if so desired. Implicit also is that if the new partner knew what his ex-partner was 'really like' it may impact on their relationship (see Pomerantz, 1986 for more on extreme-case formulations such as 'really'). But what's interesting is that A1 attempts to develop a relationship with viewers by encouraging them to 'reblog or repost' the images; presumably to increase the likelihood of his ex-partner's new partner seeing them 'so maybe he'll come across these photos'. We demonstrated the development of a similar relationship between A1 and viewers in Chapter 6 – that is, an acceptable form of revenge and homosocial exchange between men (Whisnant, 2010).

A1's aim to sexual humiliate his ex-partner for his claimed sexual promiscuity was unique in our gay dataset. What was common was for the poster to explicitly or implicitly frame his or her post as a warning to others. This serves two purposes. First, it acts as a deflection strategy, thus warding off potential criticisms, and second, the poster can frame the act of revenge seeking positively – that is, in part doing it for the benefit of others. In the following two posts, we see that A2 frames his post as a warning to others about his ex-partner's sexual infidelity, whereas A3 frames his post as a warning to others about his ex-partner's reported psychological abuses:

A2
"(anonymised) Dick Licker"
Anonymous says:
I was seeing this wanna be man (anonymised). I took him to a party and caught him in the bathroom sucking another Man's Dick. He is so disgusting, he tried to apologize saying my dick is much better than the guy I caught him with. Total fucken loser!

A2's title explicitly names his ex-partner and categorises him as a 'Dick Licker'. As we have noted throughout our analysis assertions need to be qualified if the poster is to be believed by viewers. This is achieved with a brief account of the person's reported infidelity 'sucking another Man's Dick' at a 'party'. What's interesting is that his infidelity account follows not only an orientation to their former relationship 'I was seeing this…man' but a challenge to his ex-partner's manhood, 'wanna be man'. Challenging his ex-partner's manhood achieves two things. First, it positions his ex-partner as 'effeminate' or a 'sissy' (Edwards, 2006; Hunter, 1993). Hall's (2014) data analysis of self-identified 'metrosexuals' showed that to emasculate other men, men draw on sexuality and gender. Men either categorise other men as 'homosexual' or position them as 'effeminate'. Given A2 self-identifies as gay he is compelled to position his ex-partner as 'effeminate'. Positioning his ex-partner in this way fits with his accusation of 'sucking another Man's Dick' rather than receiving oral sex from another man. In other words, his ex-partner is in the more submissive sexual position (see Walkington, 2016 for more on cultural perceptions of sexual acts).

Similarly, A2 claims his ex-partner tried to apologise 'saying my dick is much better than the guy I caught him with'. Hall's (2015) studies on genital grooming showed that penis size and shape are integral to manhood. A2 stating that his penis is 'much better than the guy I caught him with' serves two purposes. First, it adds clarity to A2's categorisation of his ex-partner as 'effeminate' since bolstering a man's penis size is a strategy deployed by some women to inflate a man's ego, whereas ridiculing a man's penis size is a means of belittlement as we showed in the previous chapter. Second, since penis size and shape are key markers of manhood, A2's claim that his penis is 'better' elevates his masculine status vis-à-vis the other man.

The final point to note is that A2 claims his ex-partner is 'disgusting'. Researchers of gay sexuality (for example, Ávila, 2015; Davies, Hickson, Weatherburn, & Hunt, 2013; Mowlabocus, Harbottle, & Witzel, 2013) note that casual gay sex is often viewed negatively in the gay community because of the increased risks associated with sexually transmitted diseases. Thus, in effect, A2 is warning others who might be interested in a sexual relationship with his ex-partner.

As we have hitherto noted in our analysis of heterosexual and homosexual posts, posters must provide an account for posting the explicit images. Unlike A1 who openly seeks revenge through sexual humiliation of his ex-partner, A2 does this via an implicit warning. What we have also shown in our analysis is that posters often do not simply seek revenge through posting the images on such websites, but also aim to regain and reposition themselves as in control and powerful. A2 achieved this through challenging his ex-partner's masculinity, claiming to terminate the relationship and revenge seeking. A3 on the other hand, works up a relatively weaker position, which serves to bolster his warning to others:

A3
"THIS GAY AND WILL PLAY YOU (HE IS ON THE RIGHT)"
Anonymous says:
Hey this is (identifier omitted) we met on a gay site and continued to talk on kik.[2] He played me into giving up my nude pictures and he wanted to meet up to have sex several times. But he didn't actually want to instead he wanted me to feel bad about myself and say hurtful things like I will never like and I will never will. He was never nice to me but the first day we met. He told me he wanted to just jerk off to my pics and that everything he said was a lie.

The first thing to notice in this extract is A3's greeting 'Hey'. Sacks (1992) identified a procedural rule for greetings, 'a person who speaks first … can choose their form of address, and in choosing their form of address they can thereby choose the form of address the other uses'. In other words, exchanges tend to occur in pairs, so that if someone says 'Hey' the response will most likely be 'Hey'. The use of a casual greeting 'Hey' then sets the tone and context of how the audience is to read the text and view the images: in a casual friendly manner. Similarly to A1, A3 is developing a relationship with viewers. This works to support references to posting in part for the benefit of others and as a deflection strategy to ward off potential critiques.

What's also interesting is that A3's post implies that physical sex may not have taken place because although the person is claimed to have 'wanted to meet up to have sex several times' they 'didn't actually' even though they did meet 'we met'. This suggests their relationship was primarily Internet-based sex or cybersex (Cooper, 2013), which has been identified as an increasingly popular form of gay (and straight) style of intimate relationship (see Race, 2015 for more detail on the various forms of online intimate relationships). As we noted in Chapter 1, such online hook-ups are often accompanied by sharing explicit images either online or through texting (Hasinoff, 2015).

A3 is also claiming to have being tricked 'He played me' into sending 'nude pictures' and being emotionally mistreated 'he wanted me to feel bad about myself and say hurtful things'. This is bolstered by the use of the extreme-case formulations 'never' and 'just' (Pomerantz, 1986). As we have noted in previous chapters, extreme-case formulations serve as discursive devices in 'defending positions against refutation, making complaints, and justifying factual claims' (Edwards, 2000), therefore strengthening his claim that his ex-partner was a charlatan 'wanted to just jerk off to my pics' who was not interested an intimate relationship. A3 positions his ex-partner as the one who was in control and thus presents posting explicit images of his ex-partner as a legitimate form of revenge.

Sexual promiscuity and explicit and implicit warnings about ex-partners were common in our homosexual (and heterosexual) datasets. In the following post A4 warns others by raising questions about his ex-partner's sexual practices:

### Sexual practices

A4
"Slimy Grindr Creep"
Anonymous says:
[Anonymised] likes nothing more than to meet as many guys as possible from Grindr and other apps usually asking for bareback sex. [Anonymised] enjoys fucking as many other desperate guys as possible behind his boyfriends back. His tiny cock doesn't leave you very satisfied.

A4 categorises this man as 'Slimy' and a 'Creep', along with the location for these categorisations 'Grindr'. Sacks (1992) pointed out that when someone is categorised he or she is presumed to be the doer of particular actions that are 'category-bound activities' and have specific characteristics as 'natural predicates'. However, 'Slimy' and a 'Creep' alone do not qualify A4's assertions (Jayyusi, 1984). A4's account centers on his ex-partner as interested in unprotected sex, 'bareback sex',[3] with other men 'many other desperate guys'. Thus, positioning his ex-partner as sexually promiscuous 'likes nothing more than to meet as many guys as possible', 'enjoys fucking as many other desperate guys as possible behind his boyfriends back'. In making 'bareback sex' and sexual promiscuity relevant, A4 indicates this is a 'risky' sexual practice (see Ávila, 2015; Davies et al., 2013; Mowlabocus et al., 2013, for more on the risks associated with casual unprotected anal intercourse). In doing so, A2 works up two contrast pairs (Smith, 1978): safe/unsafe sex; not desperate/desperate. In doing so, A4 is able to position those interested in unprotected anal intercourse as non-normative. Thus, A4's account can also be read as a warning to other men who might come into contact with his ex-partner. By framing his post as a warning, A4 is able to present his actions in a positive light, in other words, doing something for the benefit of others.

Since his ex-partner's sexual promiscuity is presented as a consequence of A2 not engaging in 'bareback sex' he implies his ex-partner viewed unprotected anal intercourse in a relationship as an entitlement. We see similarities in extract A4, Chapter 6, in which the poster blamed the posted for his action because she wouldn't engage in sexual activities he deemed his entitlement (Anderson & Umberson, 2001). Indeed, Blackwell's (2008) study of same-sex dating sites found that 43% of men expected 'bareback sex' even though it places both sexual partners at a higher risk of HIV transmission.

A4 also categorises his ex-partner as someone with a 'tiny cock' which he claims 'doesn't leave you very satisfied'. This achieves two things. First, the reference to genital size and sexual dissatisfaction works to emasculate his ex-partner. Wylie and Eardley (2007, p. 1449) point out, penis size in many cultures 'has come to symbolise attributes such as largeness, strength, endurance, ability, courage, intelligence, knowledge, dominance over men, possession of women; a symbol of loving and being loved' and, also fertility. Given this symbolism, it's understandable that some men may feel inadequate if they don't meet perceived cultural norms. Indeed, two-thirds of men in a recent UK study (Veale et al., 2013) reported some dissatisfaction with their genital size and shape. Tiggemann, Martins and Churchett (2008) reported penis size as the third biggest concern for men (behind body weight and muscularity). Second, what is implied is that A4 was willing to remain in an intimate relationship in which he was sexually unfulfilled, thus implying to others that he was emotionally invested in the relationship rather than for sexual satisfaction and presenting himself positively.

Unlike A4, A5 in the following post does not work up a positive image of himself. Instead, A5 claims his ex-partner controlled their sexual relations: 'Cunt only wants you when he does' and challenges his sexuality 'he's not straight':

## Sexuality

> A5
>
> "Cunt only wants you when he does"
>
> Anonymous says:
>
> This is my half auntie's sister's ex bf, he's a good fuck, likes to sit and ride cock, he likes piss fun, he likes his ass fucked with toys fist and cocks, he likes to cam4 pussyman00 and twitter Cumplay He loves being sucked he's from (identifier omitted) he will meet anywhere his house or car or his favourite place (identifier omitted) not far from his home or (identifier omitted) P.S he's not straight and he does take it up the arse I know I've done him in the ass since he was with my aunties sister they split up in 2011

We noted earlier that an initial address sets up the way in which others are to read the remainder of the text (Sacks, 1992). Here we can see A5's title 'Cunt only wants you when he does' immediately positions his (ex)partner as sexually selfish, controlling sexual activities and, thus the cause of the relationship breakdown. In doing so, readers are invited to read the remainder of the text with A5 as the victim and the posted as getting deserved retribution. But what is surprising is that A5 does not provide an account for the assertions; instead he provides a detailed description of how he knows the person 'my half auntie's sister's ex bf', where he's from '(identifier omitted)', where he engages in sexual activities 'his house or car or his favourite place (identifier omitted) not far from his home or (identifier omitted)', and provides a list of sexual activities he is reported to enjoy, 'likes to sit and ride cock, he likes piss fun, he likes his ass fucked with toys fist and cocks, he likes to cam4 pussyman00 and twitter Cumplay. He loves being sucked' (see Jefferson, 1991 for more on listing). Listing of sexual activities provides legitimacy and credibility to A5's account and suggests A5 has been involved in these activities with his ex-partner (Epstein, 1995).

A5's description serves two purposes. First, A5 is 'outing' is ex-partner as bisexual 'not straight' (see Schafer, 2014 for more on 'outing' and sexualities). In making his ex-partner's sexuality relevant – bisexual 'half auntie's sister's ex bf', 'he's not straight … I know I've done him in the ass' – A5 is suggesting that his ex-partner masquerades as heterosexual but is reported to be bisexual. Second, the information A5 provides about where his ex-partner is reported to live and practice these sexual activities is readable as intended for people living in the near proximity and presumably known to the victim and perpetrator.

What's also noticeable is that A5 marks the time he is reported to have had sexual relations with the person; from '2011' to 2014 when the images were posted. This suggests A5 is likely to have been emotionally involved in the relationship. Longevity given the reported misdemeanours signals tolerance and perseverance. In doing so, A5 is able to present his actions as expedient.

In the following section, we focus also on how posters account for their activities, but in female-to-female intimate relationships.

## Female-to-female accounts

When considering women-to-women posts, we followed the same data collection, coding and analytical process as those in former male same-sex relationships. We discounted those texts where terms for female-to-female sexual orientations were used as a term of abuse, for example, men claiming that women were lesbians such as 'Ex-wife lesbian slut had an affair with a girl she was working with while waitressing at a restaurant'. Similarly to male-to-male posts, less than 1% were women-to-women, which total five posts. As we noted at the beginning of the chapter the small number of posts may be a result of not wanting to reveal one's sexuality or that there were only a small number of posts in which sexual orientation was orientated to. Lesbian orientation and indexing could be seen with the deployment of specific gender and in-group terms and markers ('pretesbian',[4] 'She also stole a lot of my makeup', 'she ended up hooking up with a few other women'). We downloaded all five texts and coded these according to the three discourses: sexual promiscuity, phony sexuality and prostitution. We present an analysis of all five texts:

### *Sexual promiscuity*

> A6
> "lesbian slut! cheater! liar! thief!"
> Anonymous says:
> I met [identifier omitted] through a friend and started to hang out. long story short me and her got together a few times I was her first took her virginity n she promised to be together blablabla she ended up hooking up with a few other women behind my back and denied we even had anything going on! she had sex with 16 other women behind my back! n lied to my face! She also stole a lot of my makeup and other things … to this day she denies we had anything but these pics say otherwise [identifier omitted] bitch!

A6 begins her post by categorising her ex-partner with a list of four negative attributes 'slut', 'cheater', 'liar' and 'thief' that break social norms and imply infidelity and pilfering – that is, breaking the social norms of monogamy, honesty, truthfulness and respect for others' property (McDonald & Crandall, 2015). As noted previously, lists add clarity and weight to arguments, ward off potential counterclaims and act as devices in, and through, which to orientate (Jefferson, 1991). The items on A6's list allow for A6's ex-partner to be presented as an unsavory person thus enabling her to position herself as the victim. What is also noticeable in A6's title is that the sexuality of the person pictured is made relevant 'lesbian'. People invoke identity categories to set the tone and context in which the text or conversation is to be understood (Sacks, 1992). This means that the preceding text is readable as a 'lesbian' text because a single category is sufficient to refer to some member of a population and provide meaning for others, even though multiple other categories could be used to describe that person, for example, 'woman', 'ex-partner', 'wife', 'spouse' and so on. This is one of Membership Categorisation Analysis' 'rules of application' which was noted in Chapter 5; the 'economy rule' (Sacks, 1992, p. 238).

We have noted throughout our analysis that even though someone is categorised (for example, 'lesbian slut! cheater! liar! thief!') the person categorising is compelled to provide and account (Berkowitza & Cornell, 2005). A6 qualifies her accusation of lesbian infidelity as 'she had sex with 16 other women'; deception, 'she promised to be together'; untruthfulness, 'denied we even had anything going on!'; and pilfering, 'She also stole a lot of my makeup and other things'. What is interesting is that A6 frames posting the explicit images as providing proof of their relationship: 'she denies we had anything but these pics say otherwise'. Framing her act as proof providing rather than simply revenge is a tactic that acts as a deterrent to ward off potential criticisms and thus deflects accountability onto her ex-partner.

What's also noticeable is that A6 is claiming to have been the first person her ex-partner had a sexual relationship with: 'I was her first took her virginity'. This serves to bolster A6's position in that she perceived this to be an intimate relationship rather than casual sex. In many societies, a young woman's virginity is typically perceived as precious, and as something that is to be maintained, and given to the person they hope will remain a long-term intimate partner (Carpenter, 2015). However, as Carpenter (2015) points out, while taking a young woman's virginity is seen as a prize for some men that provides homosocial boasting rights, in more recent times with challenges to such conventional gender norms, some young women have come to see taking virginity in a similar manner. Thus, stating that she took her ex-partner's virginity in the context of revenge suggests this is boasting.

Posting, and implying, negative statements about a person's character is of course what one would expect from someone posting explicit images of another in order to seek revenge for some claimed misdemeanor. What is interesting about the following post is there are a mixture of positive and negative comments, which ironically implies A7 still has some level of affection for her ex-partner she aims to humiliate:

A7

"The womanizer"

Anonymous says:

I met her a long time ago and we dated for a little while, but she hated commitment so broke my heart and said she couldn't settle down right now, she is the perfect girlfriend but doesn't want to be anybody's. Can get any girl she wants when she wants wherever she wants but refuses to be in a committed relationship. A couple years after us dating she got married and had her heart broken just like she broke mine, except her wife really fucked her over. She got what she deserved. She is sexy, amazing in bed, and funnier than anyone I've ever met, but gets really jealous and has the worst temper I have ever seen. If you've got things to hide, steer clear because she is a fighter and will beat anybody's ass that she feels threatened by.

Dangerous and can go a little crazy when her temper gets out of control. I'm glad her life is falling apart; she broke my heart and played me like a fool. Such a whore!

A7 begins by categorising her ex-partner as a 'The womanizer', which immediately signals to the reader that this woman is sexually promiscuous and being accused of infidelity. This association occurs because of the 'hearer's maxim' (Sacks, 1974). Sacks argues that identity categories are linked to specific activities and predicates, which are then presumed members of that category. Given the 'hearer's maxim' A7 doesn't have to provide further clarification for her posting of the explicit images.

It would be easy to gloss A7's text as a person who resents her ex-partner for her unrequited love. However, focusing on this would miss some interesting details. For example, A7 begins her main body of text by marking time 'I met her a long time ago' and 'we dated for a little while', which works to position herself as someone who was interested in a long-term, stable, lesbian relationship (Kurdek, 2005). Indeed, this is stated three times: 'couldn't settle down', 'doesn't want to be anybody's' and 'refuses to be in a committed relationship' although ironically 'A couple years after us dating she got married'. Invoking relationship longevity also implies relationship stability and thus the likely impact of infidelity is amplified. Indeed, the relationship is reported to have ended some time ago 'A couple years after us dating', thus suggesting that posting is not a knee-jerk reaction to a terminated relationship. Invoking time and relating it to her own hurt 'broke my heart', A7 is able to position herself as the victim. In other words, A7 can be seen to work up an account which centres on time and emotional impact in which her needs were not met and so she is entitled to seek retribution (Whisnant, 2010).

In addition, A7 deploys several extreme-case formulations 'ever', 'really', 'worst' (Pomerantz, 1986) when describing the character of her ex-partner. As we have shown previously, the deployment of these serves to bolster accounts by squeezing out potential dissenting views. A7 also compares her actions to her ex-partner's wife: 'had her heart broken just like she broke mine, except her wife really fucked her over'. What A7's comparison does is position her action of posting explicit images of a former partner in order to seek revenge as having less impact than the actions of her ex-partner's, thus minimising A7's own actions, supported by the use of the extreme-case formulation 'really' (Edwards, 2000; Pomerantz, 1986).

In the following two posts, the posters inauthenticate their former ex-partner's sexuality:

## Sexuality

A8
"This bitch really has LOW self-esteem (Lesbian)"
Anonymous says:
I dated this girl for a few months, at the time she was into Wicca, and just about anything to upset her parents. She quickly turned into an attention

whore. One day she tried to get with one of my friends and I thought it was time to call it quits. Needless to say, the breakup did not go well and she even threatened suicide on more than one occasion. I come to find out she's what we call in the lesbian community a pretesbian. She is only lesbian because she is spiteful about men who wouldn't give her the time of day when she was younger.

Several things are immediately noticeable in A8's title. First, A8 categorises her as a 'bitch' – a malicious, unpleasant, selfish person, especially a woman (*Oxford English Dictionary* Online, 2016). The categorisation (Sacks, 1992) is qualified with the category-bound predicate 'LOW self-esteem' emphasised with the extreme-case formulation 'really' (Pomerantz, 1986) and shouting 'LOW' (see Barrett, 2012 for more on capitalising words in electronic text). Like A6, in making relevant her ex-partner's sexual identity 'Lesbian' A8 is setting the tone and context in which the rest of her text is to be understood (Sacks, 1992). What's more parenthesising '(Lesbian)' as opposed to saying perhaps 'This lesbian bitch really has LOW self-esteem' suggests this may be a delicate identity. Silverman and Peräkylä (2008) note that people qualify identities (and topics) that might be deemed socially or personally delicate such as sexuality, illness, disability and so. People do this when they anticipate others questioning their claims. As we show in our analysis below, this relates to her ex-partner's sexuality 'pretesbian'.

What is interesting is that A8 immediately begins the main body of her text by marking the time she was in a relationship with her ex-partner 'I dated this girl for a few months'. This achieves several things. First, it signals to viewers that her ex-partner's attempted infidelity 'One day she tried to get with one of my friends' occurred early in their relationship. Second, time undermines her ex-partner's actions after the relationship was terminated 'threatened suicide on more than one occasion'. A8 is implying that her ex-partner's emotional investment in the relationship was perhaps too much too soon. Combined with this, third, marking time helps to construct her ex-partner as someone who is unstable. Indeed, A8 immediately begins her text by implicitly questioning her ex-partner's mental and emotional state 'at the time she was into Wicca,[5] and just about anything to upset her parents'. Membership of the identity category 'into Wicca' is marked as rebellion 'anything to upset her parents', thus suggesting to viewers that she was not a 'real' member of this sub-cultural group (Widdicombe & Woofitt, 1990). A8 also works up an image of her ex-partner as having multiple and shifting identities, thus signaling instability. In positioning the pictured woman as unstable, A8 works up the contrast pair (Smith, 1978) of identities stable/unstable, which allows A8 to position herself as stable; later claiming her ex-partner's membership of the 'lesbian community' as 'phony' (Sacks, 1992; Schegloff, 2007) 'pretesbian'. Those who are seen to be non-normative or not having 'real' group membership are often declared 'phony' or 'defective' (Sacks, 1992).

Working up a picture of the woman as a 'phony' lesbian and as unstable, 'threatened suicide', does three further things. First, the inherent disempowerment from her ex-partner attempting to commit infidelity, 'she tried to get with one of my friends', is deflected, allowing A8 to present herself as in control. Indeed, A8 claimed to be the one who ended the relationship, 'I thought it was time to call it quits'. Second, A8 is signaling caution to viewers who might know or be interested in a relationship with this woman. Last, A8 is also able to minimise potential claims by viewers that she is purely motivated by revenge.

Overall, what A8's account shows us is that gender and sexuality identities are presumed to be stable with specific identity-bound categories and predicates. Those who are seen to contravene these conventions are thus labeled as 'phony' or 'defective' (Sacks, 1992; Schegloff, 2007). That is, transgressing conventional notions of gender and sexual identity boundaries and in this example, the posted is reported to be masquerading as lesbian to spite her parents.

A9, in the following text, draws a similar conclusion; her ex-partner isn't a 'real' lesbian since she is reported to be currently in a heterosexual relationship, thus implying that her ex-partner is 'phony' lesbian (Sacks, 1992; Schegloff, 2007):

> A9
> "[identifier omitted]"
> Anonymous says:
> Claimed she was a lesbian and now has a boyfriend she's just a whore and will take whatever she can get! Beware everyone she'll just use you

What is immediately noticeable is that A9's post is short, punchy and to the point. That is, unlike many posters A9 only states her ex-partner's name in the title, provides a single sentence stating her ex-partner's reported offence 'Claimed she was a lesbian' and follows it with a short sentence warning. These assertions are presented as factual and supported by extreme-case formulations 'she's just', 'everyone', 'she'll just' (Pomerantz, 1986). As we have noted previously, invoking these reduces the basis for others to search for an account, especially when the poster anticipates others undermining his or her claims.

An additional tact deployed is not providing any details surrounding their relationship breakup. Indeed, it is only implied that infidelity might have occurred: 'now has a boyfriend'. Thus, A9 avoids her actions potentially being seen as deriving from a scorned woman. We can thus see that A9's 'category, predicate and task' (Hester & Eglin, 1997) in categorising her ex-partner as a phony 'Claimed she was a lesbian' with the predicates 'now has a boyfriend she's just a whore and will take whatever she can get!' functions to present her post as for the benefit of others: 'Beware everyone she'll just use you' (Hester & Eglin, 1997). Given A9 presents her text as a warning to others, one might assume her anticipated audience includes those known to her and her ex-partner, presumably lesbians also since sexuality is made relevant.

Similarly to A9, A10 raises questions about her ex-partner's 'real' sexual identity. But what is different about A10's post is that her account centres on her ex-partner's reported prostitution and personal hygiene:

## Prostitution

> A10
> "Lesbian con"
> Anonymous says:
> She likes to get on plenty of fish[6] pof and say she's straight just so she can make money. Fucks any girl she can including a psychotic bitch that gave herself an abortion and bleeds all over her, a transgender and many more. Trying to join the us navy. If this is going to be protecting my country, I need to get the fuck out

A10 immediately categorises her ex-partner as both a 'Lesbian' and a 'con'. Colloquially 'con' means either a person who is a convict or someone who is a trickster (Online Slang Dictionary, 2016; http://onlineslangdictionary.com/meaning-definition-of/con). It is clear that 'con' refers to trickster when A10 makes her ex-partners sexuality relevant in order to bolster A10's claim that she is masquerading as heterosexual 'say she's straight'. According to A10 this is undertaken in order to prostitute herself 'so she can make money'. Questioning someone's sexuality in this way implies: (1) the person is inauthentic and thus (2) untrustworthy and (3) immoral and thus an unsavoury person. A10's positioning of her ex-partner is supported by a three-part list of the people her ex-partner is prepared to have sex with: 'psychotic bitch', 'a transgender' and the non-specific category 'many more' – presumably men. Listing of course, allows A10 to add weight to her assertions and present them as factual and genuine (Jefferson, 1991). Because identity categories and their bounded activities and attributes are often viewed as oppositional (Jayyusi, 1984; Sacks, 1992), this means that by indirectly categorising her ex-partner as a 'con', A10 is able to imply that she, herself, is not this type of person. That is, she works up, like A10, a contrasting pair of identity-bound attributes trustworthy/untrustworthy, which work to support her assertions as truthful (Smith, 1978).

What's also noticeable is that A10 is constructing her ex-partner as someone willing to sleep with 'any girl' – in other words, wanton. The selection of one category over another within the membership categorisation device (see Sacks, 1992 for more on the MCAs) 'gender' which includes the category 'girls' carries important implications for how the text is read. Edwards (1998) argues that these categories carry 'potentially useful conventional associations with age, marital status, and potential sexual availability'. Stokoe (2003) suggests that when the category 'girl' is invoked, it 'suggests frivolity, a lack of authority and purpose.' This 'category, predicate and task' (Hester & Elgin, 1997) serves to downgrade the type of woman the ex-partner is claimed to be willing to have sexual relations with. Indeed, the example 'girl' A10 offers readers is presented as mentally un-stable 'psychotic', medically unsafe 'gave herself and abortion' and thus ethically questionable – that is, a member of a 'disjunctive' category of person (Schegloff, 2007, p. 469). In doing so A10 is able to position her ex-partner as someone to be avoided. In other words, A8 is issuing a warning to readers about her ex-partner's sexual practices. But what is also clear is that the person's wider character is also being brought into question by suggesting that she is 'unfit' to serve as a member of the 'US navy'.

## Discussion

This chapter focused on how gay and lesbian posters accounted for posting ex-plicit images of ex-partners. The accounts show (dis)similar characteristics to those in the previous two chapters which focused on heterosexual wo/men. Unsurprisingly, all posters regardless of gender and sexuality constructed their acts as a legitimate form of interpersonal revenge, and in doing so, the posters positioned themselves as the victims. Thus, posting explicit images of their ex-partners' is arguably an equalising and empowering action and, on the whole, reported positively. Other similarities centred on infidelity, sexual promiscuity and unsafe sexual practices, selling sex, hygiene and intimate relationship con-trol. The analysis showed notions of control and dignity were similar to those in fe/male heterosexual accounts. Gay and lesbian accounts showed also that many of the alleged misdemeanours are linked, even tied to, and invested in, notions of appropriate gender and sexual interactions from masculine and feminine per-spectives, for example, gender violences, genital size, sexual performance, inti-mate relationship control, honesty, sensuality and sexual appearance. What is also interesting is that some opposite sex posters challenged their ex-partner's sexual identity by claiming they were gay or lesbian, whereas some of those in former same-sex relationships did the reverse; they claimed the other was 'straight' – that is a 'phony' (Sacks, 1992; Schegloff, 2007). Thus, the terms deployed can be seen as forms of abuse in this context.

What was also clear between all accounts despite gender and sexuality is that posting explicit images of their ex-partner was for various possible audiences: the (wo)men in question, their intimates or associates, to the victim's (and per-petrator's) own friends, an undefined viewing 'public'. Many posters framed their actions for the benefit of others through warnings about unsafe sexual practices, hygiene, sexual promiscuity and so on. Some framed their actions as providing the viewer with images to masturbate to, while others provided names and locations so that others might engage and continue the humiliation. In most cases the viewer was made complicit in the act and works as a means to deflect charges of vindictiveness for the demise of the relationship. In the next chapter, we take some of these analytical insights and discuss them within some of the more general perspectives on the contemporary phenomenon of revenge porn.

## Notes

1 Grindr claims to be the largest and most popular all-male social network spanning 196 countries worldwide. Uses include finding a date, buddy or friend.
2 Kik is a smartphone application that allows users to chat with others, share content and track the results.
3 Bareback sex refers to anal or vaginal intercourse without the use of condoms.
4 A pretesbian refers to a supposed pretend lesbian, a heterosexual female who enjoys playing the role of a lesbian (Urban Dictionary, 2008).
5 Introduced in the 1950s by the retired British civil servant Gerald Brosseau Gardner, Wicca is a modern form of paganism, witchcraft religion (Guilly, 2010).
6 Plenty of Fish is an online dating website (www.pof.com).

## References

Anderson, E. (2009). Inclusive masculinity: The changing nature of masculinities. London: Routledge.

Anderson, K. L., & Umberson, D. (2001). Gendering violence: Masculinity and power in men's accounts of domestic abuse. *Gender & Society, 15*(3), 358–380.

Ávila, R. (2015). Bareback sex: Breaking the rules of sexual health and the assumption of risks. *Sexualities, 18*(5–6), 523–547.

Barrett, M. (2012). The efficacy of interviewing young drug users through online chat. *Drug and Alcohol Review, 31*(4), 566–572.

Berkowitza, R., & Cornell, D. (2005). Parables of revenge and masculinity in Clint Eastwood's Mystic River. *Law, Culture and the Humanities, 1,* 316–332.

Blackwell, C. W. (2008). Men who have sex with men and recruit bareback sex partners on the internet: Implications for STI and HIV prevention and client education. *American Journal of Men's Health, 2*(4), 306–313.

Carpenter, L. M. (2015). Gender and the meaning and experience of virginity loss in the contemporary United States. *Gender & Society, 16*(3), 345–365.

Chan, L. S. (2016). The role of gay identity confusion and outness in sex-seeking on mobile dating apps among men who have sex with men: A conditional process analysis. *Journal of Homosexuality, 64*(5), 622–637.

Cooper, A. (Ed.). (2013). *Cybersex: The dark side of the force: A special issue of the Journal Sexual Addiction and Compulsion.* Abingdon: Routledge.

Davies, P. M., Hickson, F. C., Weatherburn, P., & Hunt, A. J. (2013). *Sex gay men & aids.* Abingdon: Routledge.

Edwards, D. (1998). The relevant thing about her: Social identity categories in use. In C. Antaki & S. Widdicombe (Eds.), *Identities in talk.* London: Sage.

Edwards, D. (2000). Extreme case formulations: Softeners, investment, and doing nonliteral. *Research on Language & Social Interaction, 33*(4), 347–373.

Edwards, T. (2006). *Cultures of masculinity.* London: Routledge.

Epstein, S. (1995). Expertise: AIDS activism and the forging of credibility in the reform of clinical trials. *Science Technology Human Values, 20*(4), 408–437.

Guiley, R. (2010). *The encyclopedia of witches, witchcraft and Wicca.* New York: Infobase Publishing.

Hall, M. (2014). *Metrosexual masculinities.* London: Palgrave Macmillan.

Hall, M. (2015). 'When there's no underbrush the tree looks taller': A discourse analytical examination of how men account for genital grooming. *Sexualities, 18*(8), 997–1017.

Hasinoff, A. A. (2015). *Sexting panic: Rethinking criminalization, privacy, and consent.* Champaign: University of Illinois Press.

Hester, S., & Eglin, P. (Eds.). (1997). *Culture and action: Studies in membership categorization analysis.* Washington, DC: University Press of America.

Hunter, A. (1993). Same door, different closet: A heterosexual sissy's coming-out party. In S. Wilkinson & C. Kitzinger (Eds.), *Heterosexuality: A feminism and psychology reader* (pp. 150–168). Beverley Hills, CA: Sage.

Jayyusi, L. (1984). *Categorization and the moral order.* Boston, MA: Routledge & Kegan.

Jefferson, G. (1991). List construction as a task and a resource. In G. Psathas (Ed.), *Interactional competence.* New York: Irvington Publications.

Kurdek, L. A. (2005). What do we know about gay and lesbian couples? *Current Directions in Psychological Science, 14*(5), 251–254.

McDonald, R. I., and Crandall, C. S. (2015). Social norms and social influence. *Current Opinion in Behavioral Sciences, 3*, 147–151.

Mowlabocus, S., Harbottle, J., & Witzel, C. (2013). Porn laid bare: Gay men, pornography and bareback sex. *Sexualities, 16*(5–6), 523–547.

Online Slang Dictionary. (2016). Con. Retrieved September 29 from http://onlineslangdictionary.com/meaning-definition-of/con.

*Oxford English Dictionary* Online. (2016). Bitch. Retrieved September 16 from https://en.oxforddictionaries.com/definition/bitch.

Pomerantz, A. (1986). Extreme case formulations: A way of legitimizing claims. *Human Studies, 9*, 219–229.

Race, K. (2015). 'Party and Play': Online hook-up devices and the emergence of PNP practices among gay men. *Sexualities, 18*(3), 253–275.

Sacks, H. (1974). On the analyzability of stories by children. In R. Turner (Ed.), *Ethnomethodology* (pp. 216–232). Middlesex: Penguin.

Sacks, H. (1992). *Lectures on conversation.* Oxford: Blackwell.

Schafer, A. (2014). Quiet sabotage of the queer child: Why the law must be reframed to appreciate the dangers of outing gay youth. *Howard Law Journal, 58*, 597.

Schegloff, E. A. (2007). A tutorial on membership categorization. *Journal of Pragmatics, 39*, 462–482.

Silverman, D., & Peräkylä, A. (2008). AIDS counselling: The interactional organization of talk about 'delicate' issues'. *Sociology of Health & Illness, 12*(3), 293–318.

Smith, D. (1978). K is Mentally Ill: The anatomy of a factual account. *Sociology, 12*, 23–53.

Stokoe, E. H. (2003). Mothers, single women and sluts: Gender, morality and membership categorization in neighbour disputes. *Feminism & Psychology, 13*(3), 317–344.

Tiggemann, M., Martins, Y., & Churchett, L. (2008). Beyond muscles: Unexplored parts of men's body image. *Journal of Health Psychology, 13*, 1163–1172.

Urban Dictionary. (2008). Pretesbian. Retrieved September 16, 2016 from http://www.urbandictionary.com/define.php?term=Pretesbian.

Veale, D., Eshkevari, E., Read, J., Miles, S., Troglia, A., Phillips, R., ... Muir, G. (2013). Beliefs about penis size: Validation of a scale for men ashamed about their penis size. *Journal of Sexual Medicine, 10*(9). doi:10.1111/jsm.12294.

Walkington, L. (2016). *Sex, gender, and power: Cunnilingus and Fellacio in casual sex.* Thesis. University of California. June. Retrieved September 8 from: http://escholarship.org/uc/item/7kn8s8j9.

Whisnant, R. (2010). From Jekyll to Hyde: The grooming of male pornography consumers. In K. Boyle (Ed.), *Everyday pornography* (pp. 114–133). London: Routledge.

Widdicombe, S., & Woofitt, R. (1990). 'Being' versus 'doing' punk: On achieving authenticity as a member. *Journal of Language & Social Psychology, 9*(4), 257–277.

Wylie R. R., & Eardley, I. (2007). Penile size and the 'small penis syndrome'. *BJU International, 99*(6), 1449–1455.

# 9

# DISCUSSION

While we have defined revenge porn as the online and offline non-consensual distribution, or sharing, of genuine or fake explicit images of someone else by ex-partners, partners, others or hackers to seek revenge, entertainment or for political motives, our analysis has focused on the posting of explicit images by ex-partners on the revenge porn site MyEx.com. We did this because we wanted to explore the interplay between pornographic interpersonal revenge and technology. Posters' accompanying texts on MyEx.com have provided a rich dataset through which to examine how perpetrators accounted for their actions by drawing on gender and sexuality discourses. Our analysis foregrounds the complex and dynamic ways in which gender and sexuality are negotiated in the context of revenge porn, and advertises the value of attending to discursive resources and practices in this way (Potter, 1996).

We have shown how posters worked up descriptions, provided accounts and blamed their ex-partner, while minimising others undermining their claims: that is, managing their 'stake' in revenge seeking (Edwards & Potter, 1992) in order to position themselves as the victim, and their ex-partner as the perpetrator. Our analysis has also shown how identity categories and their associated characteristics and activities (Sacks, 1992) were invoked to construct their ex-partner as someone who deserved punishment. Thus, the act of revenge porn could be seen or represented by the poster as supposed 'equalising' action for an alleged prior misdemeanor.

Our analysis showed similarities with how heterosexual men and women, and gay and lesbian posters drew on negative social and moralistic discourses related to gender and sexuality, for example, invoking social norms and discourses about personal hygiene, deceitfulness, notions of appropriate relationship conduct, parenthood and responsibilities, sexual objectification, sexual desires, prostitution, violence and criminality. Thus, this demonstrated the complex and nuanced ways in which gender and sexuality can be deployed in interpersonal revenge. However, the specific negative discourse or social norm deployed was, in part, determined by the poster's gender and sexuality. For example, heterosexual men drew on notions of female chastity, whereas heterosexual women drew on social norms about masculinities and penis size. Gay and lesbian posters drew on some similar norms, but could also be seen to challenge the legitimacy of their ex-partner's sexuality based on notions of authentic group membership. What was also evident in these posts was that the specific discourses or norms deployed were contextually specific. That is, they related to what the poster aimed to achieve, for example, to construct their ex-partner as a violent criminal or poor parent. Our analysis highlighted how these accounts were dependent on who the poster perceived was the audience. For example, some accounts were constructed as warnings to the victim, the victim's new partner or others (un)known.

In the remainder of this discussion we turn to some more general, cross-cutting perspectives on the contemporary phenomenon of revenge porn, and what it is and is not. The creation and display of revenge porn are part of larger social structures, cultural processes and forms of communication, with or without consent of those involved or implicated. Accordingly, here we consider: first, the reproduction of categorical gender and sexuality positions through revenge porn seen as violence; second, the various interconnected forms of ambiguity and transgression, across violation and intimacy, online and offline interaction, the public and the private and the local and the transnational; and finally, some reflections of the elaboration of rather new forms of techno-masculinities, as enacted in micro-practices.

## Binary gender and sexuality positions in doing violence

There are many ways of analysing revenge porn, and the particular posts and extracts presented, such as the expansion and affordances of information and computer technologies (ICTs), or the intertwining of the visual and the textual. However, what is clear in the previous empirical chapters is that the display of gender positions and sexual orientations, whether heterosexual or same-sex, is through antagonism, violation, power and control, or worse, towards those who have been, and maybe still are, the object of desire. As such, revenge porn is part of a whole range of gender and sexual phenomena, for example: gendered violence and abuse; sexual assault; cyberbullying and cyberstalking; normalisation of sexually abusive and misogynist online public space; and homosocial exchange within local, national or transnational communities of interest. Thus, fundamental and recurring issues concern how the violating practices of revenge porn are understandable through the lens of gender and sexual dynamics and constructions, binary gender and sexual positionings and the use of sexual meanings.

Thus, we may ask what the similarities and differences are between different gender and sexual framings of revenge porn online postings: male-to-female, female-to-male, male-to-male, female-to-female? The structure and directionality of revenge porn, and its non-consensual and probably violating and abusive forms, parallel in text those respective forms of past or present sexual relations and likely attraction. Sex, desire, even love, are structurally paralleled by attempted revenge, humiliation, abuse. This is displayed in the written text of the revenge porn, and often the accompanying visuals, in a manner comparable to the dynamics of power and control in marriage continuing after separation or divorce (Delphy, 1976).

Specific sexual orientations are here overridden by the 'logic' of desire and counter-desire, made possible in extended form by the affordances of ICTs. The virtual world becomes orientated monologically, not dialogically or interactively. Moreover, such revenges are generally explained by justifications rather than excuses (Scott & Lyman, 1968), so that the avenged person (the passive postee) becomes the one to be blamed (as active) for the actions performed towards them (the active sexual poster). This is comparable to men's explanations of their violence to women (Ptacek, 1988; Hearn, 1998).

At the same time, there are clear differences between the different sexual orientations and genres of the posts and posters. The precise textual devices by which revenge porn is differentially practiced, and justified, is then less about the affordances of ICTs and more about gendered/sexual positions and possibilities within dominant gender/sexual orders. Focusing on gender and sexuality as framing in this way is not to stereotype such practices according to sexual orientation. Different sexuality positionings, such as male-female or male-male, invoke various straight and gay conventions, respectively, as vividly shown in the appeal to known or unknown other readers and audiences of assumed similar homosocial gay or straight men (cf. Thomson, 1999; Heinskou, 2015). It is through these devices, such as the appeal to similar (to the poster) others, that the differences between male-to-female, female-to-male, male-to-male and female-to-female online postings are most explicitly enacted.

To put this a little differently, heterosexual men's practices of revenge porn, both straight and gay, and the discourses employed within and around them, can be seen as part of the dominant repertoires of men and masculinities. In this sense, they are perhaps less novel than they may appear at first sight; rather, they are extensions and elaborations of well-charted ways of dominating and abusing others, especially in the cultural context of the extensive sexist and misogynist texts online. On the other hand, women's own posts, whether straight or lesbian, tend to involve different forms, for example, of women posters as scorned revengers, or of women postees as unfaithful or not a real lesbian. Justifications of such gender/sexual positionings often rest on external referencing, for example, to the man's sexual/penile inadequacy, incapability and just desserts, or to the lesbian women's promiscuity or her inability to be a real and consistent lesbian, but rather a pretend lesbian, a so-called pretesbian, and in one case to reference to 'a transgender'.

Having said that, we note how the mass of online revenge porn seems to be very strongly based in binary, non-queer gender positionings, and in that way, despite the potentialities of virtual sexualities,[1] reproduces broader gender hegemony. Online revenge porn is another site for the performance of gender hegemony, even with the variable sexual orientations said and shown. In contrast to possible blurrings of binary gender/sexuality (cf. Monro, 2005; Roseneil, 2005), revenge (porn), it seems, is not (yet) very queer.

## Ambiguities and transgressions: violation/intimacy, online/offline, public/private, local/transnational

These gender and sexual dynamics, with their generally binary 'logic' are complicated further by the technological affordances available. In this way, it is a cliché but true to say that (online) revenge pornography is a product of its time. Revenge is ancient, but online revenge pornography needs to be placed into the wider context of contemporary socio-technological conditions, and indeed ambiguities and transgressions ... of the worlds of Twitter, Facebook, LinkedIn, What's App, Reddit, YikYak, Grindr, Tinder, Pokémon Go, SNSs, Flickr, Instagram, Snapchat, Google Plus, Dot429, 4chan, sex tapes, ... and much more, along with the desire to photograph, depict, show, receive, see, assemble and respond to 'every' social initiative, the frenetic, tick box approach to social relations and relationships, and the ever-mushrooming, unpredictable, even potentially queer, rest.

In these contexts, much of the power of revenge pornography to damage comes from both its ambiguities and its transgressions, across several boundaries. The ambiguous and transgressive nature of revenge pornography comes, first and foremost, from the fundamental paradox of revenge and intimacy, or more precisely, revenge as violation and (former) intimacy(ies). With revenge porn, intimacy precedes and/or supersedes violation; and intimacy occurs within, even as, violation. Revenge seen as violation in intimacy concerns the relations of past, present and sometimes future, intimacy, and indeed usually unequal intimacy. Intimacy might appear to *contradict* revenge as violation, but as Grandin and Lupri (1997, p. 440) note, in discussing intimate partner violence, '[t]he etiology of ... partner abuse is grounded in intimacy' (also see Hearn, 2013). Here, violence in intimacy, just like revenge pornography, occurs in contexts of (former or present) intimate relations – involving confidences, vulnerabilities, care, maybe childcare, housework, close physical proximity, conversation, silence, sexual activity and possibilities, and often a history together of experiences of similar events, maybe future contact too.

Intimacy is often ideologically afforded a (overly) positive meaning and place (see, for example, Berlant, 1998; Berlant & Warner, 1998; Sandberg, 2011), just as love and pleasure are often assumed to be beneficent, even with their operation in power and as a source of power (see, for example, Jónasdóttir, 1994; Gunnarsson, 2014; Jónasdóttir & Ferguson, 2014). The gender/sexual power relations of revenge pornography, like domestic violence and intimate partner violence, are constituted in violence *and* intimacy. Revenge occurs in association with other *knowledges* of the person, and their past, perhaps previous violations, strengths, weaknesses. Just as in-the-flesh physical and sexual intimate partner violence exploits the paradox of intimacy and violence – specifically how the person most intimate, most open, most vulnerable, can be hurt, damaged, violated through that very closeness – so does revenge pornography. The initial knownness is part of its power, and the power to violate.

This 'familiar' paradox of intimacy and violence, as in domestic violence and intimate partner violence, is now complicated by further blurrings and complex to-ings and fro-ings between public/private, offline/online and local/transnational, coupled with the enduring dynamics of sexuality and intimacy, of sexuality and violence and of violence and abuse themselves. Online revenge becomes and represents new communicative intimacies, new public intimacies, new intimate partner abuse and violence, new virtual intimate (ex-)partner abuse and violence and new virtual intimate (ex-)partner abuse and violence gathered, sometimes organised together, in encyclopaedic fashion, as in the large revenge porn sites studied.

Revenge pornography, and its diffusion, are part and parcel of the work of the normalisation of sexually abusive online environments, and of violence and abuse online more generally. Crucially, such violence and abuse is simply and unambiguously legitimate to its doers, adherents and sponsors. The routine domination of men's voices and posts in online fora (Herring, Johnson, & DiBenedetto, 1995) has in practice, and in a rather short time period, easily escalated to the greater propensity and power of men to insult and abuse, especially when there is less facial or eye contact (Lapidot-Lefler & Barak, 2012). The mass presence, even ubiquity, of sexist, racist, and abusive material on the Web is well-known and now widely catalogued, in, for example, Lori Kendall's (2002) study of the homosocial 'virtual pub'; Parmy Olson's (2012) description of sexism and racism rife in the hacking network, Anonymous and related networks; and Laurie Penny's (2014) catalogue of cybersexism in her book *Unspeakable Things*. Networked misogyny is not news any more.

This spread and diffusion can, to some extent, be attributed to the so-called 'online disinhibition effect' (Suler, 2004), coupled with processes of peer pressure, imitation, contagion, and multimodal media crossovers, in front of real or imagined audiences: to put it simply, a virtual homosocial mob. The contemporary world is, for some at least, one of oversharing, even over-communication, that comes home to roost. Escalation, persona to persona, can occur through engagement with the poster and the post, prompting further revenge and retaliation. However, such tendencies are certainly relevant for revenge porn but have to be treated with caution as full explanations of their process of development.

In contrast to some kinds of cyberbullying, cyberabuse and cybersexism, revenge porn is rather rarely totally anonymised; indeed, that can be part of its appeal for some posters, their insignificant others, and their audience(s), as part of a larger flow of online personas, to make the images, the message and the damage recognisable. While the primary victim here is the postee, the posted one, this can also spill over to friends, family, onlookers and bystanders and others, by accident or design. This follows as some posting is created in order to be viewed by the victim, the postee, while some is directed (and redirected) more to the poster's or indeed the postee's friends and acquaintances, or even a more diffuse, unknown and imagined audience. In fact, the victim postee may well not know what images and text have been posted of and about them or yet may find out weeks, months or even years later … or may never know.

Revenge porn may involve the elaboration of posters' online personas that may be or appear quite distinct from those offline. In that sense these or socially mediated selves may take a different form to those represented through, say, abusive online comments on newspaper or magazine articles. With socially mediated selves within and through revenge porn the interpersonal, not impersonal, nature of the process is vital. In this situation we can indeed ask: what is *interpersonal* about and within revenge pornography? One way of making sense of this is to see this intimacy around violence as paradoxically ambiguous 'distant intimacy' (cf. Michalski, 2004; Hearn, 2013). Moreover, social psychological processes around both disinhibition and audience-serving have to be placed into a structural context of gender domination beyond the immediate psychological processes concerned. Posters also seek to construct both their own and the postees' supposed identity or personas, implicitly or explicitly, more or less successfully.

What might be called mundane and everyday, yet still often highly damaging, teasing, bullying, humiliation and harassment to known others online may now extend to the trolling of strangers. This malevolent attention to strangers includes, for some, threats of physical abuse, attack, rape and sexual violation, as well as verbal and psychological abuse. Virtual attacks often comprise text and visuals, photographs and perhaps even videos. The violence and violation of 'only words' (MacKinnon, 1993) are elaborated further through and by visual and other senses.

Stranger attacks, online or offline, may be perpetrated against people in the public eye, mainly women, and especially politicians, journalists, sportswomen, entertainers, film stars – but in fact anyone in the public eye, such as local celebrities – as well as their family and associates. They may include the posting of the visuals of the public figure in private, personal, domestic, bodily, sexual forms; the publicness of 'the star' apparently in part legitimates the resort to these private, personal, domestic, bodily, sexual images; the public figure is, in some views, after all 'public property'.

With much revenge pornography, a *reversal* is enacted and takes place. The routines against the public domain 'star' are inverted, moved into the grasp of the private, from public realm into private realm, with the interpersonal, known relationship becoming public. Thus, we have shifted from revenges formerly typically in private, from its previous, probably fleeting, even secretive, status towards violations in public spaces.

Revenge is externalised, to become something semi-permanent, and difficult to erase and be erased, to be 'enjoyed' now or later by the posting self and crucially others too. This is not conspicuous consumption, but rather conspicuous prosumption (from the neologism combining producer and consumer). With these formerly private relations, people – participants, associates and chance viewers – becoming their own voyeurs, their own paparazzi. With online revenge pornography, what was historically and previously (constructed as) a relatively private matter of revenge is now 'out there', in the public domain(s) of the virtual world(s): local and immediate for the immediate and local followers; transnational and worldly for the strangers and unknown followers, if only by chance or proximity in the virtual space.

These distant and hostile violating intimacies may even be transnational, deterritorialised, translocal and hybrid, extending the diverse forms and processes of such transnational violences in transnational intimacy. Transnational virtual violences in intimacy are enacted in dispersion, as dispersed and distanced delocalised violences (cf. Brage, Gordaliza, & Orte, 2014). The transnational adds another dimension to intimacy, revenge and violence, and affects the form and processes of such revenges. Transnational revenges may overlap with threats at distance, abductions, 'honour violence' and forced marriage. Specifically, revenges, violences and intimacy occur in a wide variety of transnational contexts of transnational dispersed families, migration, domestic service, care chains, with various linked vulnerabilities.

## The power practices of micro-techno-masculinities

Within these broad contexts of ambiguity and transgression, violation/intimacy, online/offline, public/private, local/transnational, revenge porn can be seen largely, though not exclusively, as an example of (some) men's gendered power practices in their engagement with technological patriarchies. The co-production of masculinity and technology has been studied in many locales and forms, for example, men's gendered engagement with tinkering, craftsmanship, technical skill and simply fascination with technologies (Mellström, 1995, 2004; Faulkner, 2000; Lohan & Faulkner, 2004; Balkmar, 2012). There is burgeoning literature that charts the wider connections between men, masculinities and ICTs and other new technologies, of virtual, networked men and networked masculinities (see Poster, 2013; Hearn et al., 2013; Hearn, 2014, 2015; Zaidi and Poster, 2017).

The analysis of techno-masculinity, or techno-masculinities, has often been focused on the intersection of technology and masculinised gender power relations as a relatively new basis of power at the societal level. Such perspectives on technocracy often emphasise work-based, organisational and economically profitable contexts and sectors, that in turn bring new economo-gendered stratifications, and informational and digital divides. For example, Chang and Ling (2000, p. 27) suggest that 'technology is driving the latest stage of capitalism' through a masculine 'global umbrella of aggressive market competition', encapsulated in the term 'techno-muscular capitalism'. Here, however and in contrast, revenge porn can be seen as more immediate, seemingly personalised techno-masculinities, that are specifically channelled into personal, sexual, intimate and violent forms.

Thus, on the one hand, many issues that relate to men, masculinities, ICTs and technologies are also present in online revenge pornography. These include the presence and problematising of stereotypes around men, women and techno-logy; the paradoxically remote and invasive 'intimacies'; and the multiple techno-logical possibilities for online homosociality and abuse. On the other hand, online revenge porn can be seen as raising some new issues and creating some new phenomena around the practices of techno-masculinity, such as the globali-sation of intimacy; and the elaboration of what may be labeled 'nerd, or geek, sexualities'. These may in turn challenge and reshape the homogeneity of both hegemonic masculinity and dominant forms of patriarchal techno-masculinity. Taking this argument one step further, we might think of these developments as part of micro-techno-masculinities and micro-technologies of the masculine self, socially and technologically mediated (see Pooley, 2013), and with a some-what different form and process to those macro-techno-masculinities that figure so strongly in debates on globalisation and the place of ICTs there.

## Note

1  These online potentialities have been widely documented elsewhere (for example, Elund, 2015; O'Riordan & Phillips, 2007), and seem, at the current time at least, to be a separable aspect of online sexualities; this may well change in the future.

## References

Balkmar, D. (2012). *On men and cars: An ethnographic study of gendered, risky and dangerous relations.* Linköping: Linköping University Electronic Press.

Berlant, L. (1998). Intimacy. *Critical Inquiry, 24*(2), 281–288.

Berlant, L., & Warner, M. (1998). Sex in public. *Critical Inquiry, 24*, 547–566.

Brage, L. B., Gordaliza, R. P., & Orte, C. (2014). Delocalized prostitution: Occultation of the new modalities of violence. *Procedia – Social and Behavioural Sciences, 161*(19), 90–95.

Chang, K. A., & Ling, L. H. M. (2000). Globalization and its intimate other: Filipina domestic workers in Hong Kong. In M. Marchand & A. S. Runyan (Eds.), *Gender restructuring: Sightings, sites, and resistances* (pp. 27–43). London: Routledge.

Delphy, C. (1976). Continuities and discontinuities in marriage and divorce. In D. L. Barker & S. Allen (Eds.), *Sexual divisions and society: Process and change* (pp. 76–89). London: Tavistock.

Edwards, D., & Potter, J. (1992). *Discursive psychology: Inquiries in social construction.* London: Sage.

Elund, J. (2015). *Subversion, sexuality and the virtual self.* Houndmills: Palgrave Macmillan.

Faulkner, W. (2000). Dualisms, hierarchies, and gender in engineering. *Social Studies of Science, 30*(5), 759–792.

Grandin, E., & Lupri, E. (1997). Intimate violence in Canada and the United States: A cross-cultural comparison. *Journal of Family Violence, 12*(4), 417–443.

Gunnarsson, L. (2014). *The contradictions of love: Towards a feminist-realist ontology of socio-sexuality*. Abingdon: Routledge.

Hearn, J. (1998). *The violences of men: How men talk about and how agencies respond to men's violence to women*. London: Sage.

Hearn, J. (2013). The sociological significance of domestic violence: Tensions, paradoxes, and implications. *Current Sociology, 16*(2), 152–170.

Hearn, J. (2014). Sexualities, organizations and organization sexualities: Future scenarios and the impact of socio-technologies (a transnational perspective from the global 'North'). *Organization, 21*(3), 397–441.

Hearn, J. (2015). *Men of the world: Genders, globalizations, transnational times*. London: Sage.

Hearn, J., Biricik, A., Sadowski, H., & Harrison, K. (2013). Hegemony, transpatriarchies, ICTs and virtualization. In J. Hearn, M. Blagojević & K. Harrison (Eds.), *Rethinking transnational men: Beyond, between and within nations* (pp. 91–108). New York: Routledge.

Heinskou, M. B. (2015). Sexuality in transit – Gender gaming and spaces of sexuality in late modernity. *Sexualities, 18*(7), 885–899.

Herring, S., Johnson, D. A., & DiBenedetto, T. (1995). 'This discussion is going too far!' Male resistance to female participation on the internet. In K. Hall & M. Bucholtz (Eds.), *Gender articulated: Language and the socially constructed self* (pp. 67–98). New York: Routledge.

Jónasdóttir, A. G. (1994). *Why women are oppressed*. Philadelphia: Temple University Press.

Jónasdóttir, A. G., & Ferguson, A. (Eds.). (2014). *Love: A question for feminism in the twenty-first century*. New York: Routledge.

Kendall, L. (2002). *Hanging out in the virtual pub: Masculinities and relationships online*. Berkeley, CA: University of California Press.

Lapidot-Lefler, N., & Barak, A. (2012). Effects of anonymity, invisibility, and lack of eye-contact on toxic online disinhibition. *Computers in Human Behavior, 28*(2), 434–443.

Lohan, M., & Faulkner, W. (2004). Masculinities and technology: Some introductory remarks. *Men and Masculinities, 6*(4), 319–329.

MacKinnon, C. A. (1993). *Only words*. Harvard: Harvard University Press.

Mellström, U. (1995). *Engineering lives, technology, time and space in a male-centred World*. Linköping: Linköping Studies in Art and Science.

Michalski, J. (2004). Making sociological sense out of trends in intimate partner violence: The social structure of violence against women. *Violence Against Women, 10*(6), 652–675.

Monro, S. (2005). *Gender politics: Activism, citizenship and sexual diversity*. London: Pluto.

Olson, P. (2012). *We are anonymous*. New York: Little, Brown.

O'Riordan, K., & Phillips, D. J. (Eds.). (2007). *Queer online: Media technology and sexuality*. New York: Peter Lang.

Penny, L. (2014). *Unspeakable things: Sex, lies and revolution*. London: Bloomsbury.

Pooley, J. (2013). Sociology and the socially mediated self. In S. Waisbord (Ed.), *Media sociology: A reappraisal* (pp. 224–247). Cambridge: Polity.

Poster, W. (2013). Subversions of techno-masculinity: Indian ICT professionals in the global economy. In J. Hearn, M. Blagojević, & K. Harrison (Eds.), *Rethinking transnational men: Beyond, between and within nations* (pp. 123–135). London: Routledge.

Potter, J. (1996). *Representing reality: Discourse, rhetoric and social construction*. London: Sage.

Ptacek, J. (1988). Why do men batter their wives? In K. Yllö & M. Bograd (Eds.), *Feminist persepctives on wife abuse* (pp. 133–157). Newbury Park, CA: Sage.

Roseneil, S. (2005). Living and loving beyond the boundaries of the heteronorm: Personal relationships in the 21st Century. In L. Mackie, S. Cunningham-Burley, & J. McKendrick (Eds.), *Families in society: Boundaries and relationships* (pp. 241–258). Bristol: Policy.

Sacks, H. (1992). *Lectures on conversation.* Oxford: Blackwell.

Sandberg, L. (2011). *Getting intimate: A feminist analysis of old age, sexuality and masculinity.* Linköping: Linköping University Press.

Scott, M. B., & Lyman, S. M. (1968). Accounts. *American Sociological Review, 33*(1), 46–62.

Suler, J. (2004). The online disinhibition effect. *CyberPsychology & Behavior, 7*(3), 321–326.

Thomson, R. (1999). 'It was the way we were watching it': Young men negotiate pornography. In J. Hearn & S. Roseneil (Eds.), *Consuming cultures: Power and resistance* (pp. 178–198). London: Palgrave Macmillan.

Zaidi, Y., & Poster, W. (2017). Shifting masculinities in the South Asian outsourcing industry: Hyper, techno or fusion? In H. Peterson (Ed.), *Gender in transnational knowledge work* (pp. 119–140). Berlin: Springer.

# 10
## FUTURE INTERVENTIONS

So, to use a well-worn phrase: what is to be done? In this final chapter, we conclude with some comments on what could be done to reduce the possibilities for revenge pornography. We have already in Chapter 2 presented some of the major responses to revenge pornography, namely, legal and governmental, and technological and political responses, and some of their overlaps. Here, we continue from those reviews to consider the current legislative situation more specifically, with a focus on the United Kingdom, and weaknesses in legislation, the need for more action and interaction between governmental, not-for-profit, legislators, commercial actors, as well as victims and perpetrators. This includes support programmes for victims, punishment of crimes and re-education programmes for perpetrators, and gender and sexualities educational programmes, in schools, colleges and universities, workplaces and elsewhere, even if some of these might not be immediately feasible. We conclude on the politics of acting against revenge pornography in the changing and future fleshly/virtual cyberworlds.

## Legislative action

The UK Crown Prosecution Service's (CPS) *Violence against women and girls 2015–2016* report shows that from April 13, 2015, when the UK's revenge pornography law came into effect, to the end of March 2016, 206 people have been prosecuted for the non-consensual sharing of someone else's explicit. The CPS noted there was a growing trend in the use of social media platforms to commit these types of gender and sexual offences, which are also linked to the monitoring of phone messages, emails and the use of GPS tracking devices. The growth in these online offences has contributed to almost a 9% increase to 19% of the CPS's workload in the past six years.

Tackling the growing trend in gender and sexual offences (including men and boys) HM Government (2016a) released its *Ending Violence against Women and Girls Strategy 2016–2020* in March. The government pledged to provide £80 million in funding to help vital services and frontline work, and a dedicated Service Transformation Fund is to be launched in 2017 to "encourage new approaches, and establish and embed the best ways to help victims, and their families, and prevent perpetrators from re-offending" (HM Government, 2016a, p. 5). Their strategy targets preventing crime with pre-adult education programmes such as the *This is Abuse* (HM Government, 2015), the provision of services, partnership working, pursuing perpetrators and discussing these issues internationally with other nations and the United nations at Global Summits with the aim of setting "Global Goal targets" (HM Government, 2016a, p. 13).

While these measures may go some way to tackling revenge porn and gender violence more generally, we think there should a more specific focus on online gender and sexuality offences, given these are reported to be on the rise (CPS, 2016). Indeed, in contradiction to some of the above positive initiatives, the funding for a UK national helpline for victims of online revenge porn was due to be withdrawn in March 2017 (Laville, 2017). We discuss what else can be done specifically to tackle revenge porn in the following sections. These are likely to also have broader implications for other online offences, such as cyberbullying, cyberstalking, online aggression, 'flaming', 'happy slapping', stalking and trolling (see Hearn & Parkin, 2001).

Chapter 2 discussed responses to revenge porn. Many of these were through various types of legislation. However, universal laws to convict revenge porn perpetrators do not exist. Currently, there is a patchwork of laws that can be invoked for revenge porn offences in the United Kingdom (CPS, 2016), the United States (Goldberg PLLC, 2015), Australia (Henry & Powell, 2016), Japan (*The Japan News*, 2015), Israel (*Y Net News*, 2014), the Philippines (Franks, 2016), Sweden (*The Local*, 2014), Canada (Montgomery, 2015), India (Law Quest, 2016) and Germany (Oltermann, 2014). Some countries, such as the United Kingdom and Israel, have specific laws to making it a criminal offence to maliciously distribute intimate images without the person's consent, while in others, such as some states in the United States and Australia, other laws can be used that charge the offender for publishing indecent articles, causing offence, harassment, causing menace to another person, the distribution of an invasive images, privacy laws and so on (Franks, 2016).

Some, such as University of Miami School of Law Professor Mary Anne Franks (2016) and Dr Nicola Henry (Henry & Powell, 2016; Powell & Henry, 2016), a criminologist at Melbourne's La Trobe University, and a number of non-profit organisations (for example, Cyber Civil Rights Initiative, UK Safer Internet Centre) argue for specific revenge porn laws at the regional, national and international levels, for example, making it a criminal offence to distribute someone else's images without consent (also see Franks, 2013; Cooper, 2016; Citron & Franks, 2014).

The Philippines introduced a specific revenge porn law in 2009, which applies regardless of whether the original image was taken with permission or not (Franks, 2016). However, in some US states and elsewhere this does not apply to 'selfies', but only applies if the images were taken without the consent of the person shown. As we noted in Chapter 2, one US survey indicated that 80% of revenge porn victims took sexually explicit 'selfies' (Johnson, 2013). In addition to this, alleged offences that happened prior to the imposition of new specific revenge porn law cannot be tried under the new law. For example, the alleged revenge porn offence by Chrissy Chambers ex-boyfriend occurred before the UK revenge porn law came into existence in 2015. Thus, she must use a patchwork of prior laws to make her case (Henry & Powell, 2016).

The law firm, McAllister Olivarius, which represents alleged revenge porn victim Chrissy Chambers (Finch, 2015), suggests more should be done to stop organisations who host revenge porn images and Internet search engines linking to revenge porn. Ann Olivarius at McAllister Olivarius, said she welcomed moves by Internet search engines such as Google who have announced that it would 'stop searches linking to revenge porn images if requested by a person whose image has been posted without consent' (Olivarius, 2015, p. 1). Microsoft has already announced that they will remove links from search results when reported by victims, and Twitter, Facebook and Reddit have banned revenge porn posts. There is ongoing legal disputation on whether Facebook, and thus similar operators and operations, are liable for civil claims. A case against Facebook from October 2016 involves a 14-year-old taking the company to court in Belfast over naked images published on the social network, which 'could open the floodgates for other civil claims, according to lawyers who work with victims of revenge pornography', after a high court judge rejected Facebook's attempt to have the claim struck out (Topping, 2016).

Those Internet organisations who provide platforms for posting revenge porn, such as MyEx.com, might face future civil actions. For example, Chrissy Chambers, a woman whose ex-boyfriend uploaded an alleged revenge porn video of him having sex with her while she was allegedly drunk, is the first person to use British courts to sue the website that hosted the video footage. However, there are examples of revenge sites where intimate and explicit images of partners, ex-partners and those alleged to be involved in the infidelity can be posted without breaking any laws. For example, an urban mother in the United States who goes by the alias Ariella Alexander has set up a website called 'She's a Homewrecker' where she uploads intimate photos of women to her website, listing their full names and hometowns without their permission. The images are submitted by women, who send her images and details of their partners' alleged 'mistresses'. According to an Aljazeera report (May 2013, p. 1) she is not breaking any laws in the United States because the Communications Decency Act of 1996 means providers of interactive computer services are not liable for what their users do. Thus, in Ariella Alexander's 'About' section on her website, she makes it clear that the posts and comments are of the original poster and not

She's a Homewrecker or its owners. However, this could be an offence under specific revenge laws. But despite this, once the images have been posted, they can be distributed with in hours and so takedown might be almost impossible (Tynan, 2016). As we noted in Chapter 1, a 24-year-old victim talking on BBC *Newsbeat* (2014) said that although her ex-boyfriend posted explicit images of her on a couple of websites they are now on over 200 websites, across the globe.

McAllister and Olivarius argue that stronger civil laws should be in place so that victims can sue perpetrators for damages. Ann Olivarius is reported to have told *The Guardian* (Kleeman, 2015), 'You have to be able to go after money damages in a civil context to be able to try to stop this problem. Money is the currency of how we achieve justice, that's the measurement'. Chrissy Chambers is the first person not only pursue a criminal prosecution of her former partner, but also to seek a civil action for damages (Griffiths, 2016).

The case of Chrissy Chambers also highlights the absence of international revenge porn laws and the difficulty with bringing prosecutions for crimes committed in another country. Although Chrissy Chambers lives in the United States where the alleged offence took place, she claims her ex-boyfriend posted the videos in the United Kingdom, so she has had to pursue the case in the United Kingdom. We noted in Chapter 2 that MyEx.com is reported to be operated by several anonymous US individuals in coordination with colleagues in the Philippines, and hosted by Web Solutions B.V., Netherlands, where there was no specific revenge porn law, but has a global reach (Steinbaugh, 2014). Thus, without international and cross-border laws on revenge porn, it is likely to be very difficult for some victims to pursue perpetrators and those that facilitate these crimes.

## Education and awareness raising

According to Lundgren and Amin (2015), gender and sexual violences such as revenge porn are widespread among adolescents, which makes them vulnerable to a lifelong trajectory of violence, either as victims or perpetrators, and thus robust responses are required. We noted in Chapter 1 how the growth of sexting had facilitated revenge porn (DoSomething.org, 2015; GuardChild.com, 2015; Hasinoff, 2015) and according to McAfee (2013) one in ten ex-partners had threatened to share sexually explicit images. There is clearly a potential for revenge porn to grow in the United Kingdom (and elsewhere) given more than half of adults claim they had shared sexually explicit material through their mobile devices and stored the images online (McAfee, 2013). Thus, there is a need to raise awareness of the potential risks of revenge porn from sexting. One method of doing so is to include this on the sex and relationship curriculum (see Martellozzo et al., 2016).

Sex and relationship education is compulsory in the United Kingdom (HM Government, 2000, 2016b). This is not mirrored around the globe (United Nations Population Fund: UNPF; 2015). Sex and relationship education in the United Kingdom currently includes emotional relations and responsibilities, human sexual anatomy, sexual activity, sexual reproduction, age of consent, reproductive health, reproductive rights, safe sex, birth control and sexual abstinence. But, charities and educational groups are reported to be concerned that many teenagers are not being taught about issues like sexting, online pornography, consent and healthy relationships (Taylor, BBC, 2014) despite child sexting and revenge pornography being illegal (NSPCC, 2016). What is evident is that the primary focus of the UK sex and relationship curriculum is on sexual and health and what constitutes a healthy relationship; arguably this should also include how to deal with, and appropriate conduct when, relationships end. These might include emotion dysregulation, cognitive distortions and relationship skills deficits. Thus, problem solving, relationship skills training and emotion regulation could be included (Eckhardt et al., 2013).

Lundgren and Amin's (2015) review of school-based interventions among high school and university students in the United States, Tanzania, Spain, India and Uganda found that these had been effective in reducing gender and sexual violences. The school-based interventions address factors such as the tolerance of sexual violences, healthy relationships, nonviolent conflict resolution, communication skills, help seeking and unequal gender norms, power and control in relationships. We are not aware of any specific research that examines the impact of including revenge pornography on the UK national curriculum (see Martellozzo et al., 2016). However, an example Lundgren and Amin (2015) present is effectiveness of a school-based intervention in the United States on 'dating violence' (Wolfe et al., 2009). The study involving a total of 1,722 students aged 14–15 from 20 public schools aimed to determine the effects of an interactive curriculum that integrates a specific focus on physical dating violence within lessons on healthy relationships and sexual health. Wolfe et al. (2009) found there were fewer self-reports of physical dating violence over the two-year period that the project ran.

School-based interventions clearly go some way to help young people avoid a lifelong trajectory of violence, either as victims or perpetrators. However, given that revenge porn involves teens to thirties and upwards, information on it could and perhaps should be made more widely available to, for example, non-governmental and governmental specialist support services personnel, technical staff, legislators, educators (for example, guidelines on good practice sharing, experience sharing, networking, educators) and the general public (awareness raising on online gendered/sexualised violence, existing technical and emotional support systems, strategies for lessening opportunities of victimisation, gaining knowledge on responsible internet use and privacy keeping). Some excellent and adaptable training resource materials have recently been made available by Amber Morczek (2017) of Washington State University, Department of Criminal Justice and Criminology, setting out how to "define nonconsensual pornography (often referred to as 'revenge porn'), how it impacts victims, what is being done to address it, and how it relates to rape culture."

In addition, alternative non-violent ways of dealing with relationship break-downs could be promoted, supported by those who are seen as having credibility within specific communities. Those involved in *The Fappening* could be encouraged to talk about their experiences with the media. The print and popular visual media have to some degree covered revenge porn. For example, the British television channel ITV's soap *Coronation Street* ran a revenge porn storyline beginning November 2015 in which Rovers Return barmaid Steph Britton (played by actor Tisha Merry) is bribed by her ex Jamie, who threatens to make intimate pictures of her public in order to blackmail her brother Luke. In August 2015, the UK Channel 4's Anna Richardson uploaded naked pictures of herself to one of the most popular sites to experience some of what revenge porn victims go through. However, Ian Douglas at *The Telegraph* (2015, p. 1) argued 'It was a courageous thing to do, but potential insights were too often passed over as the programme got more and more sidetracked by showing some sexy pictures in the name of journalism'. Other visual and print media have also engaged with revenge porn, as we noted in our Introduction and Chapter 1, most notably the BBC's coverage of a 24-year-old victim talking on *Newsbeat* (2014). But despite these efforts, more focus could be given to preventative measures as well as pointing out the impact on victims.

We noted how markers of masculinity and femininity, as well as notions of 'just behaviour' were drawn upon by fe/male users in our analytical chapters. These could also be leveraged in the framing of arguments within these materials to discourage revenge porn, for example, using notions of rationality or pragmatism. Piloting these materials ahead of use will be crucial in ensuring that messages are perceived as relevant and credible by those in the target group.

## Victim support

Many programmes to support victims of gender and sexuality-based crimes tend to focus on how to reduce the risk of revictimisation, such as social support and safety behaviours (Eckhardt et al., 2013). However, as we noted earlier in this chapter and elsewhere in the book, once images are posted, it is almost impossible to retract them because of the speed of dissemination by others. The fallout may be profound, including embarrassment, reputation ruination and even the suicide of women featured on these websites (Lichter, 2013). Current support programmes tend to focus primarily on dealing with the legal process of bringing offenders to court of the removal of the images within the provisions of the Digital Millennium Copyright Act: 'to de-index websites with their photos from search engines like Google and ask the websites themselves to remove the photos, all without having to hire a lawyer' (Levendowski, 2014).

Work by colleagues at the University of Primorska, Science and Research Centre, Slovenia, in conjunction with project partners at University of Trieste (Italy), Isonomia (Spain), University of Aalborg (Denmark), University of Vienna (Austria) and local actors (such as police departments, safe internet use organisations)

(2015) suggests that the existing specialist support services and the development of protocols of cooperation between relevant authorities facing nonconsensual online sharing of sexually explicit images should be strengthened. This they argue would include mapping existing specialist support services and sharing best practices among them; promoting cooperation and multidisciplinary networking among crucial national authorities, non-governmental organisations (NGOs) and organisations that strive for safe Internet use; and tackling non-consensual sharing of sexualised images online. State-of-the-art reports to UK Home Office and non-governmental agencies such as National Stalking Training Academy and online-based revenge pornography organisations such as End Revenge Pornography, Third Parent and nobullying.com could be developed as well as the joint preparation of online advice for the victims. Also, a web page could be developed for the dissemination of learning and support materials for educators, agencies and the media.

## Perpetrator re-education

The criminalisation of revenge porn is likely to act as a deterrent for some, but not for others. Where legislation does not act as a deterrent, investigators can use software, such as EnCase, to produce an image of the alleged offender's hard drive to see deleted computer files, such as cache files, swap files, temporary files, unallocated space or slack space and left traces of their browser history, address books, date and time stamps and so on (Widup, 2014) to use as admissible evidence.

Once convicted, and punished, re-education intervention may be one possible way forward for the offender, generally male. Such interventions might include group cognitive behavioural treatment (CBT), in which offenders learn non-violence, through various techniques and exercises, such as the provision of skills in communication, assertiveness and relaxation techniques (Stover, Meadows & Kaufman, 2009). Having, said that, considerable caution is necessary around the likely success of such reforming interventions. This is partly because meta-analysis of evaluations of the success of these kind of interventions in stopping violence and violation in other contexts, notably 'domestic violence' and intimate partner violence, are, to say the least, mixed.[1]

Since revenge porn is one of the many forms of gender- and sexuality-based violences, key lessons from offender interventions should be taken up, for example, feminist re-education group treatment focusing on (largely male) power and control (Eckhardt et al., 2013). Indeed, while the success of working with violent offenders in those arenas is not convincing, there is reason to be more optimistic about broader preventive interventions against violence and sexual violence that address gender power relations more broadly and fundamentally. There is growing evidence that such latter work with men and boys that addresses directly issues of gender power and the construction of egalitarian masculinities as a central part of working against violence is a more promising route. Such approaches could be applied and modified in relation to preventing revenge pornography itself.[2] Some fairly well-established methods have been developed in anti-pornography workshops and campaigns, such as various Men Against Pornography groups, and these can be modified in working with offenders against revenge pornography. Beyond those, there is the vast array of specific methods and techniques for working with those who have committed crimes of sexual violence.

We believe therefore that in order to tackle revenge porn, a multi-faceted, multi-agency and multi-actor approach is required, locally and transnationally, online and offline. Similarly, there is a need for more research, and more action-orientated and multidisciplinary research on specific aspects of revenge porn and greater availability of funding for research-linked intervention and support work.

## Politically speaking ... and acting

Revenge porn, non-consensual pornography and online non-consensual pornography for the purposes of revenge are part and parcel of the gender-sexual-violation visual culture that, for many people and in many parts of the world, surrounds and permeates persons and social relations. As Laurie Penny (2014, p. 158) puts it clearly and directly: '[t]he biggest thing we know about sex from the Internet is this: that it happens in front of the camera'. Sexual selfies, sexting, sexual posting and cyberintimacy through the visual, and the social suffusion of sex/sexuality, especially in the cyberworld, all provide resources for further non-consensual harassment, bullying, exploitation, violation and pornography, revenge porn. The route to and roots of sexual paranoia are clear, especially for young women in the reduction of female flesh on the Net, to particular bits of body.

Faced with all this, many actions are possible – legislative, technological, support for those violated, punishment and re-education for those violating – but it is through broad political and gender-sexual-feminist political action and activism that lasting change is most likely to happen. This means a gender-sexual-feminist transformation of the Internet, of the cyberworlds, the virtual, as well as of gender-sexual power relations that reproduce violence, sexual violence and (at least most forms of) pornography. Dominating, humiliating, (hetero)sexist behaviour online is just as intolerable as offline. The Internet, the Web, is the site of struggle.

Such politics will also take and need to take new forms. Revenge porn and other online abuses are likely to continue in the current climate, and so we need to turn more attention to the *future* of gender and sexuality as an arena of policy, politics, research and action. For example, there are such key questions as: what are the implications of information and communications technologies and online/virtual/augmented reality for future genders and sexualities? Will online and virtual sex become a new norm? And how about sex robots? Will they become commonplace, and how might such a development be gendered, imbued with gender-sexual power, all the way down?

Likewise, the future of violence, sexual violence, abuse and sexual abuse will likely take different forms, with, say, the use of virtual reality, along with the deployment of robotics and even further prospects through AI, to perpetrate threat and exact revenge. How will such possibilities affect not just sexualities, but pornography and revenge or non-consensual pornography? Parallels may be useful here with the symbiotic relations of technological change and militarism. It is usually the case with the military and military violence that all new technologies are open for exploitation and deployment, and, in that sense, militarism has been a stimulus to many technological supposed 'advances'. Equally, all such technological developments are likely to be used in interpersonal sexual violence and abuse, and revenge pornography, and its successors. There may be worse to come, demanding yet more political commitment, vigilance and struggle on and around the Internet, the Web and kindred techno-virtual spaces and places. Indeed, there are strong indications that the Internet provides simultaneously and contradictorily both democratising and anti-democratic potentials. This is becoming evident in public mainstream (and populist) politics, and is likely also to be the case in body politics.

In Chapter 2, we briefly considered the growth of embodied direct action confrontations of revenge pornography by or led by feminist women. These ongoing politics against revenge porn are likely to develop further still along such lines of practice, as women, some men and further genders challenge various forms of material/virtual violation with and through their own bodies and the exposure of their bodies. These inventive interventions are part of the wider politics of gender, sexuality, feminism, bodies, embodiments and outrage, complicating some established associations of women and fleshly bodies through the affordances of advanced technologies and virtual space. Some forms of creative politics against revenge pornography thus seek to draw on both the power and use of fleshly embodiment, and the power and use of virtuality and virtual bodies, as well as the interplay of the fleshly and the virtual. Equally, opposing and stopping revenge porn demands and will demand yet more tech-savvy, political skills and feminist commitment, not just for the minority, the specialists, the nerds, the techies and the geeks, but for all, to transform the politics and practices of virtual space, and virtual space itself into a safe space.

## Notes

1 There are now several systematic meta-reviews of what are variously called 'batterer intervention programmes' (BIPs), 'men's anti-violence programmes', and 'perpetrator programmes'. These meta-reviews have concluded that there is little or no evidence to suggest that such intervention have notable effects on the reduction of violence and offending (Jackson et al., 2003; Wathen & MacMillan, 2003; Smedslund et al., 2007; Feder et al., 2008; Arias et al., 2013).

2 Preventive interventions that more explicitly address gender power and masculinities have reported as more promising than BIPs (Jewkes et al., 2015), interestingly including some located in the 'global South' and in conflict or post-conflict areas (for example, Hossain et al., 2014).

# References

Arias, E., Arce, R., & Vilariño, M. (2013). Batterer intervention programmes: A meta-analytic review of effectiveness. *Psychosocial Intervention, 22(*2), 153–160.

BBC. (2014). Revenge porn victim: I trusted him, now I'm on 200 sites. April 3. Retrieved April 2, 2015, from www.bbc.co.uk/newsbeat/26852254.

Bell, R. E. (2002). The prosecution of computer crime. *Journal of Financial Crime, 9*(4), 308–325.

Cooper, P. W. (2016). The right to be virtually clothed. *Washington Law Review, 91*, 817–846.

Citron, D. K., & Franks, M. A. (2014). Criminalizing revenge porn. *Wake Forest Law Review, 2014*(1), 345–391.

Coronation Street. (2015). Steph's revenge porn shock. November 16. Retrieved October 4, 2016, from www.itv.com/coronationstreet/extras/stephs-revenge-porn-shock-tisha-merry-interview.

Crown Prosecution Service. (2016). Violence against women and girls 2015–2016. Retrieved September 6, from www.cps.gov.uk/publications/equality/vaw/#a02.

DoSomething.org. (2015). 11 facts about sexting. Retrieved April 5, 2015, from www.dosomething.org/facts/11-facts-about-sexting.

Douglas, I. (2015). Revenge porn, review: 'Unconvincing'. *The Telegraph*. August 18. Retrieved October 4, 2016, from www.telegraph.co.uk/culture/tvandradio/tv-and-radio-reviews/11807963/Revenge-Porn-review-unconvincing.html.

Eckhardt, C. I., Murphy, C. M., Whitaker, D. J., Sprunger, J., Dykstra, R., & Woodard, K. (2013). The effectiveness of intervention programs for perpetrators and victims of intimate partner violence. *Partner Abuse, 4*(2), 196–231.

Feder, L., Austin S., & Wilson, D. (2008). Court-mandated interventions for individuals convicted of domestic violence. *Campbell Systematic Reviews, 12*(4), 1–46.

Finch, S. D. (2015). 6 Reasons why revenge porn is really f★cked Up (and how one woman is pushing back). June 16. http://everydayfeminism.com/2015/06/6-reasons-why-revenge-porn-is-actually-really-fcked-up-and-how-one-woman-is-pushing-back/.

Franks, M. A. (2013). Adventures in victim blaming: Revenge porn edition. *Concurring Opinions*, February 1. https://concurringopinions.com/archives/2013/02/adventures-in-victim-blaming-revenge-porn-edition.html.

Franks, M. A. (2016). Drafting an effective "revenge porn" law: A guide for legislators. *Cyber Civil Rights Initiative*. Retrieved March 19, 2017, from www.cybercivilrights.org/guide-to-legislation/.

Goldberg PLLC, C. A. (2015). States with revenge porn criminal laws. March 3. Retrieved April 3, 2015, from www.cagoldberglaw.com/states-with-revenge-porn-laws/.

Griffiths, S. (2016). YouTube star sues website over revenge porn. *The Sunday Times*. June 10. Retrieved September 7, 2016, from www.thetimes.co.uk/article/youtube-star-sues-website-over-revenge-porn-hs875lt2n.

GuardChild.com. (2015). Teenage sexting statistics. Retrieved April 5, 2015, from www.guardchild.com/teenage-sexting-statistics/.

Hasinoff, A. A. (2015). *Sexting panic: Rethinking criminalization, privacy, and consent.* Champaign, IL: University of Illinois Press.

Hearn, J., & Parkin, W. (2001). *Gender, sexuality and violence in organizations: The unspoken forces of organization violations.* London: Sage.

Henry, N., & Powell, A. (2016). Sexual violence in the digital age the scope and limits of criminal law. *Social & Legal Studies*, January 12. Retrieved September 7, from http://sls.sagepub.com/content/early/2016/01/11/0964663915624273.abstract.

HM Government. (2000). Sex and relationship education. *Department for Education.* Retrieved September 5, from www.gov.uk/government/publications/sex-and-relationship-education.

HM Government. (2015). This Is Abuse campaign: Summary report. Home Office. March. Retrieved from https://www.gov.uk/government/uploads/system/uploads/attachment_data/file/410010/2015-03-08_This_is_Abuse_campaign_summary_report__2_.pdf.

HM Government. (2016a). Ending violence against women and girls strategy 2016. *Home Office.* March. Retrieved September 6, from www.gov.uk/government/uploads/system/uploads/attachment_data/file/522166/VAWG_Strategy_FINAL_PUBLICATION_MASTER_vRB.PDF.

HM Government. (2016b). The national curriculum. *Department for Education.* Retrieved September 5, from www.gov.uk/national-curriculum/other-compulsory-subjects.

Hossain, M., Zimmerman, C., Kiss, L., Abramsky, T., Kone, D., Bakayoko-Topolska, M., ... Watts, C. (2014). Working with men to prevent intimate partner violence in a conflict-affected setting: A pilot cluster randomized controlled trial in rural Cote d'Ivoire. *BMC Public Health, 14*(1), 339–351.

Jackson, S., Feder, L., Forde, D. R., Davis, R. C., Maxwell, C. D., & Taylor, B. G. (2003). Batterer intervention programs: Where do we go from here? National Institute of Justice, Washington, DC. Retrieved from www.ncjrs.org/txtfiles1/nij/195079.txt.

Jewkes, R., Flood, M., & Lang, J. (2015). From work with men and boys to changes of social norms and reduction of inequities in gender relations: A conceptual shift in prevention of violence against women and girls. *The Lancet, 385*(9977), 1580–1588.

Johnson, D. (2013). 4 ways to take a stand against revenge porn. Everydayfeminism.com. December 3. Retrieved August 1, from http://everydayfeminism.com/2013/12/revenge-porn-and-internet-exploitation/.

Kleeman, J. (2015). US woman pursues ex-boyfriend in landmark UK revenge-porn action. *The Guardian.* June 3. Retrieved September 7, from www.theguardian.com/uk-news/2015/jun/03/us-woman-pursues-ex-boyfriend-in-landmark-uk-revenge-porn-action.

Laville, S. (2017). Revenge porn helpline 'to close' as government cuts funding. *The Guardian.* February 2. Retrieved February 2, from www.theguardian.com/society/2017/feb/02/revenge-porn-helpline-close-government-cuts-funding.

Law Quest. (2016). Revenge porn and the efficacy of Indian laws. Retrieved September 7, from http://lawquestinternational.com/article/revenge-porn-and-the-efficacy-of-indian-laws.

Levendowski, A. (2014). Our best weapon against revenge porn: Copyright law? *The Atlantic.* February 4. Retrieved September 8, from www.theatlantic.com/technology/archive/2014/02/our-best-weapon-against-revenge-porn-copyright-law/283564/.

Lichter, S. (2013). Unwanted exposure: Civil and criminal liability for revenge porn hosts and posters. JOLT Digest: *Harvard Journal of Law and Technology.* May 28. Retrieved April 4, 2015, from http://jolt.law.harvard.edu/digest/privacy/unwanted-exposure-civil-and-criminal-liability-for-revenge-porn-hosts-and-posters.

Lundgren, R., & Amin, A. (2015). Addressing intimate partner violence and sexual violence among adolescents: Emerging evidence of effectiveness. *Journal of Adolescent Health, 56*(1), S42–S50.

Martellozzo, E., Monaghan, A., Adler, J. R., Davidson, J., Leyva, R., & Horvath, M. A. H. (2016). *"...I wasn't sure it was normal to watch it...": A quantitative and qualitative examination of the impact of online pornography on the values, attitudes, beliefs and behaviours of children and young people*. London: Middlesex University. Retrieved November 22, from www.mdx.ac.uk/__data/assets/pdf_file/0021/223266/MDX-NSPCC-OCC-pornography-report.pdf.

May, A. (2013). Meet the suburban mom who runs a revenge porn site. *Aljazeera*. December 12. http://america.aljazeera.com/watch/shows/america-tonight/americato night-blog/2013/12/12/meet-the-suburbanmomwhorunsarevengepornsite.html.

McAfee. (2013). Love, relationships, and technology: How we expose ourselves today. December. Retrieved April 3, 2015, from http://promos.mcafee.com/offer.aspx?id=605366.

Montgomery, M. (2015). Canada's cyber bullying and revenge porn law applies to adults too. *Radio Canada International*. April 30. Retrieved September 7, from www.rcinet.ca/en/2015/04/30/canadas-cyberbullying-and-revenge-porn-law-applies-to-adults-too/.

Morczek, A. (2017). Nonconsensual pornography: Circulating sexual violence online. Hosted by Battered Women's Justice Project. Retrieved March 27, from www.bwjp.org/training/webinar-nonconsensual-pornography-circulating-sexual-violence-online.html.

NSPCC. (2016). Sexting. Retrieved September 5, from www.nspcc.org.uk/preventing-abuse/keeping-children-safe/sexting/.

Olivarius, A. (2015). Google will remove revenge porn images from search results. *McAllister Olivarius*. June 20. Retrieved September 7, 2016, from www.mcolaw.com/blog/2015/6/20/google-will-remove-revenge-porn-images-from-search-results?rq=chambers#.V8_b6IWcHIV.

Oltermann, P. (2014, May 22). 'Revenge porn' victims receive boost from German court ruling. *The Guardian*. Retrieved April 3, 2015, from www.theguardian.com/technology/2014/may/22/revenge-porn-victims-boost-german-court-ruling.

Penny, L. (2014). *Unspeakable things: Sex, lies and revolution*. London: Bloomsbury.

Powell, A., & Henry, N. (2016). Policing technology-facilitated sexual violence against adult victims: Police and service sector perspectives. *Policing and Society*, doi:10.1080/10439463.2016.1154964.

Smedslund, G., Dalsbø, T. K., Steiro, A., Winsvold, A., & Clench-Aas, J. (2007). Cognitive behavioural therapy for men who physically abuse their female partner (Review). *Cochrane Database Systematic Review, 3*, CD006048.

Steinbaugh, A. (2014). Revenge porn site myex.com sued for copyright infringement. March 7. Retrieved April 3, 2015, from http://adamsteinbaugh.com/2014/03/07/revenge-porn-site-myex-com-sued-for-copyright-infringement/.

Stover, C. S., Meadows, A. L., & Kaufman, J. (2009). Interventions for intimate partner violence: Review and implications for evidence-based practice. *Professional Psychology: Research and Practice, 40*(3), 223–233.

Taylor, J. (2014). New calls to change sex and relationship education. *BBC*. January 28. Retrieved September 5, 2016 from www.bbc.co.uk/newsbeat/article/25921487/new-calls-to-change-sex-and-relationship-education.

*The Japan News*. (2015). Police flooded with queries over revenge porn. April 2. Retrieved April 3, 2015 from http://the-japan-news.com/news/article/0002054600.

*The Local*. (2014). Sweden moves to close revenge porn loophole. May 28. Retrieved September 7, 2016 from www.thelocal.se/20140528/sweden-moves-to-close-revenge-porn-loophole.

Topping, A. (2016). Facebook revenge pornography trial 'could open floodgates'. *The Guardian*. October 9. Retrieved October 9 from www.theguardian.com/technology/2016/oct/09/facebook-revenge-pornography-case-could-open-floodgates.

Tynan, D. (2016). Revenge porn: The industry profiting from online abuse: Sites charge $100 a year to access private photos and videos of non-porn stars in the nude, usually posted by spurned ex-lovers – but it doesn't end there. *The Guardian*. April 26. Retrieved September 1 from www.theguardian.com/technology/2016/apr/26/revenge-porn-nude-photos-online-abuse.

United Nations Population Fund. (2015). Annual report: For people, planet & prosperity. Retrieved September 5, 2016 from www.unfpa.org/annual-report.

University of Primorska, Science and Research Centre, Slovenia. (2016). *Revenge porn: Tackling non-consensual sharing of sexually explicit images in cyber space.* Unpublished proposal to the European Parliament and the Council Daphne as part of the General Programme "Fundamental Rights and Justice".

Wathen, C. N., & MacMillan, H. L. (2003). Interventions for violence against women: Scientific review. *Journal of the American Medical Association, 289*(5), 589–600.

Widup, S. (2014). *Computer forensics and digital investigation with EnCase Forensic v7.* New York: McGraw-Hill Education Group.

Wolfe, D. A., Crooks, C., Jaffe, P., Chiodo, D., Hughes, R., Ellis, W., Stitt, L. A., & Donner, A. (2009). A school-based program to prevent adolescent dating violence: A cluster randomized trial. *Archives of Pediatrics & Adolescent Medicine, 163*(8), 692–699.

Y Net News. (2014). Knesset outlaws revenge porn. January 6. Retrieved April 3, 2015 from www.ynetnews.com/articles/0,7340,L-4473849,00.html.

# INDEX